David Jowitt
Nigerian English

Dialects of English

Editors
Joan C. Beal
Karen P. Corrigan
Bernd Kortmann

Volume 18

David Jowitt

Nigerian English

—

DE GRUYTER
MOUTON

ISBN 978-1-5015-2138-6
e-ISBN (PDF) 978-1-5015-0460-0
e-ISBN (EPUB) 978-1-5015-0450-1
ISSN 2164-7445

Library of Congress Control Number: 2018947833

Bibliographic information published by the Deutsche Nationalbibliothek
The Deutsche Nationalbibliothek lists this publication in the Deutsche Nationalbibliografie;
detailed bibliographic data are available on the internet at http://dnb.dnb.de.

© 2020 Walter de Gruyter, Inc., Boston/Berlin
This volume is text- and page-identical with the hardback published in 2019.
Typesetting: Integra Software Services Pvt. Ltd.
Printing and binding: CPI books GmbH, Leck

www.degruyter.com

To all my friends

Contents

List of Figures

List of Maps

https://doi.org/10.1515/9781501504600-201

1 Introduction

1.1 Preliminary remarks

Nigeria is one of the biggest 'English-speaking' countries in the world today. To say this of course implies including in the list of 'English-speaking' countries those that belong to the 'outer circle' (Kachru 1985), those where English has the functions of a 'second' language. In Nigeria, as in other such countries, English was initially a 'foreign' language; it became firmly established during the period of British colonial rule; it remains the language generally used for official communication; it is the principal lingua franca used by well-educated Nigerians, especially when they do not have another language in common; it is the language chiefly used in the education system, especially at higher levels, and in the media. It is the language most commonly used in Christian worship, at least in the cities; it is the principal language of book publication, and of contemporary Nigerian literature; it is the principal language used by Nigerians on the internet and for international communication. In Nigeria, too, a variety of English began to develop in colonial times and has continued to develop since independence.

The expression 'Nigerian English' can be taken in a narrow sense to refer to the phonological, grammatical, and lexical properties that distinguish the English used in Nigeria from varieties of English elsewhere. To describe these properties, and to suggest how widespread the use of them is among Nigerians, constitute a major task of this book. However, the broader meaning of 'Nigerian English', namely 'English as used by Nigerians', can hardly be ignored. Discussion of it cannot, in turn, ignore the still wider subject of the history, status and functions of English in Nigeria.

Werner and Fuchs (2016) speak of the 'underresearched status' of Nigerian English, and in view of the size of the country this is indeed surprising. Indicative of the meagre attention Nigerian English has received is the fact that in Melchers and Shaw (2013) it is mentioned on only six pages, comparing unfavourably even with other West African varieties (Ghanaian English being mentioned on nine pages and Sierra Leonean English on seven). In a fifteen-page article by Wolf (2010) on East and West African Englishes in Kirkpatrick (ed., 2010), it is represented by only sixteen lines.

https://doi.org/10.1515/9781501504600-001

1.2 The geographical, demographic, and historical background

1.2.1 Geography and demography

Map 1: Nigeria and West Africa

At the outset, some basic geographical, demographic and historical facts need to be presented. More substantial information of this kind is found in Falola and Oyeniyi (2015); in their book of 288 pages of main text, however, only one short paragraph is devoted to the English language.

Nigeria is a large country on the coast of West Africa, shaped roughly like a trapezium (although its politics have tended to be triangular). Its south-eastern corner lies close to the point just north of the Equator where the continent begins to bulge westwards. Its terrain resembles that of several other maritime countries in West Africa: dense forest along the coast, wooded but more open land further north, dry savannah further north still. Two great rivers trisect it, the Niger and the Benue, which after their confluence flow together down to the Atlantic Ocean, first branching out into a great delta. Except along the border with Cameroon to the east, Nigeria has no really high mountainous areas.

Nigeria's land-mass is not the biggest in Africa, but its population undoubtedly is. The claim is not so easy to prove, because although several censuses have been carried out over the course of time, the publication of the results has on each occasion been a matter of controversy. The most recent census, carried out in 2006, reported a total of slightly more than 140 million, with males exceeding females by over 3 million. According to the United Nations estimate of 2017, the total population of Nigeria is nearly 191 million and Nigeria is the seventh largest country in the world. Some other recent figures are that nearly two-thirds of the population is aged 24 or under; life expectancy is 54.5 (WHO 2017), Nigeria being 177th on the list of 183 countries; 59.6% of the population is literate (UNESCO 2015). However, these figures conceal considerable disparity between one part of Nigeria and another. Moreover, the gender breakdown of the quite impressive literacy rate is that, while 69.2% of males are literate, only 49.7% of females are.

It is also estimated that nearly 50% of Nigeria's population lives in towns and cities, of which Lagos, the former capital and still the principal commercial centre, has over 11 million people. Other very large cities are Abuja (the present capital), Kano, Ibadan, Kaduna, Port Harcourt, and Enugu. Nearly all Nigerians are adherents of one of three main religious systems: Islam, Christianity, and 'traditional' religion. Estimates of numbers are again a matter of controversy, especially as censuses have not asked questions about religion.

At one time Nigeria had a varied economy based mainly on agriculture, but in the 1960s it became a major oil producer while soon lacking the refining capacity to meet its own rapidly expanding needs. In the second decade of the twenty-first century, with the fall in the price of crude, this excessive dependence on oil exports has been called in question.

1.2.2 Ethnic groups and indigenous languages

Nigeria contains a large number of ethnic groups, differing considerably in size. Although censuses conducted over the years have not asked questions about ethnicity, the Hausa-Fulani, the Yoruba, and the Igbo are clearly the three largest groups, and one estimate shows them as making up respectively 29%, 21%, and 18%, or collectively two-thirds, of the total population (CIA 2018). According to the same source, 'minorities' – Ijo (or 'Ijaw'), Kanuri, Ibibio, Tiv, etc. – account for the rest, but the largest of them, perhaps the Ijo, with less than 10%, is much smaller than any of the big three.

Typically, each ethnic group in Nigeria is identified with a particular geographical area and a particular language, although the number of ethnic groups is undoubtedly exceeded by the number of languages; the relationship between

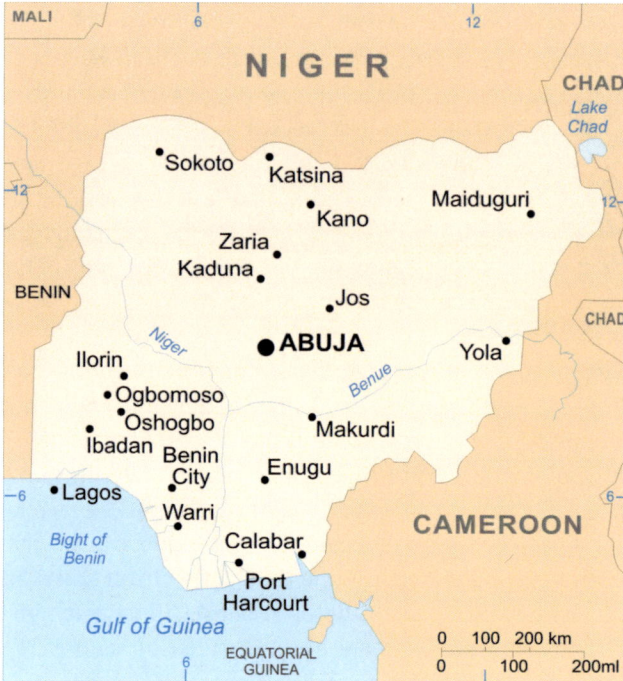

Map 2: Major cities and rivers of Nigeria

language and ethnicity is a complex one. Compounding the complexity is the fact that linguists may argue that two dialects should be regarded as one language, or alternatively that one language should be split into two dialects or even two languages; and sometimes, and not only in Nigeria, political considerations are crucial to any decision finally made. A wealth of information is provided by Blench (2014); the work is his most recent updating of an 'index' of Nigerian languages and dialects, listed alphabetically, which was first published in 1977 (the second edition, by Blench and Crozier, followed in 1992).

The classification of Nigeria's languages has undergone revision over time. Three of the four families or phyla of African languages recognized by Greenberg (1966) are represented in Nigeria: the Nilo-Saharan, the Afro-Asiatic, and the Niger-Congo. The first of these is represented by a few languages spoken in the far north-east, close to Lake Chad, notably Kanuri. Afro-Asiatic languages fall into two groups: Semitic, represented only by Shuwa (also in the far north-east), and Chadic, comprising numerous languages, of which Hausa is the most prominent, with the far North as its original 'homeland'. Niger-Congo comprises a number of groups, and to one or another of them belong the great majority of Nigeria's languages. Tone (i.e. the use of tone to differentiate lexical meaning) is one of their characteristics (although tone is also to some extent present in the Chadic languages); and among them are such important languages, mostly found in southern Nigeria, as Yoruba, Nupe, Edo, Igala, Igbo, and Ibibio. Opinion has fluctuated as to the classification of these. Greenberg placed them in the Kwa group; by the time of the Blench and Crozier *Index* (1992) they had been transferred to the Benue-Congo group as 'Western Benue-Congo'; more recent opinion is that, after all, they should be classified as Kwa languages, 'Eastern Kwa', one reason being that, unlike other Benue-Congo languages such as Tiv, they lack noun classes distinguishable by affixation. Ijo, spoken mainly in the Niger delta, is the principal member of another Niger-Congo group; while Fulfulde, the language of the still mainly nomadic, pastoralist Fulani or Fulbe, is almost the sole representative in Nigeria of another.

Estimates of the number of Nigerian languages have steadily been revised upwards, from 395 (Hansford 1976) to 420 (Blench and Crozier 1992) to 526 (Simons and Fennig eds. 2018). The number of speakers of each language as L1 is again hard to determine. The three 'majors', Hausa, Yoruba, and Igbo, are certainly in a class by themselves, each being the principal L1 in several of the country's states. Brann (1990) picturesquely labelled them 'the decamillionaires' because even at the time he wrote they were generally agreed to have at least 10 million L1 speakers each. Nearly three decades later, Simons and Fennig assign to them 33.3, 37.5, and 27.0 million each respectively.

A second tier of languages has been labelled the 'major minors', and in Brann's model they (along with the majors) were those he thought to have at least 1 million L1 speakers each: Fulfulde, Kanuri, Ibibio, Tiv, and Ijo. Fulfulde has the largest number of speakers in this group (the Simons and Fennig estimate being now 14.4 million), followed by Tiv (with 4 million). To them can now certainly, to judge by the figures provided by Simons and Fennig, be added Ebira, Igala, Nupe, and Berom. There follows the very great majority of Nigerian languages, with less than 1 million speakers each, the 'minors', but this categorization is inevitably rather misleading, since there are some languages with hundreds of thousands of speakers (e.g. Urhobo, Idoma, Mumuye, Ngas) and many with less than one thousand or even one hundred speakers. Many of the latter are endangered, and according to Ode (2015) fourteen, all but one of them in the North, face extinction.

Each of the majors has functioned as an L2 in an area beyond its 'homeland'. This is notably true of Hausa. It has been estimated that there are 15 million L2 speakers of Hausa in Nigeria, so that the number of 'speakers' (as L1 or L2) of Hausa would then be far greater than the number of 'speakers' of Yoruba or of Igbo. In the North, in fact, minority languages are endangered less by English than by Hausa, which throughout the greater part of the North serves as the 'language of wider communication' (Akinremi and Erin 2017). Hickey (2000) describes how in the twentieth century Catholic missionaries in Northern Nigeria promoted Hausa there among minority groups because of its unifying value: with the spread of Christianity among these groups, an indigenous lingua franca was needed. In contrast, Protestant missionaries, who placed less emphasis on manifest ecclesial unity, favoured using the languages of the minority groups themselves, and translation of the Bible into these languages became, and remained, one of their priorities. Much of this work, which has perhaps saved some languages with small numbers of speakers from extinction, has been carried out by the Summer Institute of Linguistics (SIL), based in Texas, USA, and by the Nigeria Bible Translation Trust (NBTT).

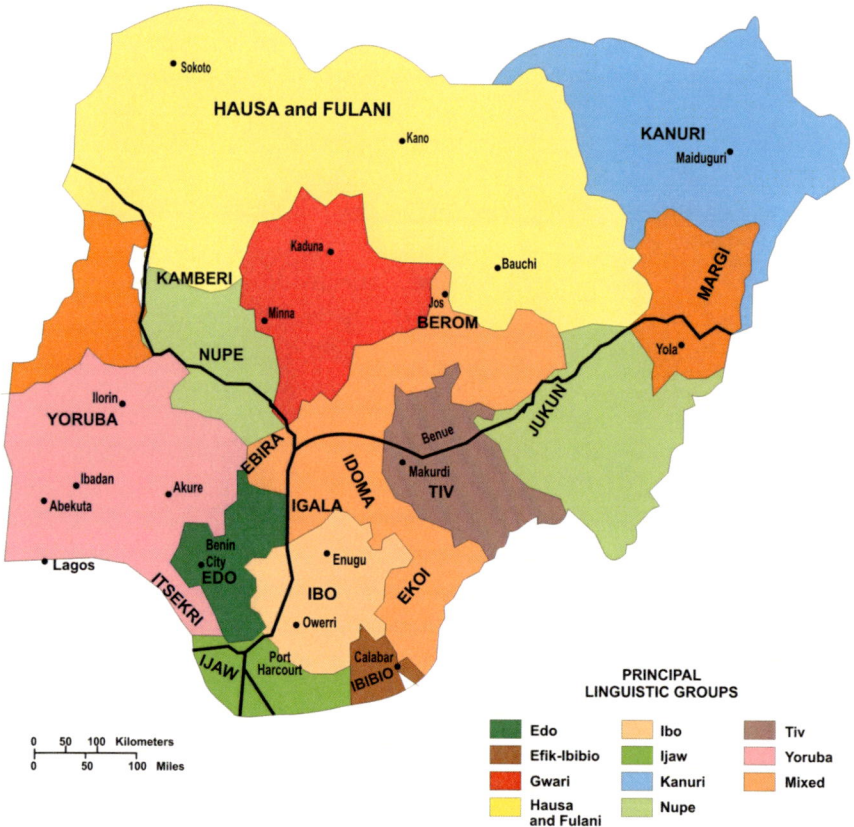

Map 3: Languages of Nigeria

1.2.3 The North and the South, and political developments

(a) General

As must be already apparent, it is difficult for the expressions 'the North' and 'the South' to be avoided in any discussion about Nigeria. Some facts need stating here because of the bearing that they have on the different ways in which the two different areas (to use this word for lack of a less misleading one) have experienced the English language and on differences in their attitudes to it. The North comprises the whole of the land north of the great rivers and some to the south of them. Kano and Kaduna are its biggest cities; Abuja, the Federal capital, lies approximately in the centre of the whole country. The North is predominantly Muslim (but with a large Christian minority), and the Hausa are its principal ethnic group. The South lies entirely to the south of the rivers, is predominantly Christian (but with a large Muslim minority, especially in the south-west), and its two main ethnic groups are the Yoruba (in the south-west) and the Igbo (in the south-east). In both the North and the South there are numerous other ethnic groups.

(b) A brief history

The North-South divide has much to do with Nigeria's history, and more is said about this, as well as about the history of English in Nigeria, in Chapter Five.

First, in both North and South indigenous kingdoms and cultures flourished for many centuries before modern times. In some places, notably Nok in the North and Ife, Benin, and Igbo-Ukwu in the South, impressive works of art were produced, in terra-cotta, brass, or bronze. A farming economy was everywhere the norm; but in the extensive savannah lands of the North it was complemented by grazing, especially when the nomadic Fulani moved into the area with their cattle in the eighteenth century.

The North, especially Hausland and Borno, was affected from about 1000 AD onwards by the spread of Islam, which arrived via the Sahara desert. In the nineteenth century the jihad of the Fulani Usman dan Fodio resulted in the subjugation of the Hausas to the Fulanis, the establishment of the caliphate of Sokoto, a more thorough Islamization, and the further spread of Islam, especially to the area now often called 'the Middle Belt' (roughly the southern part of the North). Many Fulanis settled in the cities and towns of Hausaland, and began to intermarry with the Hausas. This is the main reason why today the two peoples together are often referred to as 'the Hausa-Fulani'.

In the South, in complete contrast, the white man made his first appearance on the coast in the fifteenth century. Soon, the trans-Atlantic slave trade began. The indigenous kingdoms decayed. In the nineteenth century, the slave trade was replaced by 'legitimate' trade, and Christian missionaries brought Christianity, Western education and the English language.

In the last decades of the end of the century Britain asserted sovereignty over the polities of the entire South and then over those of the North as well. After 1914 there was a single government for the whole area, but the contrast between its two parts endured. In the North, the British operated a system of 'indirect rule' (as in India), which allowed the existing ruling-class to remain in place; in the South, where political authority had traditionally been far more fragmented, this system could not work. In the South, an English-speaking educated class rapidly developed, and it was chiefly from its ranks that nationalist opposition to colonial rule and agitation for independence grew.

After the Second World War the British began to devolve power to Nigerians, and the North-South divide was built into the new constitutional arrangements. A Federal government at the centre was established, along with three regional governments, in the North, the West, and the East respectively. Each region was controlled by one of the three main ethnic groups (the Hausa-Fulani in the North, the Yoruba in the West, the Igbo in the East). The North, supported by the British, obtained representation equal to that of the other two regions combined in the new Federal legislature. It enabled the North to control the Federal government in the period immediately after independence, which came in 1960.

The aspirations of various 'minorities' in all three regions led to the creation, first, of the Mid-West Region out of the West in 1963, then to the re-division of the entire country into twelve States in 1967. Resisting this move, the Igbo-dominated Eastern Region made an abortive attempt to secede from the Federation, proclaiming itself the Republic of Biafra, and a protracted Civil War (1967–70) ensued. Later, continuing agitation by minority and other groups resulted in the creation of more and more states: at present there are thirty-six. In ethno-linguistic composition they range from those that are fairly homogeneous, such as Oyo, Ogun, Osun, Ondo and Ekiti (Yoruba), Anambra, Enugu, Ebonyi, Abia and Imo (Igbo), and Kano, Katsina, Jigawa, Zamfara, and Sokoto (Hausa-Fulani) to those that are highly multilingual, such as Edo, Cross River, Rivers, Plateau, Bauchi, Kaduna, and Adamawa. The Federal Capital Territory (FCT) contains the Federal capital, Abuja, and is therefore even more heterogeneous, as is Lagos State for a similar reason. Benue is an example of a state that comes in the middle of the range, with two relatively large ethnic groups (Tiv, Idoma) and a few smaller ones.

Some official recognition has been given in recent years to the grouping of the states into six geopolitical 'zones', although these have no legal existence. Their compound names (North-West, South-East, etc.) suggest that the concepts 'the North' and 'the South' continue to have considerable psychological force among Nigerians.

Map 4: Contemporary Nigeria: the thirty-six states

At independence the government of Nigeria, like that of other former British colonies, was based on the Westminster model. In 1966, in the first of a series of coups, this was replaced by military rule, which lasted until 1979. A presidential system was adopted for the brief Second Republic (1979–83), which ended in another coup, followed by a second long period of military rule. Presidential democracy was restored in 1999.

1.3 English, Pidgin, and other languages

1.3.1 English: numbers

The number of English speakers in Nigeria is hard to determine, partly because in Nigeria as in other ESL or EFL countries the concept 'speaker of English' has no clear denotation. Such a 'speaker' might be a well-educated person to whom English comes at least as naturally as the mother tongue, or someone of little education with a very limited English vocabulary. In the past, in the period before and well after independence, the paucity of the number was emphasized, and English was, understandably, considered to be a hallmark of membership of the numerically small elite. Bamgbose (1971) suggested a lower estimate of 5% of the population, roughly representing those who met 'the standard expected of a secondary-school leaver', or a higher estimate of 10%, representing those who had a 'level of proficiency generally attained by primary-school leavers'. However, the 1970s and 1980s, the era of the oil boom, witnessed a huge expansion in the number of Nigerians undergoing education at all levels, and estimates of the number and the percentage of English speakers were accordingly revised. Jibril (1982) put the percentage at as much as (but 'not more than') 30%, while Emenanjo (ed. 1990), who like others before him regarded English as 'elitist'in Nigeria, suggested 20%, as did Igboanusi (2002a).

Although Omoniyi (2006) oddly suggests only about 1% (one million speakers out of an estimated population of 97 million), most recent estimates give a much higher figure than those advanced down to 1990, and fundamentally this is due to the continued expansion of education services. A Euromonitor report produced for the British Council in 2010 (Pinon and Harden 2010) claimed that 53% of Nigerians could speak English at least to intermediate level and that in the three years 2006–09 the number of speakers grew by 6%, higher than the rate of increase of the population. Udofot (2010) presents the results of some telling research carried out in the main market in Uyo, the capital of Akwa Ibom State: although Ibibio (one of the 'major minors') is generally understood in the state, 76.7% of the respondents preferred to use English for business transactions. These claims are supported by casual observation: throughout the country, but perhaps especially in the South, conversation in English – in a language that may contain imperfections but is certainly English – can be had with mechanics and bus-conductors and peasant farmers, as well as with students and academics and civil servants. It is doubtful whether English deserves any longer to be called 'elitist' in Nigeria.

1.3.2 Pidgin: numbers

Nigerian Pidgin English (NPE, henceforth 'Pidgin') has a mainly English lexical superstratum, while various indigenous languages account for the grammatical substratum. Like those of (Standard) English, it is impossible to determine the number of the 'speakers' of Pidgin with any certainty. Many Nigerians, especially the more educated, understand it but prefer not to speak it because of its demotic, anti-bourgeois connotations, although many other Nigerians use it for just those reasons. Many Nigerians consider Pidgin a debased form of English, or confuse it with 'broken' (English), defined by Elugbe (1991) as 'a mixture of pidgin and imperfect English'. Banjo (1996) says, neatly, that 'Nigerian Pidgin is related to English but is not a dialect of it'. The contemporary poet Eriata Eribhabor is among those who write in it, and he promotes a standardized form of it.

One striking fact is that for historical reasons, alluded to above, it was in the South that, a long while ago, Pidgin began to develop and spread. It has become creolized in some parts of the South (notably in the coastal area of Delta State), but its principal function is as a lingua franca, especially where numerous first languages are spoken and therefore also in cities. It plays this role also throughout the country in other environments where the population tends to be heterogeneous, such as higher institutions (especially among students), and police and military barracks. Its presence is well-established in some Northern cities; but it does not play the same function in the North as in the South. Fundamentally this is because, as already demonstrated, Hausa is a principal L2 in the North, and has been a major lingua franca there since colonial times. In some important ways Hausa is in fact to the North what Pidgin is to the South. For this reason the estimate given by Faraclas (2008), that 'well over half of the ... inhabitants of Nigeria are now fluent speakers of the language [i.e. Pidgin]' should be treated with caution; while the remarks of Crystal (1997) are decidedly misleading. In a seven-line paragraph about Nigeria he says that about half of the population 'use pidgin or creole English as a second language', as if to say that Pidgin is not only a form of English but is the only form of English that Nigerians speak. In contrast, he says that about 1 million out of 16 million Ghanaians use English as a second language (which seems a low estimate). The Lewis et al. (2016) estimate of Nigerian speakers of Pidgin (as L1 or L2) is about 30 million, which may be on the conservative side.

1.3.3 The status of English and other languages

Nigeria inherited English as its official language at independence; yet it could be called Nigeria's "unofficially official" language. This is to say that no explicit declaration as to its official status has been made, in the present Constitution of the Federal Republic, which came into effect in 1999, or in any other form. Some Nigerians have expressed surprise at the idea that such a declaration might or should be made. The widespread assumption is that the role that English actually plays is so pervasive and indispensable that it does not need reinforcement through a constitutional statement. In this respect Nigeria resembles the United Kingdom. The Constitution, which dates from 1999, comes closest to officially endorsing the role of English when it says that 'the business of the National Assembly shall be conducted in English'.

Since independence the minds of Nigerians have been exercised by the National Language Question, perhaps more in the immediate post-independence decades than subsequently. Patriotic Nigerians have argued that Nigeria should have a national language that is truly part of its culture and expressive of its identity, and that, whatever its current usefulness might be, a language imported from outside, by 'Europeans' whose objectives were fundamentally exploitative, cannot fit that requirement. An extreme view is that of Unegbu (2015), who calls English in Nigeria 'a necessary evil'. In contrast, many Nigerians have not hesitated to stress the benefits of English and have even referred to it as at least *a* national language, even when they themselves have championed the use of indigenous languages. Many today wholeheartedly endorse the assertions of Afolayan (1984):

> It is unrealistic for anybody in Nigeria today to think that national unity can be forged in this country without recourse to the utilization of the English language.... Furthermore, the fact that it is now functioning as the language of Nigerian nationism cannot be denied.

An early balanced summary of the various arguments is provided by Bamgbose (1971).

Among the candidates for the role of national language, predictably, have been the three major languages, or one of them; but advocacy here bristles with political implications. Spokespersons for 'minor' languages have moreover attacked the idea of privileging the major languages that it implies. Other suggested candidates include one of the 'minor' languages themselves, such as Igala (Sofunke 1990) or Edo; Swahili (a proposal once made by the distinguished writer Wole Soyinka but discounted by Bamgbose 1989); or an artificial language such as the 'Guosa' of Alex Igbineweka, which he describes in Igbineweka (1981) and still promotes. This is an amalgam of the three major languages, and such an amalgam is often jokingly referred to by Nigerians as 'Wazobia', once the title of a popular television programme; *wa*, *zo*, and *bia* are the translation of English 'come' into Yoruba, Hausa and Igbo respectively. The impracticability of Igbineweka's idea has been pointed out by several Nigerian linguists.

Pidgin also has its advocates. A major problem here is that the lexis of Pidgin is largely borrowed from English; if Pidgin were used for various official purposes, requiring the use of much abstract vocabulary, it would look so much like English itself that the case for adopting it in place of English would be weakened. This view would naturally be challenged by its supporters. Another strong argument against it is that, as pointed out above, Pidgin is not widely used as a lingua franca in the North, where it contends to its disadvantage with Hausa.

The attitudes of Nigerians to the National Language Question have been investigated by, among others, Akinjobi (2004). Her one hundred 'educated' subjects were taken in equal numbers from four groups: those with Hausa,

Yoruba, Igbo, and a 'minority' language respectively as their L1. Among the questions put to them was whether, in their opinion, any of the three major languages should replace English as the country's 'national language'. (The study did not distinguish between 'official' language and 'national' language.) Of the Hausa speakers, 75% felt that one of the three majors should assume that role, and that it should be Hausa. In sharp contrast, 86% of the Yoruba speakers, 94% of the Igbo speakers, and 70% of the 'minorities' speakers felt that none of the three majors should, and that English should retain that role. Linguistic chauvinism is clearly strongest among the Hausas.

Some steps have nevertheless been taken in the direction of official recognition of the three majors. The Constitution, referred to above, stipulates (section 55) that the business of the National Assembly 'shall be conducted in English, and in Hausa, Ibo and Yoruba when adequate arrangements have been made therefore'; but English remains the only language used. The Constitution also (section 97) allows for the use of indigenous languages in state houses of assembly, and in some of the more purely monolingual states debates are conducted partly in English, partly in the principal indigenous language of the state in question; but in the houses of multilingual states, such as Plateau, English is invariably used.

Concern over the threat posed by English to indigenous languages has also inspired efforts to ensure that these are taught in schools and used as the medium of instruction. The National Policy on Education, first introduced in 1977 and revised several times since then, stipulates that the mother tongue should be used as the medium of instruction in the first two of the six years of primary school and that where possible literacy should be attained in it, while English should become the medium of instruction in the third year of primary school. It also requires that one of the three major languages should be taught at junior-secondary level (i.e. grades 7–9 in the American system), in addition to the mother tongue and of course English; and that at senior-secondary level 'one Nigerian language' should be studied.

The operation of the Policy has been hampered by many practical difficulties. Only a small number of mother tongues have reached a sufficient level of development, even in terms of possessing a standard orthography, for them to be taught as school subjects. In many areas, especially cities, pupils in schools even at primary level come from different mother-tongue backgrounds. Only a few languages (but including the major three) can be studied at tertiary level for the purpose of obtaining teaching qualifications. Teachers are often unwilling to go to teach a language in an area where it is not the mother tongue. Above all, defenders of the minority languages have attacked the Policy because it discriminates against them and, in the words of Ker (2002), is 'at variance with the tenet of "equal educational opportunities"' enshrined in the Policy. He points out that a child speaking (i.e. as L1) a major language can comfortably handle two languages (e.g. Hausa and English); but a child speaking a minority language has to grapple with three (e.g. Etulo, Igbo, and English).

Much interest was aroused by the Ife Six Year Primary Project of the 1970s, under which pupils attending schools chosen for the project underwent instruction entirely in their mother tongue, in this case Yoruba. According to Fafunwa (ed. 1989), the policy was highly successful, leading to 'greater result in permanent literacy and numeracy'. Yet for various reasons it has not been officially adopted, or copied elsewhere in Nigeria.

Of other non-indigenous languages known to Nigerians, Classical Arabic is the most notable since it is the language of the Holy Book of Islam and the main language for the expression of the Islamic faith. It was first brought to the North across the Sahara Desert hundreds of years ago by Arab missionaries, explorers and traders, and today has a conspicuous presence in parts of the country where there is generally a substantial Islamic presence, such as large parts of the North, and of the South-West. Arabs long ago used the Arabic script to devise an alphabet for the Hausa language, known as *ajami*; as a result there existed some literacy in Hausa before the coming of Western education. Arabic is widely taught, in Government schools in Muslim-majority States, in non-Government-funded *Islami-yya* schools, and in Quranic schools of a traditional sort.

French is taught as a foreign language in Nigeria in schools and universities, and it is important for communication between Nigeria and francophone African countries, although there must be more francophone Africans learning English than anglophone Africans learning French. The military regime of General Sani Abacha in the 1990s declared French an official language alongside English, but there is little to show for the policy.

Nigeria's multilingualism is epitomized in the language of its currency notes (those in circulation in 2016). On each note representing a lower denomination (N5, N10, N20, N50), the denomination is given in English and also in each of the three main languages. On the N100 note it is given in English only, while on each higher-denomination note (N200, N500, N1,000) it is given in English and in Arabic. Other details, such as 'Central Bank of Nigeria', are given in English only.

1.3.4 Linguistic repertoires and language functions

To compose a sociolinguistic profile of Nigeria is clearly a complex matter. A national profile ultimately summarizes the linguistic profiles or repertoires of a multiplicity of individuals, and in Nigeria there is a great variety of these.

At the simplest extreme, an individual Nigerian knows only an indigenous mother tongue; the next simplest repertoire is that someone knows two languages, most often an indigenous mother tongue and a second language which may be another indigenous language, or Pidgin, or English. Various combinations are possible when three or more languages are learned – three indigenous languages; two indigenous languages and English; one indigenous language, Pidgin, and English, and so on. At the level of just two or three languages the complexity is intensified: if, for example, dialects as well as languages are considered (thus an individual may know an Igbo dialect, Standard Igbo, and English); or if the left-to-right sequencing is taken to indicate the temporal sequence in which the languages are learned but not a necessary increase in proficiency. Thus in the sequence Yagba (a dialect of Yoruba) – Standard Yoruba – Pidgin – English, one speaker with this repertoire might be more proficient in Standard Yoruba than in the other three, another with the same repertoire might be more proficient in English than in the other three, and so on.

Familiarity with several languages is different from the mixing of languages, or hybridity. This has become an important topic of interest in international discussion of New Englishes (Rubdy and Alsagoff 2013). It has become a striking fact of language use in Nigeria too, especially among peers of younger, educated age groups. It goes far beyond the classic situations of bilingualism, of either the coordinate or the subordinate type. In Nigeria's sociolinguistic profile Adegbite (2011) identifies monolinguals, bilinguals, and polyglots, and as suggested by the above sketch of possible individual repertoires, there are many polyglots in Nigeria today. In a particular discourse they often freely operate code-switching and code-mixing, and the mix or the switch usually involves (Standard) English and Pidgin, or English and an indigenous language. Defenders of indigenous languages often complain that it is difficult for their more educated fellow-Hausas, -Igbos, etc. to utter a sentence without introducing at least one English word into it. Akinremi (2016) is a recent interesting study of the insertion of English lexical items into the grammatical framework of Igbo discourse.

Adegbite nevertheless also, citing Baker (2001) and Dada (2006), draws attention to the emergence in Nigeria of a category of 'limited' bilinguals or 'semilinguals', apparently knowing only parts of two or more languages. It is a local aspect of an inevitable worldwide contemporary trend, as described by Blommaert (2010), who sees the individuals concerned as having 'truncated repertoires' – which means that the languages constituting a repertoire have become truncated. Since it is particularly observable in cities, Otsuji and Pennycook (2010) label the development 'metrolingualism'. It is certainly observable among younger Nigerians living in towns or studying in higher institutions: their repertoire usually today includes what Akinremi and Dajang (2015) call the Nigerian Pidgin-based Youth Variety, with many unique vocabulary items. To those concerned about the future of indigenous languages the development is naturally considered a danger; but English is also endangered by it, because a young Nigerian's knowledge of English is usually limited, in spite of the great fluency in the use of the language that he or she may possess. This is especially true of Standard English vocabulary, large parts of which may eventually cease to be used in Nigeria at all. The theory may help to account for the deterioration in English performance in Nigeria, which is of great concern to many observers (see below).

This pessimism apart, the likelihood is that the number of Nigerians who not only speak English, but speak it more proficiently than any other language, must have steadily increased in the decades since independence. An increasing number of Nigerians moreover learn English before they learn any other language, and the fact is increasingly remarked on (Akere 1982; Udofot 2005). The pattern more often occurs among the elite than among social groups, and often occurs because the parents come from different ethnic groups. Akere observes:

> Children born into such homes would first of all acquire the English language in order to be able to communicate with their parents. Although they may acquire either of their parents' languages later on, for the most part the general elements of the indigenous culture and the patterns of social relations are acquired and practiced through the medium of the English language.

It remains true that the languages belonging to the repertoire of the average Nigerian tend to be used in different domains. Principal domains and the languages used that correspond to them are summarized in the following table (adapted from Jowitt 1991).

Table 1: Domains of language use, and languages used

Domain	Language(s) used
1. OFFICIAL (official pronouncements and correspondence, official discussion in the civil service, educational institutions, the armed forces, ecclesiastical institutions, etc.; proceedings in courts of law)	English; mother tongue (MT) (in lower courts of law)
2. EDUCATION: medium of instruction in: lower primary school upper " " secondary school tertiary institutions	 MT, Pidgin, Hausa (in the North), English " " " " " (but English according to Government policy) English English
students' assignments, and examinations	English (in all subjects except other Ls)
textbooks	English (but also the three major Ls in primary school)

Domain	Language(s) used
3. MASS MEDIA:	
radio and television	majority of programmes in English; some in the three major Ls and Pidgin; news broadcasts in a variety of MTs
published books	majority in English, a few in the three major Ls
newspapers	" "
video films	English and the three major Ls; a few in other MTs
advertisements	English, the three major Ls, Pidgin
popular music lyrics	some English; indigenous languages (esp. Yoruba, Hausa); Pidgin
4. RELIGIOUS OBSERVANCE:	
i. Christian	some services and prayers in English, some in Nigerian Ls, notably Hausa in the North (but not in Benue, Kogi, Kwara)
ii. Islamic	Arabic for formal prayers; MT or Hausa (as L2) for other purposes (e.g. sermons)
iii. traditional	MT
5. INFORMAL INTERPERSONAL RELATIONS:	
i. home and family	MT; Pidgin; some English (among the better educated); some Hausa even as L2 in the North
ii. peers, and other (i.e. spanning different age groups)	as for (i), but a Nigerian L where this is known (as L1 or L2) by both speakers, esp.Hausa in the North; or Pidgin; or English (among the better educated); and in fresh social contacts one or another L will be tried out to ascertain which will be the most suitable for communication.
6. CREATIVE WRITING	mainly English; extensive writing in Hausa; some in Yoruba; very little in any other language

1.4 English as the language of education, the media, and literature

1.4.1 The teaching and learning of English

As the table suggests, the average Nigerian child learns to speak and write English chiefly in a formal setting. The process begins at primary school (six years) and continues through junior-secondary school (three years) and senior-secondary school (three years). The teaching of the subject is thus linked to the school timetable, and this means that at secondary level six lessons per week are assigned to it, each lasting for forty minutes; thus the formal learning of English is confined to four hours per week, and is never intensive. On the other hand, in theory if not always in practice, English is the medium of instruction from the third year of primary school upwards, and this exposure to English outside the English classroom must help to promote proficiency in it. The teachers, who today are nearly always Nigerians, are produced by university departments of English or Education or by Colleges of Education, although many university graduates of other disciplines (such as Mass Communication) are also assigned to teach English. Teachers are rarely the beneficiaries of workshops or other in-service programmes. Professional bodies such as the English Language Teachers' Association of Nigeria (ELTAN) that might have helped in this regard have very limited resources, especially in view of the size of the country and the vast number of schools and teachers; and the same can be said of the British Council in Nigeria, which in the past has played a role in seeking to raise teaching standards.

In the final year of secondary school students sit for a public examination, that of either the West African Examinations Council, WAEC, or the more recently-established National Examinations Council, NECO. As long ago as 1963 a pass in English ceased to be a requirement for the award of the WAEC's School Certificate; however, for most programmes today universities require candidates for admission to have credits in English and Mathematics. In universities and other higher institutions students also compulsorily take a General English or Use of English course intended to improve their communication skills. Its effectiveness is hampered by huge numbers of students and shortages of staff: Adegoju (2012) reports a class size of 6,000 students at Obafemi Awolowo University, Ile-Ife (where the course was first introduced in the 1970s).

1.4.2 English in the Nigerian media

The table shows that English is widely, but by no means exclusively used in Nigeria as the language of book publication, newspapers, radio and television, films, and advertisements.

The overwhelming prominence of English as the language in which books are published in Nigeria conceals the fact that for many years the Nigerian publishing industry has been in poor shape. Moreover, as Ike (2004) shows, primary and secondary textbooks account for 90% of all books published.

The reading of newspapers is also on the decline in Nigeria as it is in other parts of the world; Garba (2016) claims that 'most Nigerian newspapers belong to a dying breed'. About twenty daily English-language papers are still published in print form, but about fifty are now available online. In either form they purport to be directed at a nationwide audience, but some tend to give special attention to issues pertaining to a particular part of the country, and to attract readers there: thus the *Daily Trust* is widely read in the North, *The Nigerian Tribune* in the South-West. The number and variety of papers and their readiness to criticize the authorities (such as it may be) help to promote the development of civil society in Nigeria.

The early 1990s saw the beginning of the dramatic rise of the Nigerian home-video film industry, to which the sobriquet 'Nollywood' was soon given. A United Nations News Centre report shows that in 2006, with 872 films produced that year, Nigeria's production was nearly twice as great as that of the USA's 'Hollywood' and second only to that of India's 'Bollywood'. The report also shows that 56% of the films were produced in indigenous languages (Hausa, Igbo and Yoruba naturally accounting for most of these) and 44% in English (although the indigenous-language films also have English sub-titles). Nigerian films are highly popular in other African countries, being accessible on the various African Magic channels. Some Nigerian critics have nevertheless deplored the negative image of Nigeria that they allegedly often convey (with excessive prominence given, it is said, to certain unsavoury aspects of traditional religion, such as witchcraft). Some critics in other African countries have also attacked the quality of the English used in the films.

The number of television channels and radio stations has steadily increased in Nigeria over the decades. Some are owned by the Federal Government (the Nigerian Television Authority, NTA, and the Nigerian Broadcasting Corporation, NBC, which have a presence in every state) or by State Governments; others are privately owned (AIT, Channels, Silverbird, etc.). All of them mainly feature English-language programmes, but some state television channels and some local radio stations also air programmes in indigenous languages. At certain times of the day in some states the news is presented in several languages spoken in the state, as well as English; thus the Plateau Radio and Television (PRTV) news is broadcast in eleven local languages.

Nigerian popular music has been represented since the 1960s by a number of styles and artistes, one of the most famous, especially in the 1970s and 1980s, being 'the king of Afro-beat', Fela Anikulapo-Kuti (or just 'Kuti'; originally Fela Ransome-Kuti). The majority of those who have achieved nationwide or international renown are Yoruba. As the table shows, the lyrics use a mixture of an indigenous language (most often Yoruba), Pidgin, and English, with much code-switching (Babalola and Taiwo 2009).

1.4.3 Nigerian literature in English

As the table also indicates, creative writing in Nigeria is carried out mainly in English, although the production of short, cheap novels in Hausa is a thriving industry in the North, especially in its biggest city, Kano.

Over the decades an impressive corpus of works of Nigerian literature in English has come into being. This is testimony to the extent to which, in spite of the inadequacies of the formal system of learning it, the English language has permeated the psyche of Nigerians and is used by creative minds among them to convey all aspects of their experience. Some writers have attained international fame and recognition, and the books of a few of them have become set books in examination syllabuses in the UK and elsewhere outside Nigeria. In Nigeria itself, they are the staple of Literature programmes in university departments of English, and have for long been so. Alarm is nevertheless constantly being expressed over the decline of the reading culture among Nigerians, which probably affects books even more than newspapers, and is not a uniquely Nigerian problem.

In the middle of the twentieth century Nigerian literature in English barely existed. Within a short time the scene became so crowded with published writers that even to list all their names would be a challenging task. They include Chinua Achebe, Cyprian Ekwensi, Flora Nwapa, T.M.Aluko, Gabriel Okara, Elechi Amadi, Isidore Okpehwo, Buchi Emecheta, Chukwuemeka Ike, Festus Iyayi, Kole Omoto-sho, Ken Saro-Wiwa, Ifeoma Okoye, Zaynab Alkali, Abubakar Gimba, Ben Okri, Biyi Bandele, Eme Akpan, Chimamanda Ngozi Adichie, Sefi Atta, Adaobi Tricia Nwaubani, Helon Habila, Lola Shoneyin, and Chigozie Obioma (novels and short stories); John Pepper Clark Bekederemo, Gabriel Okara, Christopher Okigbo, Mabel Segun, Funso Aiyejina, Niyi Osundare, Odia Ofeimun, and Tanare Ojaide (poetry); and Ola Rotimi, 'Zulu Sofola, Femi Osofisan, and Tess Onwueme (plays). Wole Soyinka is in a class by himself because he has written in each of the three main literary genres, as well as autobiography and a prison diary, and because in 1986 he became the first African to be awarded the Nobel Prize for Literature. Some of the other writers just mentioned are also notable for their versatility: thus the late Achebe, primarily a novelist, also wrote short stories, poetry, and criticism. Other international prizes for literature that have been won by Nige-rians include the British Booker Prize (won by Ben Okri for *The Famished Road*, 1991) and the Commonwealth Writers' Prize for Best First Book Overall (won by Chimamanda Ngozi Adichie for *Purple Hibiscus* in 2005). Words of Achebe from an influential essay in a collection (Achebe 1975) have become both a classic defence of the Nigerian writer's choice of English – Standard English – as his medium of expression, and a complementary justification for the emergence of 'new', Nigerian English:

[The African/Nigerian writer] should aim at fashioning out an English which is at once universal and able to carry his peculiar experience....it will have to be a new English, still in full communion with its ancestral home but altered to suit its new African surroundings.

Banjo (1996) speculates that the term 'New Englishes', now used worldwide, may well owe its origin to this remark by Achebe.

The implications of this two-fold programme have placed a question mark over certain non-Standard types of writing that attracted attention especially in the early days of the growth of Nigerian literature. They include the Onitsha market literature written in the 1950s and 1960s by Igbo authors of limited education, and catalogued and analysed by Obiechina (1972); and the picaresque fiction of the semi-educated Yoruba Amos Tutuola, notably *The Palm-Wine Drinkard*, which was published in 1952 and attracted attention outside Nigeria, notably from the British poet Dylan Thomas. At the time, Nigerians spotted, and understandably resented an implied assumption that the book should be taken as representative of Nigerian writing in English. Three decades later saw the publication, with less controversy, of Ken Saro-Wiwa's *Soza-Boy*, which has a poorly educated first-person soldier-narrator and is deliberately also written in non-Standard English, called 'rotten English' by the author. Extracts from both Tutuola and Saro-Wiwa appear in Chapter Five.

As the names in the list above indicate, most published Nigerian writers are men; yet the number of women writers has steadily increased, and central characters who are self-determined, modern young women now feature frequently in their novels. The great majority of Nigerian writers in English have always come from different parts of the South, but rather belatedly the North also began to produce some novelists, those already mentioned being Alkali, Gimba, and Habila. Many writers represent the second or third generation in an educated family; many have attended a good school or a university. Some, perhaps finding life in Nigeria difficult for a writer, have taken up residence in the UK or the USA (Okri, Bandele, Adichie, Habila), one danger of which is separation for too long from one of the principal sources of one's inspiration.

Nigerian writers are expected by their fellow-Nigerians to have, and often do have a progressive ideology and reformist aims. Some have engaged themselves in political activity: notably Soyinka at the beginning of the Civil War, and Saro-Wiwa, who campaigned against the degradation of the environment in his native Niger delta region and was put to death by the military regime of Sani Abacha in 1997.

A great variety of themes feature in Nigerian writing: conflicts in traditional society (Achebe, Amadi), corruption and mismanagement in the post-independence era (Achebe, Clark Bekeredemo, Iyayi, Osofisan), the predicaments of women (Nwapa, Okoye, Alkali, Adichie), the impact of the Civil War (Okpehwo,

Adichie), care of and the threat to the environment (Osundare), children's experience (Omotosho, Akpan, Obioma), the supernatural in everyday life (Okri), the uses of history (Habila), internet scams (Nwaubani). Nigerian writing is also marked by a considerable variety of styles. In the novel, plain realistic prose is the most common type, becoming more daring and sometimes sensational in more recent writers such as Bandele and Adichie, while Okri, with his juxtapositions of the probable and the improbable, is an isolated representative of magic realism. Okara in *The Voice* represented a lone attempt to render in English the syntactic patterns of Ijo, his mother tongue. In poetry, Okigbo and Soyinka are marked by modernist opacity, Clark Bekeredemo and Osundare by relative simplicity and clarity.

No prominent Nigerian writer has followed the call of Ngũgĩ (1986) for a return to an indigenous language as the right language for an African to use for literary expression.

1.4.4 Nigeria's complaint tradition

The explosive growth of Nigerian literature in English and of the readership it has attracted outside Nigeria constitutes a remarkable story; but contrasting with it is the disquiet frequently expressed by certain Nigerians about the quality of the English spoken and written in the country. No paradox lies here, since it is still true that only a few Nigerian users of English both undertake the writing of books and succeed in having them accepted by publishing houses inside or outside the country. Many other books (literary works, inspirational books, self-help books, textbooks, and so on) are in fact written by Nigerians and then published privately: the authors put up the finance and later 'launch' them. Not having been adequately edited, they are usually marred by a greater or lesser number of various linguistic blemishes. The Nigerian Liquefied Natural Gas (NLNG) project awards an annual prize for literature; but sometimes no award is made because, in the view of the judges, the quality of the writing is considered too poor.

A 'complaint tradition' concerning English language matters has been in existence for a long time in Nigeria, and it is similar in some ways to the tradition in the UK described by Milroy and Milroy (1998). Like their counterparts in the UK, the Nigerian 'complainers' draw attention to the deficiencies of their fellow citizens in grammar, spelling, pronunciation and vocabulary. The complaints often assume that there was a time when educated persons invariably used the language correctly; the object of the complaints is to maintain or to recover the purity of the Standard.

The Nigerian 'complainers' usually occupy university posts, and have been voicing their complaints over a period of several decades. They include Salami (1968), Ubahakwe (1979), Adejare (1984), Omodiaogbe (1997), Fakoya (2004), Adesanoye (2004), and Eyisi (2015); Ayo Banjo, the doyen of Nigerian professors of English Language from the 1970s onwards, added his voice in Banjo (2014). Adejare wrote at a time when most Nigerian users of English had at most undergone secondary education and there were as yet relatively few students in higher education:

> ...the nation's huge investment in the English language appears not to be yielding any substantial dividends. The percentage and quality of passes in the subject at the primary and secondary school levels are disconcertingly low nation-wide.

Banjo argues thus:

> Perhaps for too long we have looked on helplessly as the spoken and written English of recent products of Nigerian education of all tiers has become an embarrassment to the system and a source of frustration to would-be employers in the private and public sectors of the economy of our country.

Achebe (1984) gave his own authoritative expression to the anxiety many years ago in these words:

> I am convinced that a major flaw of our political culture is the inefficient and half-baked language in which we conduct our national affairs. The quality of the English language spoken and written in Nigeria has been falling rapidly and will fall more dramatically in the next few years.

The linguistic malaise has been linked to moral malaise and political malaise: thus the first part of the title of a paper by the playwright Osofisan (2001), with an echo of Saro-Wiwa (see above), is 'Rotten English, Rotten Nation'.

Attention is also increasingly being focused on the grammatical shortcomings of university lecturers, although this is a delicate, even hazardous undertaking since these are the very people whom society regards as educated above all. Adesanoye's 2004 article partly relates the history of his personal growing dismay. In his doctoral thesis, written thirty years earlier (Adesanoye 1973), he had upheld the usage of persons of the graduate class as a standard. By the 1990s, when he was Director of the Ibadan University Press, he saw a number of professors' inaugural lectures, and found the English of many of them defective. The data he actually presents in the 2004 article are taken from more recent inaugurals, and in them too he finds much to question. He still affirms that the English of the majority of them is impeccable; on the other hand, he expresses the fear that, to the extent that in some of the lectures it is not impeccable, Nigerian academics might be 'going the way that our students (undergraduate and postgraduate) have already gone', so that the 'model' once provided by persons of this class is indeed 'vanishing'.

A special type of alarm is frequently expressed today in Nigeria about the impact of the language of SMS (Short Message Service) texting and of the social media, with its deletions, number homophones, disregard of punctuation marks, etc. (Rotimi 2012; Faleke 2015). The fear is that the 'new innovative orthography' is further corrupting the use of Standard English in the country.

Not by way of palliation, Azuike (2011) reminds his fellow Nigerians that similar concerns are currently being expressed in countries around the world, including the UK and the USA. Schneider (2007) shows that a complaint tradition has long existed and remains alive in ESL countries such as the Philippines, Hong Kong, Malaysia, Singapore, India, and Kenya; and in Singapore public anxiety has produced the Speak Good English Movement (SGEM) described by Rubdy (2001). In Nigeria it has not yet reached this public level; however, an initiative with presumably the same kind of aims as the SGEM is the English Language Clinic started at the University of Ibadan in 2012 (Akinjobi ed. 2014). It includes a walk-in clinic where experts 'treat' pathological conditions of individuals' language use, a Facebook clinic with similar aims and with 45,000 members as of 2016, a quarterly lecture series, and several other programmes.

1.5 Nigerian English

1.5.1 General perceptions and attitudes

The claim that the quality of the English spoken and written by Nigerians is generally deteriorating raises questions about Nigerian English, and to this subject our attention can now be given.

It should first be pointed out that Nigerian English is a subject that has been under discussion in Nigeria, and by no means only by scholars, over a long period. It has also been a highly controversial subject, encountering many different attitudes among Nigerians, and these range from emphatic rejection to enthusiastic acceptance, with various intermediate positions. The same dichotomy of opinion is found in other ESL countries; thus Sailaja (2009) observes that 'the term "Indian English" is not one that all Indians are comfortable with'. Paradoxically, Bamgbose (1982) shows that some Nigerians include elements of Nigerian English in their speech in the very act of expressing great hostility to it.

Jowitt (2013) calls the contending parties 'the rejecters' and 'the accepters' respectively, although many accepters actually do more than 'accept'; they positively welcome and promote. Rejecters, many (but not all) of whom today belong to the older generation, but who are often still influential, uphold an 'exoglossic' or 'exonorma- tive' Standard (invariably Standard British English) as the model for usage in Nigeria. Some of their names are mentioned above in 1.4.4; they regard any kind of recog- nition of Nigerian English as tending towards the mere endorsement and encour- agement of errors. Accepters, in contrast, all fundamentally accept that a Nigerian English variety exists, with distinct characteristics; that it is one of the considerable number of 'outer circle' varieties found in the world today; and that it is likely in time to evolve its own, 'endoglossic' or 'endonormative' Standard. Banjo (1979, 1993) here occupies a somewhat cautious, conservative position, stressing the need for Nige- rian English to be 'internationally intelligible' as well as 'internally acceptable'. In contrast, Adetugbo (1979), writing in the same forum and manifesting the interest in communicative competence that had become fashionable in the 1970s, urged:

> Why should Nigerians care whether, if Nigerian English has forms like *He is not on seat* or *Master, they are looking for you* and these are perfectly acceptable in the Nigerian context, they are unacceptable and unintelligible to native speakers of English? Should we not worry first about acceptability, especially of the spoken medium, within our immediate language environment before we set the too high goal of international acceptability? And were we to do this shouldn't communicative competence take precedence over grammatical competence?

A problem that soon arises in any discussion of Nigerian English, and other New Englishes, is that the word 'standard' is ambiguous. Jowitt (1991, 2007a) shows that it has two principal meanings and that they can work in opposition to each other. With a capital 'S', the word implies a level of quality, a model to follow, as in 'Standard English'; but with a small 's' it can mean that which is average, or normal because generally used, and so common. The investigation of Nigerian English seeks to recognize linguistic items that are commonly used and so are 'standard'; but that does not automatically mean that they are to be regarded as 'Standard' (correct, prescribable) forms. A representative example, much used below, is *barb* meaning "cut and dress the hair of someone", which may be described as 'standard' – being used by numerous Nigerians – but can hardly yet be considered 'Standard'. Confusion often arises in Nigerian English studies because writers do not make clear in which of these senses 'standard' is being used. Thus Igboanusi (2002a) devotes a section of his Introduction to 'Features of Standard Nigerian English', and he uses 'Standard NE' twice in the first paragraph of this section and once elsewhere; otherwise in the Introduction and in the main part of the book he uses only 'NE'. This important terminological issue has not been resolved, but partly as a way of resolving the ambiguity, Jowitt (1991) proposed use of the word 'popular', and the expression 'Popular Nigerian English', to refer to distinctive Nigerian usage in the sense expressed by 'stand- ard' but not in the sense of 'Standard'.

The related concept of 'standardization' has been discussed by Bamgbose (1998). He identifies five measurements of the degree of standardization of linguistic items, of which the most important are 'codification' and 'acceptability'. The codification of Nigerian English must be regarded as being still at an early stage (with, for example, no generally accepted dictionary of Nigerian English being available), and this is true also of its 'acceptability', since this would require extensive tests of the acceptability (to Nigerians, presumably of pre-determined qualifications) of hundreds of linguistic items. For these reasons, it can hardly be denied that, where Nigerian English is concerned, Quirk's answer to Kachru in their famous dispute of the early 1990s (Quirk 1990; Kachru 1991) remains on the whole justified: non-native varieties are not yet institutionalized.

The contrast and tension between rejecters and accepters of Nigerian English correlates to a high degree with the familiar contrast of prescriptive and descriptive approaches to discussion of language issues. Those who reject Nigerian English are almost inevitably prescriptivists, because if they are teachers of English part of their concern is to maintain standards of 'correct' usage and adherence to forensic rules, which they consider Nigerian English to threaten. Those who accept or promote are typically also descriptivists, since their general advocacy inevitably involves them in describing 'Nigerianisms' (a useful way of referring to the commonly occurring forms of Nigerian English), in seeking to identify its sub-varieties, and so on. Nevertheless, the accepters or promoters may have an ultimate prescriptive agenda: thus Odumuh (1987) says, with clear reference to the Nigerian variety that he describes, 'the need has often been expressed for a variety of English which can be used prescriptively in our schools and colleges'.

Although moves to recognize the existence of Nigerian English and encourage its development began spontaneously in Nigeria soon after independence, the terms now often used to express some kind of approval of it are ones made familiar through the rapid growth of interest in New Englishes internationally that marked the 1980s. Nigerian English is English which has become 'nativized', 'domesticated', 'indigenized', and so on; it has taken on distinctively Nigerian qualities. Thus Adegbija (2004) says:

> The term "domestication", in the context of English in Nigeria, connotes "home-grown", "made native", "adapted and tamed to suit the Nigerian environment"... There is a sense in which domestication implies that English has become Nigeria's property.... We may then say that English in Nigeria has been nativized, Nigerianized or has been given Nigerian citizenship... English is now made to do precisely what Nigerians want it to do.

It is a small step from there to say that English is no longer a foreign language in Nigeria, but has become a Nigerian language.

Numerous scholars writing over a period of over half a century have supported the assertions expressed in the advocacy of Adegbija, or implied that they do so. They include Banjo (1971, 1979, 1995, 1996), Adekunle (1979), Bamgbose (1971, 1982, 1995), Akere (1982), Adetugbo (1977, 1979), Jibril (1982a, 1982b, 1986), Awonusi (1985, 1990, 2004), Eka (1985), Kujore (1985), Odumuh (1987), Jowitt (1991, 2008), Bamiro (1994), Udofot (2004), Mustapha (2011), Okoro (2011), Gut (2012), Fuchs et al. (2013), Adegbite et al. (2014), and Kperogi (2015). Only a few of their relevant publications are here mentioned. It is worth adding that more than half of the Nigerian scholars mentioned come or came from the South-West, with Yoruba as their mother tongue. If the interest in Nigerian English is greater there than elsewhere, the possible explanation is that it was there that English first began to be taught and learned (details are found in Chapter Five), so that English has had more time there to become 'nativized' and 'domesticated'. Most of the other Nigerian scholars who feature in the list come from 'minority' groups. Nigerian English has attracted less interest from those whose mother tongue is Hausa or Igbo, Jibril being a notable exception.

It may be added that, as subsequent chapters reveal, the 'Nigerianness' of Nigerian English is by no means only a matter of necessary or desirable adaptation to the Nigerian environment, to Nigerian culture, nor does it just reflect 'mother-tongue interference'; it has broader dimensions in which such adaptation is not easy to identify. There are abundant signs of the creative, spontaneous use of English in ordinary, everyday discourse in Nigeria which lacks specific cultural references. To take one illustrative anecdote: at a university Senate meeting where the question of asking some outside figure to give an annual public lecture was being discussed, one senator's objection to a certain name was: 'Remember that he is very old, and at that age anything can happen'. The remark provoked spontaneous laughter, and the fact that it did so surely demonstrates that English has been established for so long in Nigeria that its mature users have a keen responsiveness to figures of speech such as euphemism.

1.5.2 Errors and variants

Discussion of errors cannot be avoided in discussion of Nigerian English, and *a fortiori*, one might say, of any outer circle or expanding circle variety. For some 'rejecters' the matter is simple: any linguistic form that is not acceptable in Standard British English is an error, and should be corrected. In contrast, and in line with much contemporary thinking, some 'accepters' seem to play down the gravity of errors (e.g. Bamgbose 1998).

For many 'accepters', however, it is essential in a description of 'Nigerianisms' to distinguish between 'errors' and 'variants', with the implication that the latter are 'legitimate' and so potentially or already acceptable. The distinction was made in the early days of the development of Nigerian English studies by Walsh (1967), who spoke of 'Nigerian English' (i.e. variants) and 'imperfect English' (i.e. errors). It has been maintained by, among others, Banjo (1996). Jowitt uses interlanguage theory (Selinker 1972, Corder 1981) to offer an explanation for the incidence of common English errors in Nigeria. According to this theory, such errors are 'fossilized', and the process of fossilization began in the past at an unspecifiable time (but see Chapter Five), in the usage first of individuals and subsequently in the wider society. Sometimes analogy is the strategy falsely adopted. *Barb* can thus be plausibly accounted for as a back-formation by analogy with *sing-singer*, etc.

Adegbite (2010) usefully discusses errors and variants in the usage of Nigerians in terms of acceptability, using 'features' as a neutral term in place of 'errors' and 'variants'. 'Pragmatic and creative' features are tolerated more than 'linguistic' features, he says, and among the latter 'lexico-semantic' and 'phonological' features are tolerated more than morphosyntactic features. Among phonological features, 'lapses pertaining to sound segments and syllables are... frowned upon more than lapses at the stress and tonal levels'. Adegbite also asks: 'If ... a non-native speaker of English commits one or two lapses in a 15-minute speech or a writer commits such in a 20-page article, does that make the speaker/writer incompetent?'. He rightly implies that the answer is 'no'; but for some extreme rejecters it would be 'yes'.

The subject of the attitudes to grammatical errors adopted by Nigerian scholars from different points of view is taken up again in Chapter Three.

1.5.3 Sub-varieties

A major concern of several of the scholars referred to has been the identification of varieties within Nigerian English, i.e. of sub-varieties. It was perhaps more of a concern in earlier decades than more recently, for reasons suggested below. In addition, and again in line with worldwide trends, it seems that 'accepters' have felt more confident in asserting the autonomy of Nigerian English as a whole, and are therefore less interested in identifying sub-varieties.

1.5.3.1 The ethnic parameter

Several schemas of sub-varieties have been proposed over the years. Jowitt (1991) classifies them according to the parameters 'ethnic', 'educational', and 'linguistic', with 'occupational' as a possible extra. On the ethnic parameter, sub-varieties have been proposed that correlate with ethnic groups, and can be distinguished as 'Hausa English', 'Yoruba English', 'Igbo English', etc. Jibril (1979, 1982, 1986) is notable for this kind of differentiation, although he identifies and specifies just two such sub-varieties, 'Hausa English' and 'Southern English', and he is interested mainly in segmental phonology. More details are presented in the next chapter, but it is worth adding here that, to the extent that sub-varieties of Nigerian English have been differentiated according to the ethnic parameter, differentiating features have been identified almost exclusively in the area of phonetics and phonology, hardly at all in lexis and semantics, and not at all in morphology and syntax.

1.5.3.2 The educational parameter

The educational parameter has attracted more interest than the ethnic parameter. The first proposed schema was that of Brosnahan (1958), who identified 'levels' of usage, albeit in southern Nigeria only, and correlated them with educational attainment. Pidgin features in the schema as Level I and is said to be the English of those with no formal education, while the three higher levels, II, III, and IV, correlate with those who have completed primary, secondary, and tertiary education respectively. Since Pidgin has increasingly been recognized as a language in its own right, only Levels II–IV of Brosnahan's schema are relevant to an analysis of Nigerian English. It is worth adding that, whereas in his day the great majority of Nigerian users of English had not progressed beyond primary school, so that their English could be categorized as 'Level II', sixty years later, with thousands of graduates now being produced, not to talk of those who have undergone secondary education only, the picture is very different.

Banjo (1971) sought to categorize varieties (sub-varieties) of spoken Nigerian English, and used a parameter which can be called linguistic, since in its phonology, syntax and semantics each of his four varieties marked off a certain 'distance' from the British Standard; however, each was also correlated with educational attainment. Variety IV was the least distant from this Standard, Variety I the most. A major concern of Banjo's in this analysis was, like Odumuh's, prescriptive: to identify the variety which could serve as the model in the teaching of English. The choice really lay between Variety III and Variety IV, but in Banjo's view Variety IV, used by Nigerians who had studied in Britain, sounded unnatural in Nigeria and was therefore unsuitable. As pointed out above, he wanted to identify a variety of Nigerian English that was both acceptable within Nigeria and intelligible internationally, and it was only Variety III that could fulfil these roles and also serve as a classroom model.

Adesanoye (1973), using an extensive corpus of written texts, proposed three 'varieties' and correlated them with occupations: Variety 3 users were superior judges, senior civil servants, academics, and newspaper editors; Variety 2 users included magistrates and some journalists (i.e. not of editor rank); Variety 1 users were low-grade workers. Yet this 'occupational' schema turns out to be indistinguishable from an educational one, since in Nigeria, as elsewhere, the kind of occupation one succeeds in obtaining (if any) is fundamentally determined by the level of education one has attained. Thus the occupational groups constituting Adesanoye's Variety 3 users also constituted the class of graduates.

Three was now established as the number of Nigerian English sub-varieties requiring to be recognized, and it is surely significant that in the 1970s and subsequently the model of a triad of 'lects' (basilect, mesolect, acrolect), which Bickerton (1975) had used to characterize 'post-Creole' English usage in the Caribbean, became influential in New English studies. Bamgbose (1982) endorsed this tripartite categorization, and at the same time fused the schemas earlier proposed: thus his 'Variety 3', the acrolect, represents the Variety 3 of Adesanoye, the Variety III of Banjo, and the Level IV of Brosnahan, and perhaps, for clarity's sake, could be labelled 'neo-Variety 3'. Bamgbose also – and unexceptionably – identified the new Variety 3 as 'Standard' Nigerian English and also as 'Educated' Nigerian English, two expressions which henceforth featured prominently in Nigerian English studies; and he gave numerous phonological, syntactic, and lexical examples.

This updated tripartite schema represented the orthodox approach to Nigerian English sub-varieties for many years. A lect-based triad is used by Ugorji (2010). Udofot (2004), however, proposed a fresh kind of triad: 'Non-Standard' (Variety One), 'Standard' (Variety Two), and 'Sophisticated' (Variety Three). Each variety was associated with a group of exponents, defined according to the degree of formal education in English, and with phonological features. Exponents of the 'Sophisticated' variety included lecturers or graduates in English or Linguistics, who would have had the benefit of undergoing some formal training in English pronunciation, or persons who had 'lived in mother tongue areas'; among its phonological features were the ability to make all phonemic distinctions (in effect meaning those of British or American English) and the 'flexible' use of intonation.

The specifications that Udofot gives for her 'Sophisticated' variety are actually more like those for Banjo's Variety IV, which he rejected as a possible Standard. Its exponents clearly constitute a tiny percentage of the speakers of English in Nigeria. Therefore it seems hardly to need recognition at all among the sub-varieties. Of Udofot's triad we would then be left with two varieties, Standard and Non-Standard, to represent the English that most Nigerians speak. These two could be related to the Banjo-Bamgbose Varieties 1, 2, and 3 (which means that their Variety 2 would correspond to either Udofot's 'Non-Standard' or to her 'Standard', or to both).

Two varieties is in effect the proposal of Odumuh (1986). He actually mentions three, but one of them is Pidgin, which can be discounted. The two that remain are designated 'Nigerian English' ('NE') and 'Non-Standard Nigerian English' (NSNE) respectively; his 'Nigerian English' is thus 'Standard Nigerian English'.

1.5.3.3 A critique of the educational parameter

Jowitt in several publications (1991, 2007a, 2008, 2015) has pointed out that the various proposals for identifying and differentiating educational or developmental sub-varieties encounter several objections. These have also been recognized by Banjo (1971, 1996).

Fundamentally there is a logical problem, arising out of the tension between defining a set of linguistic features on the one hand, and defining a social group on the other who are exponents of the set of linguistic features. The former is a relatively simple task, but the latter is much harder. Thus while 'educated Nigerian English' can be taken to mean 'the English of educated Nigerians', it is not clear whether or not Nigerian undergraduates today generally count as being 'educated'. (A common view today is that an educated Nigerian is one who holds at least a first degree or its equivalent. In contrast, in the past, at the time of independence, for example, someone who was 'Standard Six' – i.e. held only a primary-school-leaving certificate – could count as being educated because he or she was likely to be able to read and write adequately.)

Even if this fuzziness were overcome, a problem would remain: the ambiguity not only of 'educated Nigerian English', but also of 'Standard Nigerian English'. Each may refer to the defined set of linguistic features, or to the usage, whatever it may be, of the defined social group. If the latter is meant, then most certainly we would find so many cases of what elsewhere is called 'divided usage' that it would be difficult to claim that a particular social group is characterized by a certain set of linguistic features. An approach which sought to regard as 'Standard' just that usage characteristic of graduates in formal contexts would encounter the same problem, since there is usage which is used by some graduates in some formal contexts but would not be used by other graduates in the same contexts. Examples of usage which some would consider to be too informal appear in Chapter Four, section 4.4. The problem is complicated by the fact that there is not a simple dichotomy between features which are 'accepted and not used' and others which are 'not accepted and not used': between them is another category, those which are 'not accepted, but used'. In any variety, moreover, there is a difference between features that are 'Standard and formal' and features that are 'Standard and informal'.

To take one example, already mentioned, *I'm going to barb my hair* is an utterance frequently heard in Nigeria where British or American English would say *I'm going to get my hair cut*. It entered the literature with Bamgbose (1971), and it features under the headword *barb* in Adegbite et al. (2014). There is no established procedure, however – except consultation of the 'exonormative' standard – by which we can confidently 'assign' it to the 'less educated' ('non-Standard') sub-variety or the 'more educated' ('Standard') sub-variety. If it is labelled a 'non-Standard' form, it is undeniable that it is used by a considerable number of more educated people, by graduates, even if they would not accept it as 'Standard'.

Another example, very familiar to any student of Nigerian English, is *'I'm coming'*, which as a complete statement usually means "I am going away but will not be away long" and is clearly a translation from L1s (cf. Hau. *Ina zuwa*, Igb. *Ana m abia*, Yor. *Mo mbọ*). Jowitt (1991) says that it breaks no grammatical rules, and its meaning could be regarded as a useful addition to the meanings of *come*, since it concisely expresses what in Standard English requires more words. Eyisi (2003), on the other hand, treats it as an error, 'a sheer semantic blunder'. Accepted or not, it is widely used at all levels of Nigerian society.

Where pronunciation is concerned, Udofot's data (2004) also illustrate the problem. She suggests that the 'ability to make all phonemic distinctions' is associated with the class of graduates. We are likely to find that if we take exponents from the class of undergraduates and another from the class of graduates, some exponents from either class realize the TRAP vowel as [æ] and the BATH vowel as [ɑː]; let us call them sub-group A. However, some from either class – sub-group B – will realize the vowels as [a] and [ɑː] respectively, some others – sub-group C – as [a] and [aː] respectively, and some others – sub-group D – will realize both vowels as [a]. Moreover, different realizations will be found in the usage of one individual, even in a single stretch of discourse. The conclusion must be that the sub-varieties are not discrete, and they are not stable.

It is plausible to suggest here that, with regard to any given linguistic item about which there is a division of usage or a division of opinion among Nigerians, two standardizing forces are at work: one pulling in the direction of the existing 'Standard' (which turns out to be still the same as the 'exonormative' British or American Standard), the other pulling in the direction of a developing, distinctively Nigerian 'standard'.

1.5.3.4 Conclusion: acrolectal and non-acrolectal levels

One conclusion that the preceding discussion leads to is that even to propose just two sub-varieties of Nigerian English is problematic, not to talk of more than two. The truth is that there is a lectal continuum rather than a set of discrete lects or varieties. Nevertheless, it would surely be intellectual cowardice, and would represent a disservice to Nigeria, if no attempt were made to distinguish

between the English of relatively more educated and that of relatively less educated persons in Nigeria. For this reason, the somewhat cumbersome expressions 'acrolectal' and 'non-acrolectal' are in this book subsequently much used.
They will be applied in the areas of phonology, morphosyntax, and lexis alike.
'Acrolectal' is equivalent to 'more educated' and 'non-acrolectal' to 'less educated'; and 'non-acrolectal' arises out of the desirability of fusing the Nigerian
English basilect and mesolect which, as argued by Jowitt (2015), is suggested by
the lect-based model of Ugorji (2010) (for details, see Chapter Two). 'Level' (as in
'acrolectal level' and 'non-acrolectal level') is also used in place of the problematic 'variety' and 'sub-variety', and obviously implies that differences in English
usage among Nigerians (where they are not differentiated according to the ethnic
parameter) are considered to be chiefly conditioned by level of education. The
attribution subsequently of a Nigerian English expression to this or that 'level' is
of course impressionistic. It is bound to be so, unless for purposes of research a
corpus of texts almost unimaginably large is brought into existence.

1.5.4 The influence of American English

While many Nigerian scholars have been busy seeking to identify and specify
Standard Nigerian English, the actual operative Standard remains the British
Standard, as it has been since colonial times. One obvious indication is the fact
that most English dictionaries used in Nigeria are ones based on this Standard,
with the *Oxford Advanced Learners'* topping the list. Nevertheless, it has been
claimed, sometimes as a matter of concern, that American English has had a
growing impact on Nigerian usage (Adetugbo and Awonusi 1982; Awonusi 1994;
Kolawole 2004; Kperogi 2015). The reasons for this influence are fairly obvious:
the model presented in the past by American teachers of English; the influence of
American films, especially today those viewed on television; the fact that numerous educated Nigerians have spent long periods in North America. A few common
examples are the realization in speech by some Nigerians of 'o' as [ɑ] in such
words as *God*, and of post-vocalic 'r' as [r] in words such as *Lord*; the use of *gotten*
as the past participle of *get*; the use of *–or* in the spelling of words where British
English has *–our*. Other examples from morphosyntax are given in Chapter Three.

Some Nigerians today are not aware of the differences between these two
Standard varieties. Thus Umar (2015) administered a test of lexical items to
seventy students of English at the University of Maiduguri, who were asked to
identify which of the two the items belonged to: she found that the majority of
them could not make correct identifications.

1.5.5 West African Englishes

Geography and history combine to make it appropriate to consider Cameroonian English, Nigerian English, Ghanaian English, Sierra Leonean English and Gambian English together as 'West African Englishes'. This is the title of a chapter by Omoniyi (2006) in a compendium of World Englishes, although on the whole Nigerian English is given disappointingly little attention in the book.

As Banjo (1996) points out, the expression 'West African English (WAE)' is capable of two interpretations. The first has just been presented: WAE is the aggregation of all the national varieties. The other is that the varieties are treated as dialects of one WAE variety. This 'unitive' approach is found in, for example, Trudgill and Hannah (2008), which lists a number of features of the phonology, grammar, and lexis of 'West African English' in the few pages devoted to the subject. The specifications can be misleading, however: thus it is suggested that /apʊl/ is the 'West African' pronunciation of *apple*; but, to consider just Nigeria, although in Nigeria the introduction of /ʊ/ in some syllabic consonants marks out Yoruba speakers of English, as Akinjobi (2009) shows, it is not a general Nigerian characteristic. *Rice water* is listed in Trudgill and Hannah as an example of 'West African' lexis, and is defined as "rice porridge"; but this is an item of Ghanaian but not of Nigerian cuisine.

In their comparison of lexical items in Nigerian English and Cameroonian English, Wolf and Igboanusi (2003) maintain, as does Wolf (2010), that 'the commonalties are small compared to the differences', and that their study 'lends support to viewing the different national varieties of West African English in their own right'. Ultimately, political considerations decide such an issue: surely so when, for example, Canadian English is distinguished from US English. Nevertheless, 'politics' could work towards either 'unity' or 'diversity'. There exists some strong sentiment in West African countries – found in francophone as well as anglophone countries – in favour of regional cooperation; but on the whole greater emphasis is given today to the recognition and expression of national identities, in language and in other contexts.

1.5.6 Nigerian English research

The present century has witnessed certain important developments in research into Nigerian English and other varieties of English around the world.

One criticism that has been made of the work done on Nigerian English in the past is that it merely recycled existing findings, or the data used were 'impressionistic', resulting from the writer's own observations and judgments. Many studies, nevertheless, were truly data-based. The data were sometimes supplied by a mini-corpus of written texts (such as students' essays or newspaper articles) or, in the case of phonology, by a mini-corpus of recordings of speakers, usually reading prepared texts.

Even with the arrival of bigger data-bases, and so of electronic corpora as a major aid to language researchers worldwide, this kind of resource did not quickly become available to researchers into Nigerian English. It was in 1995, under the inspiration of the late Sidney Greenbaum and the direction of Ayo Banjo and Funso Akere, that work to produce a Nigerian component of the International Corpus of English (ICE) began; but adequate funding was unavailable for many years.

Thanks to the efforts of Ulrike Gut and her colleagues at the University of Augsburg and later at the University of Münster, with the support of Nigerian scholars at universities in the South, ICE-Nigeria was at last released in 2013. An introduction to it was provided for the benefit of Nigerian researchers by Gut (2012). It has some limitations, especially the fact that its approximately one million words express mainly 'educated' and so 'acrolectal' usage, when so much of what is distinctively Nigerian in the use of English by Nigerians is found at 'lower' 'levels'. A disproportionate number of the contributing speakers and writers come from the South. But there is a fair prospect that ICE-Nigeria, and other corpora such as the Brigham Young University Corpus of Global Web-Based English (GloWbE) (Davies 2013; Davies and Fuchs 2015), will transform Nigerian English studies in the years ahead. Some studies based on ICE-Nigeria have already been published (Fuchs, Gut and Soneye 2013; Gut and Fuchs 2013; Werner and Fuchs 2016), and some of their findings are presented in later chapters. The corpus is also subsequently used to provide examples of various usages and to suggest their frequency of occurrence. 'The corpus' refers henceforth to the ICE-Nigeria corpus.

Another important tool that has become available in comparatively recent times to researchers into Nigerian English is the *Electronic World Atlas of Varieties of English* (*e-WAVE*) (Kortmann and Lunkenheimer 2013); and a great part of its interest lies in the possibilities it opens up for cross-varietal comparisons. It assigns 'ratings' in 76 varieties for 235 features. These represent morphosyntax only, however, and for this reason *eWAVE* is given more attention in Chapter Three.

The nature of subjects for research into Nigerian English has also changed in recent decades. As the number of universities has grown, and in line with worldwide trends, Nigerian scholars have increasingly investigated relatively newer areas of language study, such as discourse analysis, women's language, pragmatics, stylistics, ESP and therefore registers such as those of politics, religion, the law, medical practice, the media, and so on; and typically texts produced by Nigerians are used as sources of data. Thus the general focus of study is Nigerian English in the broader sense. Particular areas of interest are the functions and status of English in Nigeria, the teaching and learning of English, and the language of literature, now usually studied against the background of literary stylistics.

The range of all these older and newer concerns is impressive, and can be regarded as a sign of the current sophistication of English Language studies in Nigeria today. It also perhaps reflects a diminished interest in describing the distinctive forms of Nigerian English. Significantly, of more than 280 presentations made in 2015 at the 31st Conference of the Nigeria English Studies Association (NESA), now renamed the English Scholars' Association of Nigeria (ESAN), not more than ten could be said to be clearly relevant to this issue.

2 Phonetics and Phonology

2.1 Some preliminaries

Serious study of the distinctive forms of spoken Nigerian English began as a response to classroom requirements, and to the difficulties of learners. Awareness of these grew in Nigeria in the 1950s and 1960s, as the number of secondary schools greatly increased and the first Nigerian universities and university departments of English took shape, but also reflecting the attention being given in contemporary linguistics and language teaching to the spoken language.

2.1.1 The phonologies of English and Nigerian languages compared

At that time, too, contrastive analysis (CA) was in vogue as a resource of potential use to teachers of English as a second or foreign language. The forms of the target language (TL), English, were contrasted with those of the learners' mother tongue (MT), and, on the assumption that MT forms influenced the production of TL forms, learners' difficulties could then be predicted, as a first step towards the overcoming of them. With regard to Nigerian MTs, Dunstan (1966) was an important early work of this kind, contrasting the sounds of the three major languages with those of English. More recently, with the increasing recognition and study of New Englishes, the continuing role of 'mother-tongue influence' in shaping the distinctiveness of a New English has been re-affirmed. Thus Schneider (2003) agrees that the phonology of such a variety contains features 'which in many cases linguists will be able to identify as transfer phenomena from the phonology of indigenous languages'.

Most discussion by Nigerians of 'the pronunciation of English' has hitherto assumed the existence of a permanent, static norm, which has almost universally been taken to be British 'Received Pronunciation' (RP). RP contains twenty vowel phonemes (or twenty-two if two phonemic triphthongs are added) and twenty-four consonants, while the General American (GA) system has sixteen vowels and the same number of consonants. In comparison with each of these major pronunciation varieties, every Nigerian language has a reduced set of vowels. Hausa has five monophthongs, or rather five pairs of monophthongs, each pair having short and long members with phonemic significance, and two diphthongs, making a total of twelve (Jibril 1982b); interestingly, too, in Hausa the short and long forms of /a/ account for nearly half of all vowel tokens. Yoruba has seven oral vowels and four nasal vowels, a total of eleven (Bamgbose 1965). Igbo has eight vowels, divided into two vowel-harmony sets. Where consonants are concerned, Hausa,

https://doi.org/10.1515/9781501504600-002

according to Sani (1989), has thirty-four phonemes, more than English, although Sani's list includes clusters of phonemic importance such as [kw] and [gw]. Igbo also has more consonants than English, some dialects having considerably more, as Emenanjo (2015) shows. Yoruba, however, has eighteen consonants, fewer than English. All three languages possess certain consonant phonemes which are absent from English.

Another major contrast is that Nigerian languages are tone languages, tone being of major importance for lexical differentiation, and to some extent also having grammatical functions; English on the other hand is an intonation language, tone extending over groups larger than the word and thus having various functions (grammatical, attitudinal, etc.). Nigerian languages possess tone, but they lack stress; English, in contrast, has stress but lacks (lexically significant) tone. The absence of stress in Nigerian languages also means that they contrast with English in terms of rhythm: if languages are given a position on a continuum between two polarities, 'stress-timed' and 'syllable-timed' (Dauer 1983), English tends to be more stress-timed, Nigerian languages more syllable-timed.

It is commonly assumed by students and teachers in Nigeria (and perhaps not only in Nigeria) that 'the pronunciation of English' refers to the 'correct' articulation of segmental sounds; formerly at least the prosodies or suprasegmentals – especially stress, rhythm, intonation – were neglected or ignored in the classroom. This could be explained as the practical outcome of syllabus provisions and time constraints: it has always seemed logical to teach the segmentals first, and often there is no time left to teach the suprasegmentals. Word-stress might be taught, but rhythm and intonation tend to be left out entirely. At the scholarly level, too, the study of the suprasegmentals of Nigerian English for some time lagged behind that of the segmentals. Since the 1980s, however, as the relevant section below indicates, increasing attention has been given to the suprasegmentals also.

2.1.2 Received Pronunciation (RP) as the norm in Nigeria: history and current attitudes

As the English pronunciation norm in Nigeria, RP continues to be given at least nominal public endorsement. It is used by the West African Examinations Council, by school syllabuses, by the English textbooks based on these, and by the materials used to teach English phonology at tertiary level.

The circumstances in which this situation came about, in Nigeria as in other parts of the former British Empire, are well-known. In colonial times RP was the typical native accent of the British-born senior officials of the government, and of officers in the Army and the police. Usually they came from the upper classes who ruled Britain itself, and had attended one of Britain's 'public' (independent) schools. 'Education officers', i.e. teachers in government secondary schools, often came from the same class, as did many Anglican missionaries and missionary teachers. Their RP accent was naturally passed on to the new Nigerian elite that emerged after the Second World War, and to some extent, especially in the North, as Jibril (2000) shows, it was deliberately inculcated in the Northern elite. Thus the accent came to enjoy the same prestige in Nigeria as in Britain itself. However, the once large number of British personnel employed in government steadily departed from the country before and after independence, and before long there ceased to be a sizeable number of British exponents of RP in the country. The original Nigerian exponents of it also began to die off. It is worth noting here that, unlike South Africa and parts of East Africa, Nigeria was never a country of white settlement, a fact which limits the applicability to Nigeria of Schneider's (2007) Dynamic Model (also see Chapter Six).

The desirability of retaining RP as the norm for Nigeria has been questioned, notably by Awonusi (2004), who rightly points out that the accent has lost prestige in Britain itself, that it has been undergoing certain changes, and that there are various types of it. Nigerians, like the rest of the world, have come to realize that the BBC has ceased to regard using the accent as an indispensable qualification for its newsreaders, and those who today view the BBC World News, for example, are exposed to a variety of accents of which RP is just one (Melchers and Shaw 2013).

Nevertheless, in Nigeria no suitable and agreed substitute for the RP model has been found. Some television and radio presenters in Nigeria continue to be trained to speak with this accent. Many of them do so, albeit with varying degrees of success and consistency. In the current absence of any RP-speaking social group, Adegbija (2004) and others have proposed that the accent of Nigerian Television Authority (NTA) newsreaders be regarded as expounding the desired endonormative standard. In the wider society, however, there is no great move to promote it, and it continues to be regarded as 'un-Nigerian'. Some younger Nigerians today derisively call English spoken with an RP-type accent *fone* ([fo.ne, L.H]), a word clearly derived from 'phonetics' (also see Chapter Four, under 'slang').

Apart from the special training given to newsreaders, it has for long been obvious that the ability of Nigerians to realize RP-type sounds increases according to the degree of formal education. Today, graduates are relatively more likely, and those with only primary education are relatively less likely to realize the full range of these sounds; and 'mother-tongue influence' (or 'transfer') is stronger at the 'lower', non-acrolectal level. Many other factors come into play, however, especially family background. Thus children from educated families might have acquired English before starting school and before learning any other language; and some might have RP-type sounds in their pronunciation.

2.2 Varieties of spoken English in Nigeria

Recognition of these differences in phonological proficiency inspired efforts to distinguish varieties of Nigerian English usage, as outlined in Chapter One. The Brosnahan (1958) and Banjo (1971) models are each primarily based on phonological data, as is that of Jibril (1979, 1982b, 1986). With data supplied by sixty informants, this is chiefly notable because, in contrast to Banjo, Jibril distinguishes 'Northern' from 'Southern' pronunciation. In the full-blown version of the model (Jibril 1982b, 1986) the 'Northern' accent has become the 'Hausa' accent, characteristic of what today are the states of the 'far' North. The 'Southern' accent is used by large numbers of non-Hausa Northerners, and features of it are also present in the speech of younger Hausas. Jibril then recognizes three influential pronunciation 'types' in Nigeria: RP is 'Type 1', 'Southern' is Type 2, and 'Hausa' Type 3. While admitting that differences exist within the 'Southern' type, he believes that these are less significant than the differences between Type 2 as a whole and Type 3.

Jibril at the same time incorporated a major educational or developmental dimension into his model. Each of the two local varieties, 'Hausa' and 'Southern', was to be viewed as a continuum of usage, between the polarities of 'Sophisticated' (or more educated) and 'Basic' (or less educated), Sophisticated Hausa and Sophisticated Southern being close to each other and also to RP. All these arguments are neatly captured in pictorial form as a triangle:

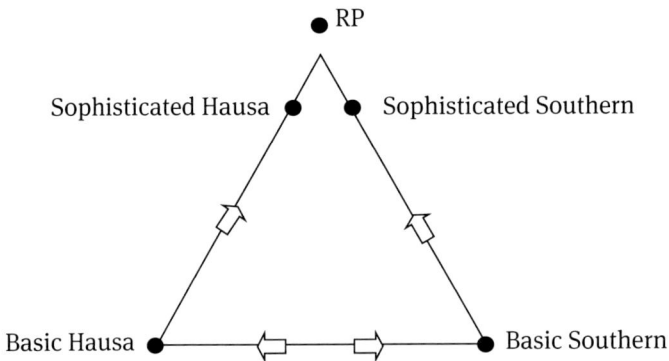

Figure 1: Jibril's model of varieties of Nigerian English

As with other models that emphasize the idea of a continuum of usage instead of discrete varieties, Jibril's model can be understood – correctly – to mean that features that might be expected to occur at the 'Basic' level might also occur at the 'Sophisticated' level, and vice versa. It also supports the thesis, presented in

Chapter One, of two standardizing forces in contention: one pulls in the direction of RP, the other in the direction of 'Basic' (Hausa or Southern). If we take one example of the operation of the model, the STRUT vowel is commonly realized as [a] in Basic Hausa and as [ɔ] in Basic Southern; but at the Sophisticated level of each variety, [ʌ] is more likely to be used in place of these Basic variants.

Jibril's work might have marked the beginning of an 'ethnic' or region-based differentiation of varieties of Nigerian English. However, as observed in Chapter One, little further work of this kind has been published. Some studies that have been published focus on the difficulties with English pronunciation of different groups. They include Ojarikre (2007), Essien (2011), Opanachi (2013), and Okunsebor (2015), which relate to Urhobo, Ibibio, Igala, and Esan speakers respectively. Anyagwa (2015) reasserts the importance of recognising ethnically-differentiated varieties; her work on suprasegmentals is also referred to below.

A more recent developmental model, rivalling Jibril's model in comprehensiveness, is that of Ugorji (2010). Adopting the familiar 'lectal' triad (basilect-mesolect-acrolect), Ugorji uses as a data-base recordings of 405 'educated' Nigerian informants, divides them into three groups (presumably on the basis of level of educational attainment), and treats the collective utterances of each group as representing one of the three lects. The informants are broadly representative of the ethnic composition of Nigeria, but Ugorji is not concerned with an 'ethnic' differentiation of varieties or lects. He specifies the vowel and consonant phonemes which occur in each lect, each having a most frequent variant and one or more less frequent variants. Thus, at the basilectal level /i:/ is the most frequent realization of the vowel of both *live* and *leave*, with /ɪ/ as a 'free variant', but at the mesolectal and acrolectal levels the two are in principle differentiated.

Reviewing the full range of such specifications, Jowitt (2015) points out that the basilect has seven monophthongs, the mesolect eight, and the acrolect twelve – the same number as RP. Complex vowels and consonants respectively follow the same kind of trend, towards identity in number with RP. Moreover, for each of these groups there is just a slight increase in number from the basilect to the mesolect, while the increase is much greater from the mesolect to the acrolect. This suggests that the basilect and the mesolect might be collapsed together.

Like so many Nigerian linguists, Ugorji is interested in possible prescription as well as description, since he wishes to identify which one, among the variants of a particular phoneme, should qualify for adoption in the phonology of an endonormative Standard Nigerian English. For this purpose he makes use of optimality theory (Kager 1999) and its hierarchy of evaluative parameters, which a particular sound either satisfies or violates. Thus in his discussion of the GOAT vowel, /o/ 'wins' over /əʊ/ (the RP variant) and over /ɒ/ (/ɔ/) because it satisfies all six parameters while the other two sounds violate three or four of them. This use of optimality theory with the aim of attempting to establish an endonormative Standard Nigerian English is a new departure and gives the model special interest.

Besides Jibril and Ugorji, a number of other scholars over the years have compiled inventories of the phonemes of Nigerian English, including Dunstan (1966), Eka (1985, 1987), Jowitt (1991), Banjo (1995), Simo Bobda (1995), Udofot (2004), Adetugbo (2004), Awonusi (2004), and Gut (2008). More than twelve such inventories (but not including those of Dunstan, Ugorji and Gut) are collectively analysed by Josiah and Babatunde (2011). Their paper needs handling with some care. More than once they label /ɜ:/ as 'mid-front', when it has always been regarded as a central vowel. In their list of the RP phonemes, /a:/ appears as representing the long, back, open BATH vowel; but /a:/ belongs to the older, Daniel Jones method of the transcription of RP, and today the Gimson-Cruttenden /ɑ:/ is rightly preferred.

Josiah and Babatunde are in the tradition of seeking to define a Standard variety of English that as a classroom model can replace RP. In their analysis of the various inventories of phonemes, they point out the 'disharmony' among these, and consider it unfortunate, since such an inventory purports to 'accurately describe the standard spoken English in Nigeria'. Some of the particular features of their own 'harmonized' model are that RP /i:/ and /ɪ/ are conflated to /ɪ/ (by which they surely mean /i/); /æ/ is replaced by /a/; /əʊ/ is replaced by /o/ or /ou/; and so on. The long, back, open RP /ɑ:/, appears not to be represented, unless /a/ is intended to do duty both for this and /æ/. In a number of cases a 'basic' vowel and several 'variants' are recognized – RP /ɜ:/ is replaced by four variants, for example – but in the view of the writers this is necessary so that the diversity of standard realizations of different phonemes in Nigeria can be taken into account. More controversial is that in the area of consonants /t/ and /d/ are proposed as 'basic' in place of RP /θ/ and /ð/ (surely intended in place of their indicated '/ŋ/'), a substitution stigmatized by more educated speakers; /θ/ and /ð/ are proposed as 'variants'. But these problems and mistakes apart, the recommendations generally make much sense, if a Standard Nigerian English phonology is not forever to be merely a replica of RP. In line with their recommendations, but working independently and utilizing the work of Ugorji (2010), Jowitt (2015) proposes that in a 'Nigerian Received Pronunciation' /o/ and /e/ should be 'officially' recognized in place of RP /əʊ/ and /eɪ/ respectively. Interestingly, [o] is specified as 'basic' or a 'variant' in seven out of the thirteen vowel inventories examined by Josiah and Babatunde; /ou/ is specified in four, but /o/ is clearly the 'winner'. It is also the realization of the GOAT vowel in several varieties of English around the world.

2.3 The Nigerian English Accent (NEA)

2.3.1 The NEA: segmental sounds

A 'working' descriptive review of the English phonemes as Nigerians realize them will now be presented. It represents the current collective understanding that emerges from the data found in the work of the various scholars mentioned above. In it, and in line with some current work (Awonusi 2004; Anyagwa 2015), the totality of Nigerian realizations of English sounds will be referred to as the Nigerian English Accent, NEA.

Like 'Nigerian English' itself, 'NEA' can be understood in both a wide sense and a narrow sense. In the wide sense it refers to all the commonly occurring phonological forms used by Nigerians in speaking English, and therefore including all the RP forms, since all of these feature in the speech of some Nigerians. In the narrow sense, primarily used here, it means Nigerian forms that differ from RP forms.

In line with the arguments presented towards the end of Chapter One, an attempt is made, inevitably impressionistic, to indicate the 'level' at which the use of a particular NEA form is common. As there stated, such levels, 'acrolectal' and 'non-acrolectal' are distinguished; and henceforth, in order to avoid constant repetition of these expressions, the symbols (+) and (–) are respectively used: (+) indicating the acrolectal level, or suggesting that the form in question is found in and is more characteristic of acrolectal speech; (–) indicating the non-acrolectal level, or suggesting that the form is more characteristic of non-acrolectal speech.

In support of the argument, now familiar in the discussion of World Englishes, that RP should cease to be taken as a benchmark for specifying the sounds found in other English accents, the lexical sets invented by Wells (1982), which are comparatively innocent of any built-in 'ideological' bias, are used in this review to specify the vowels. Comparisons with RP and also with the vowels of General American (GA) are nevertheless also included, since very detailed descriptions for these accents are available. The transcription system used is that of Gimson and Cruttenden (Cruttenden 2001). In line with the practice of Anyagwa (2015), and also with that of Jowitt (1991), 'NEA(Hau)', 'NEA(Yor)', and 'NEA(Igb) are used to refer to the distinctive English phonology of each of the three main ethnic groups (Hausa, Yoruba, Igbo). The names of other ethnic groups will be given in full when their distinctive English sounds deserve mention.

2.3.1.1 Vowels

1. FLEECE; and 2. KIT

The FLEECE vowel is a high, tense [i:] generally in NEA, as also in RP and GA; it also features in all the indigenous languages. The NEA(Yor) and NEA(Igb) realization is often shorter than in RP (–).

The KIT vowel, a lax [ɪ] in RP and GA, is frequently realized in NEA as [i] or [i:] but also not infrequently as [ɪ]. The tensing to [i:] may be the result of stressing. The vowel of suffix –*(l)y* is invariably tense, even with pluralization. Thus in 'broadcast talks'-1 (btal_1) of the corpus, the speaker discusses events of past decades, which are mentioned in turn as the *sixties … seventies … eighties*, etc., and in each case the final syllable is realized as [iz].

Ugorji (2010) suggests that the non-lax variants are more characteristic of (–) speech; but among many (+) speakers the two sounds are in free variation. The lack of observance of the distinction leads to common spelling confusions (–): of *live* and *leave*, *sit* and *seat*, *this* and *these*. Since realizing [ɪ] seems to be the fundamental difficulty, the tense-vowel member of each pair might be expected to occur more often; but, for example, **this books* also occurs in writing.

Where the length of vowels generally is concerned, Eka (1987) argues that NigE long vowels are often shorter than in RP; nevertheless, 'educated Nigerian speakers maintain length differences in English', and make phonemic distinctions between long ones and short ones.

Arguably, [ɪ] is more likely to occur in NEA (Hau) because Hausa has a phonemic distinction between short /i/ and long /i:/, and the short form is used as the KIT vowel and sometimes laxed. Igbo has a phonemic distinction between /i/ and /ị/, which are both high and front, but the second of the two, which Jowitt (1991) calls 'pharyngealized', has a retracted root position and narrow pharynx size (Emenanjo 2015), and is therefore different from [ɪ]. This may explain why NEA(Igb) speakers also often do not distinguish between [i:] and [ɪ]. Yoruba and several other languages (e.g. Edo) have only one vowel, /i/, in this region.

In RP and GA, /ɪ/ frequently occurs in 'unstressed' syllables, though not as frequently as [ə]. In NEA, especially NEA(Yor, Igb), spelling often determines the pronunciation: *market, wanted* are respectively [maket], [wanted]. The quasi-suffix –*age* of *garage, language, message*, etc. is often [edʒ] (RP and GA [ɪdʒ]); the –*ach* of *spinach* is usually [atʃ] or [adʒ].

One exceptional form is the [ʊ] used by some NEA(Igb) speakers in *been*, possibly influenced by Igbo *bụ*, which translates English existential *be*.

Some NEA(Igb) speakers further centralize [ɪ] so that it approaches [ə], as in *this* ([ðəs]).

Where [iː] occurs as the vowel of a stressed, word-final, open syllable, some NEA(Igb) speakers both shorten this and convert it to an Igbo-type [i̩], e.g. *three* ([θri̩]).

3. DRESS; and 4. FACE

The DRESS vowel, phonetically [ɛ] in RP and GA, is generally also [ɛ] in NEA, with [e] as a variant. In NEA(Yor), /e/ sometimes occurs (in 'Yes', for example), and the reason may lie in the fact that, although Yoruba has a phonemic distinction between /e/ and /ɛ/, represented orthographically by 'e' and 'ẹ' respectively, Yorubas when writing their language often ignore the diacritic of the latter; hence when an English word contains 'e' it may be assumed to represent either /e/ or /ɛ/.

Hausa lacks /ɛ/ but has a phonemic distinction between short /e/ and long /eː/, so that [e] tends to be used to realize the DRESS vowel and [eː] to realize the FACE vowel. At the same time, in NEA(Hau) the DRESS vowel may be realized as [a(ː)] (*recommend*, for example, may be pronounced [rakəmand]), which can be explained by the very high frequency of [a(ː)] and the low frequency of [e(ː)] in Hausa.

In Igbo, [ɛ] and [e] are allophones (both represented by orthographic 'e'; in NEA(Igb), [ɛ] is more common than [e] as the realization of the DRESS vowel.

Generally in NEA, speakers rarely use [ɛ] as the realization of the vowel of *says* and *said*, instead using the FACE vowel; this could be regarded as an example of spelling pronunciation.

Much has already been said about the FACE vowel in the last section. In RP and GA it is a centering diphthong, [eɪ]; in NEA it is variously a monophthongal [e] or a diphthongal [eɪ], with the incidence of the diphthong increasing among (+) speakers. Speakers who use [e] virtually conflate pairs such as *get-gate* and *let-late*; this can be heard in NEA(Hau) speech. Some (+) speakers, probably conscious of the difference between [e] and [eɪ] and aiming at an RP-type sound for the FACE vowel, prolong the second element of the diphthong, so that the sound becomes something like [ej].

NEA speakers (+, −) use [a] in a number of words where RP and GA usually have [eɪ], represented in spelling by 'a'. The words include the following: *Abel, Abraham, available, Cambridge, capable, cater, chamber, crayfish, data* (NEA is here close to the usual GA pronunciation), *fatal, fragrant, Jacob, label, laden, ladle, latent, nasal, naval, papal, patent, plagiarize, radiant, sacred, stabilize, stadium, status, vacant.* No convincing explanation has been offered for this phenomenon. 'Spelling pronunciation' seems the most plausible; but in many other words with the same kind of environment – e.g. *able* – [eɪ], not [a] is used.

5. TRAP

In NEA (+, –), and as in many parts of Africa, the TRAP vowel is a front, open [a]. It features in all indigenous languages. In RP and GA it is [æ], which does occur in some NEA(+) speech, if not consistently. It is perhaps rather more frequent in NEA(Hau), perhaps because [æ] occurs in Hausa as an allophone of [a]. Some older NEA(Hau) speakers make the TRAP vowel much closer, so that it resembles [ɛ], as in conservative RP. A plausible explanation is the influence of native speakers of RP who, as earlier noted, very deliberately many decades ago imparted their accent to members of the Northern elite; they would have been exponents of what today is regarded as a very conservative type of RP.

In NEA, [a] is a heavy-duty vowel, realizing not only the TRAP vowel but frequently also that of BATH (i.e. of RP *bath*), STRUT, NURSE, and LettER (and CommA). The [ɑ:] of RP *bath* is particularly liable to be fronted, shortened, and conflated with [a]; in spelling, as a result, pairs such as *match-march*, *pack-park*, and *impact-impart* are often confused, especially at (–) levels.

6. BATH

As just observed, the BATH vowel is generally [a] in NEA. In RP it is a back [ɑ:], and this is used by some (+) speakers; however, it is one of the RP vowels that sound unnatural or affected to many Nigerians and no doubt would feature in the specifications of Banjo's Variety IV. But perhaps recognizing the length of RP [ɑ:], many speakers (+) make an effort to distinguish the TRAP vowel from the BATH vowel, the latter being realized as [a:].

7. STRUT

The vowel of STRUT is realized variously in NEA as [ʌ] (as in RP and GA), [a], and [ɔ]. [ʌ] does not occur in Nigerian languages, is comparatively rare in NEA (–) speech, but becomes more frequent in (+) speech. The [a] realization is more characteristic of NEA(Hau) speakers, [ɔ] of NEA(Yor) and (Igb) speakers.

In RP and GA, [ʌ] is also present in a number of common words in which it is represented in spelling by 'ou', 'o', or 'oo' (*young, enough; one, other; blood, flood*, etc.). In NEA, the same strategy is adopted for these spellings as for the 'u' of *strut*, i.e. in NEA(Hau) the pronunciation is [a]; in other NEA varieties, [ɔ].

Some speakers use [aʊ] for the 'ou' of *country* and *southern*, no doubt following the model provided by *count* and *south* respectively.

As is well known, [ʌ] occurs in RP in many words where the spelling reflex is 'u' because of the lowering of [ʊ] a few centuries ago in England. Many NEA (+) speakers instead use [ʊ] in many words of this type when the vowel is stressed, such as *cucumber* ([kukʊmba]), *buffalo*, ([bʊfalo]), and *incumbent*.

8. CLOTH; and 9. THOUGHT

The CLOTH vowel is a rounded [ɔ] in NEA(Yor) and NEA(Igb), as in GA, and is therefore also close to the rather more open RP [ɒ]. It is realized very differently in NEA(Hau). Hausa lacks back, half-open vowels, but has the back, half-close pair /o/-/o:/; in much NEA(Hau) speech the CLOTH vowel is realized as [o]. Where orthographic 'a' represents the CLOTH vowel and this follows [w] in RP, NEA (+, –) often uses [a] (in, e.g., *dwarf, quality, squash, squat, swan, swallow, what*), presumably influenced by the spelling.

The THOUGHT vowel is [ɔ:] in NEA(Yor) and NEA(Igb). It is close to, but shorter, less rounded, and less tense than RP [ɔ:]; it is close to, but longer than GA [ɔ]. As it is the long counterpart of the NEA realization of the CLOTH vowel, it is often difficult to perceive that a distinction is being made between members of pairs such as *pot-port, shot- short*. The pair *other-order* make for an interesting spelling confusion, i.e. *other* is used in place of *order*, especially in the phrase *in order to...* This is common at (–) levels, where the two words are often pronounced [ɔda] and [ɔ(:)da] respectively, with just a slight lengthening of the vowel of the second word. Similar observations apply to NEA(Hau), where the THOUGHT vowel is realized as [o:].

It can thus be seen that in all NEA varieties the THOUGHT vowel is the long counterpart of the CLOTH vowel, though the quality of the vowel in both its forms is different in NEA(Hau) from what it is in NEA(Yor) and NEA(Igb).

In some words where this vowel is spelled 'au', e.g. *daughter*, some NEA(Hau) speakers use [aʊ], perhaps influenced by orthographic Hausa 'au' (/aʊ/); and generally in NEA [aʊ] is realized as the vowel of *laud(-able)* (perhaps by confusion with *loud*).

In *roar, hoarse* and other words where RP [ɔ:] has the spelling reflex 'oa', some NEA speakers produce a diphthong, [oa], which does not appear to feature in any other inventory of English sounds.

10. GOAT

The GOAT vowel, a diphthong in RP (today usually [əʊ]) and in GA ([ou] or [oʊ]), is commonly realized as a monophthongal, long, back [o:] in NEA (+ and -), although a diphthong, [ou], is also observed by some scholars (e.g. Eka 1985). The frequency of [o:] can be explained because it is salient in every Nigerian's auditory experience, featuring in all Nigerian languages. The RP diphthong is realized as a variant in some (+) speech (especially in the speech of persons consciously aiming at an RP accent), but, like [ɑ:] if not more so, it sounds affected to very many Nigerians (as to many non-RP speakers of British English); the GA type of diphthong sounds less so.

Since [o:] is also used by NEA(Hau) speakers as the realization of the THOUGHT vowel,such speakers tend to conflate members of pairs such as *boat-bought*, *flow-flaw*, etc. The contraction of *will not* to *won't* (with a diphthong, [wəʊnt] in RP, [woʊnt] in GA) could be expected to become [wont] in NEA; in fact, [wʊnt] is usually heard, and the pronunciation is almost the same as that of *wouldn't* [wʊdnt]. Linked to this phonological issue is a grammatical or lexical one: as discussed in Chapter Three, *will* and *would* often seem to be used interchangeably.

In several words NEA uses [o(:)] where RP has [ɒ] or [ɔ:], e.g. *follow* ([folo]), *glory* ([glori]), *story* ([stori]).

11. FOOT and 12. GOOSE

The FOOT vowel is sometimes [ʊ], as in RP and GA, but sometimes [u], especially in NEA(Hau) and (Yor) speech (e.g. *full* is [ful] rather than [fʊl]). Mother-tongue influence is the ready explanation: Yoruba has only one high, back vowel, /u/, while Hausa has the short-long distinction of /u/ and /u:/, which may be used to correspond to RP /ʊ/ and /u:/ respectively. In NEA(Igb) speech [ʊ] is the usual realization of the FOOT vowel, undoubtedly because Igbo has a distinction between /u/ and /ụ/ and the latter is almost identical to [ʊ].

The GOOSE vowel is generally realized as [u:], as in RP and GA, although it is somewhat shortened in NEA(Yor) and NEA(Igb).

A word example of conflation of the FOOT vowel with [u] is *input* (often [input] in NEA; RP and GA [ɪnpʊt]), and the NEA realization may even be [inpjut], suggesting a confusion with *impute*.

13. NURSE

This vowel has various realisations in NEA. The long, central RP and GA vowel, [ɜ:], does not exist in Nigerian languages, and for Nigerian speakers spelling tends to determine the realization, according to this table:

Table 2: Realization of the NURSE vowel

Spelling reflexes	word examples	NEA(Yor), NEA (Igb) realisation	NEA(Hau) realisation
-ir-	*sir, first, girl*	[a]	[a]
-er-, -ear-	*her, heard, earth, learn*	[a], [ɛ]	[a]
-ere	*were*	[a], [ɛ]	[a]
-ur-	*burn, turn, church*	[ɔ]	[a]
-or-	*work, world, worse*	[ɔ]	[a]
-our-	*courteous, journey*	[ɔ]	[a]
-eur	*amateur*	[(j)ua]	[(j)ua]

An RP-type realization of the NURSE vowel becomes more common in NEA(+) speech.

14. PRICE
The PRICE vowel is a diphthong, [ai] generally in NEA, almost as in General RP and in GA, with a fronted first element.

15. CHOICE
This is generally [ɔi] or [oi], almost as in RP and GA. However, some NEA(–) (Yor, Igb) speakers simplify the diphthong by introducing [j], so that *oil* may be heard as [ɔjil].

16. MOUTH
This is generally [au], almost as in less conservative RP and in GA. The more conservative RP [ɑʊ] is very seldom heard.

17. NEAR
NEA often realizes the NEAR vowel as a diphthong, [ia], which is close to RP [ɪə] but with characteristic opening of the second element (see no.22 below). Other realizations include [ie] (Eka and Udofot 1996). In certain words what probably represents a spelling pronunciation is used, for example, *zero* [zero] and *theory*, [θeori]. The vowel of the second syllable of *Nigeria* is realized as [i] in Jibril's Type 2 (hence *Nigeria* is [naidʒiria]), but sometimes as [a] in his Type 3.

18. SQUARE
In NEA(–) the SQUARE vowel, which is [ɛə] in RP, is conflated with another diphthong, [ia] (the NEA realization of no.17). Hence the pairs *tear* ('water coming from the eye')-*tear* ('rend'), *cheer-chair, fear-fair, steer-stair* are commonly conflated. At the (+) level [ɛa] is more likely to be heard. At all levels a reduction to [ɛ] is common, as in *Mary* ([mɛri]).

19. CURE
When final the CURE vowel, [ʊə] in RP, is generally realized as [ua]. In non-final positions it is often reduced to [u], as in *rural* (commonly [rural]), *Europe* ([jurɔp]).

20. POWER
The triphthong, [aʊə] or [ɑʊə], which occurs in some types of RP (not types which today would be considered 'affected'), is rarely heard in NEA. For the RP sound the glide from the first element to the second, and then from the second to the

third, is marked by a very slight movement of the lips; for the second element of the NEA sound there is a much more pronounced rounding of the lips, i.e. the second element is often consonantized to [w]. This produces [awa] (or [awə] in more (+) speech).

21. FIRE

Much the same kind of observation can be made about the FIRE vowel as about the POWER vowel. A triphthong, [aɪə], is rather rare in NEA; instead, the central element may be consonantized to [j], which produces [aja] or [ajə], or even [ajɔ], as in *iron*. This is more typical of Jibril's Type 2 speakers. Non-finally it may be reduced to [ai]; hence *Ireland* may be indistinguishable from *island*, as in 'broadcast discussions'-1 (bdis_01, speaker 1) in the corpus. Some Type 3 speakers (including non-Hausas in the North) reduce it to the diphthong [ɛə], becoming [ɛa], as in *entire* ([entɛə], [entɛa]). A more detailed discussion of triphthongs, with some reference to the Nigerian variants, is provided by Jowitt (2001).

22. LettER, commA

At issue here is the realization in NEA of the vowel which in RP and GA is a very short, central [ə], is the most frequent of all vowels, only occurs in 'unstressed' syllables, and is more frequent in such syllables than other vowels which can also occur there. This vowel does not feature in Nigerian languages, although some (for example, minority languages of Plateau State) have mid vowel phonemes that are close to it (such as /œ/and /ɤ/). In Hausa it can occur as an allophone of /a/, which probably explains why [ə] more often occurs in NEA(Hau) than in NEA(Yor) and NEA(Igb) speech.

In (−) speech, especially in NEA(Yor) and NEA(Igb), spelling often determines how the vowel is realized, as the following table shows:

Table 3: The realization of the LettER, commA vowel

Realization as	Word example	Pronunciation of word		
		in NEA		in RP
		(Yor, Igb)	(Hau)	
[a]	appeal	[api:l]	[api:l]	[əpi:l]
[e]	recent	[ri:sent]	[ri:sant]	[ri:sənt]
[ɔ]	actor	[aktɔ]	[akta], [akto]	[æktə]
[u]	bonus	[bonus]	[bonas]	[bəʊnəs]

As indicated, in NEA(–)(Hau), the vowel of the unstressed syllable in each of the examples in the table is quite likely to be [a], although in the -*or* suffix it may be [o].

In NEA (+) speech, [ə] occurs much more frequently, but it contends with the typically (–) realizations. In the spoken texts of the corpus, both [ə] and the corresponding 'unreduced' vowels seem to alternate freely and unpredictably, even in the speech of a single speaker.

Where –*ure* is unstressed and in current RP is pronounced [jə] (e.g. *failure*, [feɪljə]), some NEA speakers use [jua]. More precisely, this is a characteristic of NEA (Hau) speech; and it may have resulted from the modelling provided in the North decades ago by native speakers of what today would be considered highly conservative RP.

A summary of NEA realizations of English vowels is shown in these diagrams:

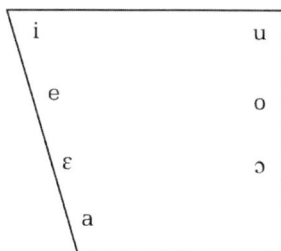

1. NEA (Igb, Yor) : Monophthongs   2. NEA (Hau) : Monophthongs

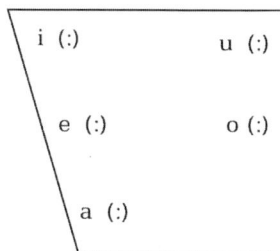

3. NEA : Diphthongs

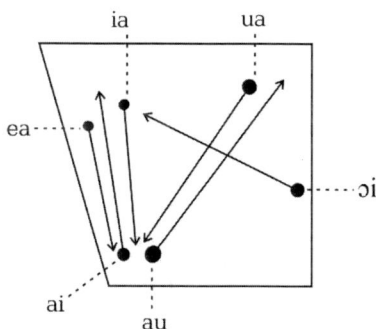

Figure 2: Vowel charts: Nigerian realization of English vowels

2.3.1.2 Consonants

The consonants of NEA are easier to specify than the vowels; hence each will be introduced by the usual IPA phoneme symbol.

1. /p/; 2. /b/

The voiceless bilabial stop is [p] in NEA as in other varieties. However, Hausa (and Kanuri) speakers may realize it alternatively as [f] or [ɸ], undoubtedly because these, along with [p], are allophones in their mother tongues of /p/ (or of /f/). Yoruba has no /p/; it does have /kp/, a doubly articulated voiceless plosive, but this does not seem to interfere with the realization of [p] in NEA(Yor). The voiced bilabial stop is [b] in NEA, as in other varieties.

3. /f/; 4. /v/

The voiceless labio-dental fricative is generally [f]; but see the remarks on no.1. The voiced labio-dental fricative is generally realized as [v]. However, /v/ is absent from the consonant system of Hausa and of Yoruba, and especially at (–) levels it is often realized differently. In NEA(Hau) [v] is often conflated with [b]; in NEA(Yor), with [f], which probably explains the confusion that may appear in spelling (*safe* and *save*; *belief(s)* and *believe(s)*).

5. /t/; 6. /d/

The voiceless alveolar stop is generally [t], although Igbo speakers may give a more dental colouring to it (i.e. [t̪]). There is a tendency among some speakers to adopt a spelling pronunciation for the past tense/participle –*ed*, i.e. to realize it as [d], which may account for the confusion in spelling (especially at the (–) level) of *ceased* and *seized*, which both become [si:zd], and for the general confusion of these two verbs. /d/ is generally [d].

7. /θ/; 8. /ð/

Many (–) speakers have difficulty with dental fricatives and the obvious reason is that these sounds do not exist in indigenous languages. The realizations differ, however, between Type 2 and Type 3 in Jibril's model: in NEA(Hau), i.e. Type 3, the tendency is to realize them as [s] and [z] respectively; in NEA (Yor, Igb), i.e. Type 2, as [t] and [d] respectively. More attention has been given to the latter in the literature, and the substitution of alveolar stops for dental fricatives often seems to be taken as one of the key indicators of a Nigerian English accent (and also of Pidgin speech). Yet, as shown above, it occurs among speakers from the more southerly parts of the country; moreover, it is severely stigmatized by (+) speakers and occurs relatively less often in their speech. Nevertheless, pairs such as *faith-fate* can be confused by more educated users (e.g. students), at least in writing, and deviant spellings such as *authomatic* can likewise be attributed to the confusion of /θ/ and /t/ (and, here, to the model presented by *author, authority*). The common misspellings *lenght* and *strenght* may be due to realizing /θ/ as [t], or they may be influenced by the occurrence of *-ght* in some quite frequently used words.

With regard to the voiced counterpart of /θ/, Okoro (2011) observes that for 'th' in the words *filthy*, *healthy*, and *wealthy* (but not in *filth*, etc.) some Nigerians use /ð/ instead of /θ/. A possible explanation is that the whole '-lth-' cluster is assumed to require intervocalic voicing.

9. /s/; 10. /z/

/s/ is realized as in RP and GA; but among certain speakers it also does duty for certain other consonantal sounds, as shown below. /z/ is generally realized as in RP and GA. However, certain indigenous languages do not possess /z/, notably Yoruba, Igala, Ibibio, and the tendency for speakers of those languages is to realize it in English as [s], the voiceless counterpart. This tendency is predictably more common at (–) levels.

11. /ʃ/; 12. /ʒ/

The voiceless palato-alveolar fricative is generally realized as in RP and GA, but it does not feature in some Yoruba dialects and other indigenous languages, and being close to /s/ it may be realized as [s]. Its voiced counterpart, no. 12, is a rare sound in English and does not exist in most Nigerian languages, although it does exist in some Igbo dialects. As the frequent misspelling of *occasion* as *occassion suggests, it is often replaced by [ʃ], or [dʒ], or [z].

13. /tʃ/; 14. /dʒ/

The voiceless palato-alveolar affricate is generally realized as in other varieties, but it does not feature in Yoruba, Igala, and other languages; in English, L1 speakers of these languages tend to conflate it with /ʃ/, producing [ʃɔʃ] for *church*, for example. The voiced counterpart, no.14, features in all three major Nigerian languages, and is realized as in RP and GA. However, it does not feature in some other Nigerian languages. At (–) levels, L1 Ibibio speakers may realize it as [j] (as in *major*, [me:jɔ]); Ijo speakers as [z].

15. /k/; 16. / g /

/k/ is realized as in other varieties, but NEA(–)(Hau) speakers labialize it (i.e. as [kʷ]) before the orthographic 'o' (itself realized as [a]) of the initial unstressed syllable in such words as *condition*, *committee*. No.16, / g /, is generally realized as in RP and GA. It does not feature in Ibibio, and at (–) levels x may in English words replace it with [k]. Where '-ng-' occurs medially in spelling, [g] may be inserted after [ŋ], as in *hanging*, [haŋgin].

17. /h/

It is widely realized as in RP and GA, as a syllable onset. However, many NEA(Y) speakers both delete [h] when it occurs in other varieties (as in *house*, [aus]) and insert it when it does not so occur (as in *eye*, [hai]). This was one of the findings of Awonusi (2007), and of Soneye and Gut (2012), whose data are drawn from the corpus. They also showed that a large and ethnically diverse number of their informants operated /h/-deletion, although while approximately 62% of Yorubas did so, only 38% of Igbos and 29% of Hausas did so. In certain cases, such as *hour, honour, vehicle*, the insertion of /h/ can be explained as due to spelling pronunciation, and it is also common among Nigerians of a variety of MT backgrounds. The name for the letter 'h', *aitch*, is generally in NEA pronounced [heitʃ] or [hetʃ].

18. /r/

NEA is generally non-rhotic, i.e. /r/ does not occur in syllable-coda, only in syllable-onset position. Among (+) speakers it is generally pronounced as in RP, i.e. as a post-alveolar frictionless continuant, [ɹ]. However, a lingual roll, [r], can be heard in the English speech of certain ethnic groups, notably minority groups in Northern states such as Plateau and Adamawa. A post-vocalic retroflex /r/ is not infrequently inserted by speakers who have presumably been influenced by GA, in some cases because educated by American missionaries. This consonant does not feature in some Nigerian languages, notably Tiv, Idoma, and Ebira, and in certain Igbo dialects; /r/ then tends to be conflated with /l/ in the English speech of the speakers concerned, although this is highly stigmatized by (+) speakers.

19. /l/

It is generally realized as in RP and GA, with the distribution of the allophones [l] and [ɫ] as found there, although sometimes "dark" 'l' ([ɫ]) is used in syllable-onset position and sometimes "clear" 'l' ([l]) is used before a consonant. In Urhobo there is no /l/; some speakers replace it in English words with /n/, e.g. *London*, [nɔndɔn]. Some remarks on 'syllabic' /l/ appear below.

20. /j/

The palatal semi-vowel is generally realized as in RP and GA. Some differences concern 'cluster' /j/, i.e. preceding RP /u:/ or /ʊə/. In (–) speech [j] is sometimes omitted, as in *fuel, furious*; at all levels [j] is usually inserted after liquids where RP has lost it, as in *blue, blew, flew, grew*, probably by analogy with *new, few*.

21. /w/

The voiced labio-velar semi-vowel is generally realized as in RP, GA. A notable variant is that some speakers use the voiceless [ʍ] in words spelled with an initial 'wh-', such as *why, when*, which has virtually disappeared from RP. There are two likely sources in NEA: (1) the continuing impact of the teaching of conservative RP to earlier Nigerian generations; (2) the earlier influence of Irish Catholic and Scottish Presbyterian missionaries, especially in the South-East and parts of the South-South (Akwa Ibom and Cross River States) respectively.

22. /m/
The labial nasal is realized as in other varieties. In NEA(Igb) it is sometimes protracted finally (as in *them*), perhaps owing to MT influence (Igbo having syllabic /m/ as in *Nye m*, 'Give me').

23. /n/
The alveolar nasal is realized as in other varieties.

24. /ŋ/
The velar nasal features as a phoneme in several Nigerian languages, and in Hausa as an allophone of /n/ finally; in Yoruba marginally as a realization in some dialects of the unemphatic pronoun *mi*. Its rarity in Yoruba probably accounts for a tendency in NEA(Yor) to conflate it with [n], or to delete it entirely and nasalize the preceding vowel. This may happen to [n] itself; hence *sin, seen*, and *sing* may all be realized as [sĩ].

Consonant clusters
English is famously rich in two- or three-consonant clusters, occurring both as syllable onsets and syllable codas, where a few four-consonant clusters are also found; and clusters also occur at junctures. In Nigerian languages, (C)V could be called the default syllable structure, in many languages there are no closed syllables at all, and clusters when they feature at all do so as onsets. The articulation of clusters is therefore one of the difficulties faced by a Nigerian learning the sounds of English. The natural tendency is to simplify, or rather to facilitate, by either insertion (epenthesis) or deletion, sometimes by substitution.

Insertion (e.g. [heləp] for *help*, [sitiriti] for *street*) is more highly stigmatized by (+) speakers than deletion, which itself is not a rare occurrence in (+) speech. The final consonant of a coda cluster is commonly deleted, a few examples being [kɔntak] for *contact* (deletion of the second consonant of a two-consonant cluster, common among certain speakers of Plateau State origin), and [atist] for *artists* and [advans] for *advanced* (deletion of the third consonant of a three-consonant cluster). The frequent omission of –*s* or -*d* in the writing of –*sts* noun plurals or the –*(e)d* of the past tense or participles may be an indication of the deletion of these morphemes in speech. Examples of the deletion of the first consonant of coda clusters are given by Akinjobi (2010): all of her fifty subjects deleted the /k/ of the /ks/ of the words *mixture* and *expected*. The simplification of onset clusters is less common, but even some (+) speakers, especially those whose mother tongues lack /kw/, have difficulty with words with an initial [kw] cluster, such as *equip* and *quarter*, which may be realized as [ikip] and [kɔta] respectively.

Substitution is also a less common tendency. One example is that *characteristics* is realized by some speakers as [karastaristiks], [st] presumably being easier to articulate than [kt].

Syllabic consonants

At phonetic level in RP, some consonant clusters result from the presence in a word of a syllabic consonant, /l/ or /n/, as in *table* [teɪbl], listen [lɪsn]; an epenthetic [ə] may precede this consonant, which thus ceases to be syllabic (Roach et al. 2006). In NEA, epenthesis is quite often operated (–), and other vowels may appear in this position, such as [u] or [e], so that *table* and *listen* may become [tebul] and [lisen] respectively. A prominent-sounding [a] is frequently inserted in the –*al* suffix, e.g. *legal* [legal], *national* [naʃɔnal]. It seems that [u]-insertion is particularly common in NEA(Y). An interesting study by Akinjobi (2009a) of 300 educated Yoruba speakers showed that the words *principle* and *principal* were realized differently and reflected the spelling, [u] being introduced before [l] in the first word, [a] in the second word; moreover, in some words the [l] was omitted.

2.3.1.3 Spelling pronunciation

Several examples have been given above of 'spelling pronunciation'. The hypothesis is that, where a word commonly has a pronunciation in NEA different from that of RP and GA, often this is because spelling has been used as a guide to the pronunciation; and that generally learners assume that English words are pronounced as they are spelled. This may mean that a particular grapheme is always associated with a particular phoneme. Though they may occur in educated usage, many spelling pronunciations are considered to be clearly erroneous by educated Nigerians, who look to the Standard dictionaries as the only reliable guide. The very common errors can be regarded as the result of fossilization.

In addition to the examples given above, the following is a list of common examples of spelling pronunciation, with one common NEA realization of the word (sometimes out of more than one possibility) also shown.

above, [abo:v] (+), i.e. the GOAT vowel, not the STRUT vowel is used. The "dictionary" pronunciation of – *ove* words in English is generally unpredictable. In other such words, NEA is in line with RP and GA, although as pointed out earlier, the STRUT vowel is widely realized as [ɔ] or [a].

architect, [a:tʃitekt] (+).

aren't, [arnt] (–). The 'r' is also realized as [r] in weren't (commonly [wernt]).

awe, [awe] (–); highly stigmatized by (+) speakers; and it is often cited by them jokingly as an example of spelling pronunciation (possibly because of its orthographic resemblance to an indigenous-language word).

brochure, [brokjua] (+, –).

cleanse, [kli:nz] (+, –). In some other words '-ea-' is realized as [i(:)], e.g. *peasant*, [pizant]; *weapon*, [wipɔn] (–).

climbing, [klaimb...]; 'b' is likewise realized as [b] in other derivatives of verbs where it occurs at the end of the verbal stem, e.g. *bombing*, *plumber* (+, –).

debt, [dɛbt] (–); 'b' is also realized as [b] in *subtle*.

favourite, [fevərait]; likewise, *elite* is frequently [ilait] (+, –).

fiery, [fiari] (–).

legal, [legal] (–).

leopard, [liopad] (–). The 'eo' of *Geoffrey*, *Leonard* is also thus realized.

listen, [list(e)n] (–). The 't' of a number of other words is also realized as [t] where it is 'silent' in RP and GA, e.g. *castle*, *epistle*, *fasten*, *whistle*. The pronunciation is highly stigmatized by (+) speakers.

mayor, [mejɔ] (+, –).

prayer, [preja] (+, –).

quay, [kwe] (–).

shepherd, [ʃefad] (–).

sword, [swɔd] (+,–).

tier, [taja] (+).

tortoise, [tɔtɔis] (–).

towel, [towel] (+,–).

vineyard, [vainja:d] (+,–).

Wednesday, [wednesde] (+,–).

In words containing [ð], orthographic 'th', and where 'th' is followed by '-es' or '-ed', this morpheme is sometimes realized as a separate syllable, e.g. *clothes*, [kloðez]; *breathed*, [briðed] (+,–).

Words which have been 'borrowed' into English from other languages, and which in RP and GA still retain features of their original pronunciation, are often more thoroughly 'anglicized' and given a spelling pronunciation by NEA speakers (+, –), for example:

apostrophe, [apɔstrɔf]. Likewise other words of Greek origin: *catastrophe*, [katastrɔf], *epitome*, [epito:m], *hyperbole*, [haipəbol], *psyche* [saik].
bona fide, [bona faid].
en masse, [en mas]. Likewise, *en route*, [en rut]; *en suite*, [en swit]. NEA eschews the use of the French nasal vowel [ã] in such expressions as used in English, as also in *genre*, often pronounced [dʒenri].
Jamaica, [dʒamaika].
Renaissance, [rənaisans].
Sophocles, [sofoklz]. Likewise other Greek proper names ending in '-cles'.
vitae, [vite, vitae]. It is commonly used thus in *curriculum vitae*.
Volkswagen, [vɔlkswadʒen].

2.3.2 The NEA: Suprasegmental sounds

As earlier remarked, the segmental sounds of Nigerian English were at first given more attention than the suprasegmentals or prosodies; the distinctiveness of Nigerian English phonology was associated with the former rather than the latter. Moreover, word-level stress attracted attention earlier than stress in connected speech, rhythm, and intonation. This sequence of focuses of interest is undoubtedly natural enough, especially in the description of the phonology of a New English.

Worth mentioning at the beginning of this section is the hypothesis that Nigerians speaking English tend to apply to English the pitch-level patterns of Nigerian languages, and so to treat English itself as a tonal language. The hypothesis was first advanced by Amayo (1980) and Jibril (1982), but it has been developed and tested experimentally by Udofot (2007) and Gussenhoven and Udofot (2010). It is argued that the relatively high pitch of the 'stressed' syllable(s) of a word when uttered in isolation or declaratively in native-speaker English is equated with the high pitch (or tone) (H) that may accompany a syllable in a word in a Nigerian language, while 'unstressed' syllables are equated with low pitch (L); moreover, like every word in a Nigerian language, every English word is assumed to have a fixed 'tonal' pattern of pitch levels. One interesting manifestation of the tendency is that, although a given English word, for example *knowledge*, thus has an inherent pattern (here, H.L), it sometimes has to function interrogatively instead of declaratively, as suggested in punctuation by *knowledge?*; but the inherent pattern will be maintained. A native speaker uttering *knowledge?* has more than one option, including H.LH and L.LH; but the Nigerian speaker is likely to always prefer the first of these options, in order to preserve the H of the first syllable.

2.3.2.1 Stress in simple words and compounds

(a) Simple words

'Stress' is used here as the well-established term used to refer to what is really a cluster of factors that collectively serve to define 'accent' or 'prominence' and include, along with 'stress' (or 'force' or 'volume') itself, pitch, length, and vowel quality. In English words uttered in isolation, a 'stressed' syllable normally has greater volume, is higher in pitch, is longer, and has full vowel quality. Stress is nevertheless relative, and phoneticians differ as to the number of different levels or degrees of stress that need to be recognized in English. Cruttenden (1997) recognizes primary, secondary, tertiary, and 'unstressed' levels.

In the teaching of English sounds at a relatively advanced level it seems unfortunate that at least secondary stress should not be recognized, in addition to primary stress. In Nigeria, the teaching of stress usually confines itself to presenting two levels, 'stressed' and 'unstressed'. Learners are encouraged to identify the 'stressed' syllable in any particular word, when what is really meant is the syllable carrying primary stress.

This lack of recognition of degrees of stress other than primary is reflected in the work of scholars. The first published work to give major attention to Nigerian English stress placement was Kujore (1985), and differences between RP and Nigerian English in primary-stress placement take up one large section of the book. His presentation of data chiefly takes the form of a long list of words, with capital letters used to indicate the 'stressed' syllable in each case; here, a prime (′) placed before the relevant syllable is used.

Concentration on primary stress is also found in Jowitt (1991). His more analytical approach attempts a grouping of data into these categories:

(1) Disyllabic words or compounds. In certain words where RP has the stress on the first syllable, NEA places it on the second (e.g. *cha'llenge*, *ma'dam*, *fire'wood*).

(2) Single words of more than two syllables, which fall into several sub-groups:
   (i) verbs ending in the suffixes *–ate*, *-ize/-ise*, *-y*, or *–ish*, where in NEA the stress falls on the final syllable (e.g. *congratu'late*, *adver'tise*, *modi'fy*, *distin'guish*);
   (ii) *-ism* nouns, where in NEA the stress falls on the syllable preceding the suffix (e.g. *capi'talism*);
   (iii) 'medical trade names' (e.g. *aspi'rin*);
   (iv) 'other examples', including *agri'culture*, *An'thony*, *Eu'ropean*, *pre'ferable*.

(3) Compounds of more than two syllables (e.g. *sitting-'room*, *grammar 'school*).

Jowitt also points out, however, that Nigerians do not consistently place stress as indicated: thus *'Florence* and *Flo'rence* may variously be heard as realizations of this girl's name. The variation suggests that, as proposed in Chapter One, two standardizing forces are at work in Nigerian usage. Here, one pulls in the direction of RP (*'Florence*), the other in the direction of NEA (*Flo'rence*).

These early accounts of Nigerian English word-stress placement were largely descriptive, but Jowitt, like Kujore, hints at the possibility of a more 'explanatory' approach by remarking that what stands out from the data is 'delayed primary stress', i.e. the tendency in Nigerian English to place primary stress further to the right than is the case in RP. Such an approach is developed by Simo Bobda (2007, 2010), supported by experimental data. His work is a study of both Nigerian and anglophone Cameroonian usage.

Essentially, Simo Bobda suggests that, to cope with the complexity of English word-stress, speakers unconsciously employ strategies relating to various rules or constraints, and that the set of strategies employed by Nigerian and Cameroonian speakers on the one hand is somewhat different from that of native speakers on the other. The two sets of speakers share certain constraints, such as word class, syllable weight, and affix stress property, and they likewise share associated rules, such as 'move stress backward', especially to the antepenultimate syllable if there is one, and alternatively 'move stress forward'. These two rules compete with each other even in native-speaker usage (where on the whole there is a predilection for backward stress): thus in RP *'controversy* and *con'troversy* both occur. In addition, however, Nigerian and Cameroonian speakers have developed 'autonomous' strategies of their own, such as 'I-stress' and 'N-stress', the operation of which Simo Bobda appears to be the first to have suggested.

In either case – 'shared' strategies and 'autonomous' strategies – variant pronunciations result. This is to be expected where autonomous strategies are applied, but it also comes about where constraints are shared, because NEA may apply a different balance of constraints, and it may ignore exceptions. Thus the 'backward' rule produces NEA *'acute* and *'canoe*, and in these examples it prevails over the constraint by which many loan words retain their original stressing, here the final-syllable stress found in RP *a'cute* and *ca'noe*. The NEA application of the 'antepenultimate' version of the backward rule produces *'apparent*.

Backward stress in NEA can sometimes be explained as combining with and reinforcing (or being reinforced by) the 'noun-verb alternation constraint', i.e. the rule that says that in disyllabic noun-verb pairs nouns are stressed on the first syllable, verbs on the second. Hence in NEA *'distress*, *'exchange* and *'respect* are usually thus pronounced as nouns, while in RP they have the same stress as the corresponding verbs. Likewise, the nouns *'success* and *'applause* are usually pronounced thus in NEA, even though in their structure they differ somewhat from the corresponding verbs *succeed* and *applaud*. Another example is *'despite*, and here, as with some of the other examples, it is tempting to feel that in fact the two syllables are equally stressed, especially as high pitch is assigned to each. To Simo Bobda's examples could be added *comfort*: in RP backward stress is applied to both noun and verb, but in NEA the noun-verb alternation constraint is applied (noun – *'comfort*; verb – *com'fort*).

In NEA, the 'syllable weight constraint' may cause 'forward' stress to prevail over 'backward' stress. In effect this means that when a syllable is heavy (by containing a long vowel or diphthong, or a short vowel followed by a consonant cluster) it attracts stress. This is true of the –*ate*, -*ise*/-*ize*, and –*y* verbs that feature in the Kujore and Jowitt lists; Simo Bobda also mentions *an'cestor*, *ca'lendar* (where the final syllable is not heavy, but the penultimate is) and also *plan'tain* and *cha'llenge*. *Cha'llenge* is interesting since frequently the noun as well as the verb is given final-syllable stress.

Where Simo Bobda's 'affix property constraint' is concerned, NEA has the derivative *A'rabic* (in contrast to RP *'Arabic*), in accordance with the Standard rule by which the –*ic* affix causes stress to fall on the preceding syllable. The nominalizing suffix –*ism* behaves like –*ic* in NEA, producing *capi'talism*, *Catho'licism*, etc. In NEA, in contrast to RP, -*ative* becomes stress-bearing, as in *represen'tative*. In other derivatives the base bears stress, which is not altered by affixation or by the backward stress rule (e.g. NEA *pro'testant*). All these examples can be explained in terms of a preference for forward stress over backward stress, and this is also found in the stressing of many personal names (e.g. *Chris'topher* and *Mo'nica*; *Jo'nathan* is another example). Yet the –*ean* affix, which bears stress in RP (on the first of its two syllables), causes backward stress in NEA (*Eu'ropean*, *Ga'lilean* in addition to Simo Bobda's *Ca'ribbean*); possibly in NEA -*ean* is regarded as a one-syllable affix like –*ic* or -*ism*, causing a shift of stress in the base.

The 'autonomous' constraints developed by Nigerians and Cameroonians, according to Simo Bobda, include 'I-stress', i.e. the tendency to stress a final syllable containing /i(:)/ or /ɪ/, as in *bi'scuit* and *Israel'i,* to which *distin'guish* and *estab'lish* could be added; and 'N-stress', another constraint, which is reflected in the tendency to place stress on a final syllable containing coda /n/, as in *plan'tain*, *aspi'rin*, *bulle'tin*, and names such as *Jose'phine*. The 'final obstruent' constraint produces the rule that stress is placed on a final syllable with a coda obstruent, as in *bi'as*, *inter'pret*, *exhi'bit*.

The idea of 'constraints' to explain differences in stress placement between Nigerian English and British English is also developed by Omachonu (2011). His analysis is generally compatible with that of Simo Bobda, but fundamental to his work is his conscious use of Optimality Theory (OT), which, as mentioned above, Ugorji has also used and applied to the analysis of the English segmentals. In OT, constraints determine which one of several possible 'candidates' should be taken as the optimum phonological form, and constraints are themselves ranked in a hierarchy. Omachonu plausibly suggests that the two varieties concerned differ in their ranking of constraints and that different rankings result in different stress patterns. For example, a 'non-finality' constraint, which ranks high in the British English hierarchy, ensures that *'madam* is thus stressed in British English; in the Nigerian English hierarchy, on the other hand, an 'uneven iamb' constraint ranks higher than the non-finality constraint, and makes *ma'dam* more acceptable.

Little investigation has been carried out to determine whether or not Nigerians speaking English manifest any differences in the placement of word-stress that correlate with L1 or ethnicity. As observed by Atoye (2005), studies of Nigerian English stress placement have largely assumed homogeneity of usage across Nigeria. A study by Anyagwa (2015), however, referred to earlier, perhaps marks the beginning of the recognition of regional or ethnic differences in this area. Anyagwa suggests that there are significant differences between Yoruba speakers and Igbo speakers of English: thus in certain disyllabic words, such as *protein*, *schedule*, *crayon*, her Yoruba informants had a general preference for final-syllable stress, while the majority of Igbo speakers preferred penultimate stress (as in RP). Possibly the differences could be explained as differences in adhering to constraints. On the other hand, a number of words were stressed in the same way by both groups, including those with an *–ate*, *-ize*, or *–fy* suffix, the stress falling on the suffix itself, as has often been pointed out.

On the whole, and so despite the evidence for a preference for 'backward' stress in some words, it can be said that the studies carried out so far support the claim that Nigerian English has a tendency to prefer 'forward' stress. A convincing explanation of the reasons for it has yet to be offered. It is also difficult to see how the tendency might be related to the hypothesis, outlined above, that Nigerians at a certain level of learning treat English as a tonal language.

(b) Compounds

As pointed out above, in studies of Nigerian English it is the assignment of primary stress in simple words which has mainly received attention. Jowitt's analysis extends to compounds and phrases, but a more substantial study of compounds has been carried out by Sunday (2011), using fifty subjects and a native-speaker control. Some of the examples he uses actually seem to be phrases rather than compounds (e.g. *local government*), but the distinction between compounds and phrases is notoriously difficult to draw. More problematic are some of the findings. Thus for 'compounds' with two bases, such as *house-fly*, *mealtime*, *national anthem* and *gold medallist*, the claim is made that stress was given to the first base in 94.5% of cases. This seems counter-intuitive, and informal testing of other subjects, both Nigerian and British, showed a unanimous preference for giving the stress to, for example, the second base of *gold medallist*.

Part of the problem is that, as first pointed out by Amayo (1980), and as remarked above, in the understanding of Nigerians who have an explicit awareness of stress, this seems to be associated with high pitch. Hence because if in *gold medallist* the pitch of *gold* is made higher than that of *me-* (as often in RP), *gold* is assumed to have greater stress. In RP (but not in NEA) *gold* may in fact be uttered variously on a low pitch or a high pitch, but *me-* will always have the greater stress unless emphasis is given to *gold*, and if *me-* is uttered on a low pitch because a question is intended it will still have the greater stress.

The likelihood that higher pitch is assumed to be equivalent to greater stress was put to an informal test when some university students were asked to listen to three different pronunciations of *part time*, illustrated by the interlinear method of transcription as follows:

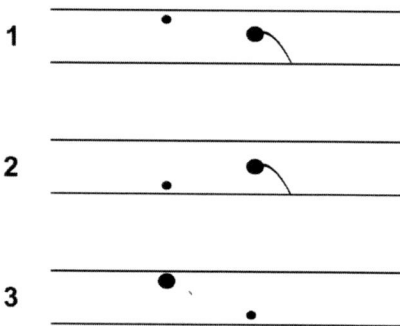

Figure 3: Three pronunciations of *part-time*

The students were certain that in 1, as well as in 3, the 'stress' was on *part* and that only in 2 was it on *time*.

2.3.2.2 Stress in connected speech

(a) Preliminaries

Stress in Nigerian English connected speech – in sentences as well as in phrases – has also received less attention than word-stress, and rather less than intonation. This is perhaps partly due to the complexity of the general subject-matter, to which the ambiguity in the word 'stress' itself contributes. This sentence as uttered in RP can serve as an illustration:

> She can speak Hausa better than I can

Are we to say that it contains four 'stressed' syllables (*speak, Hau-, bet-, I*), the concept of 'stress' actually representing four factors that contribute to 'accent' or 'prominence' (pitch, etc.); or are we to say that there are five 'stressed' syllables, because the second *can*, with its full vowel quality, also bears stress, albeit secondary stress? If the latter, our analysis becomes more delicate and more accurate, and to classify the syllables into a dichotomy of 'stressed ~ unstresed', 'strong ~ weak', begins to look too simple, as well as misleading. In connected speech, as in words and compounds, there are really degrees of stress or prominence.

Yet it makes sense to begin a brief analysis with this dichotomy. Using the noun phrase *the 'President of the 'Federal Re'public of Ni''geria* as an example, we find that it has the same stress patterning in NEA as in RP and GA. In each case, 'strongest' stress or 'end stress' (here indicated by a double prime, ") falls on the last stressed syllable of the phrase. Other such phrasal examples are *the 'value of 'human ''life, 'many 'married ''couples, Ah'madu 'Bello Uni''versity*. Sentence examples include:

> You are 'very ''welcome.
> I will be a'vailable 'next ''week.
> 'Thank you for your 'prayers and your en''couragement.

In contrast, there are several cases where RP and GA give the extra stress to a stressed syllable that is not the last, as in *''motor 'cycle, 'Water ''Management 'Board*. The names of Nigeria's states also receive non-final stress when uttered by RP and GA speakers: thus *''Kano 'State, ''Lagos 'State, 'Cross ''River 'State*. Hogg and McCully (1987), explain the apparent anomaly by suggesting that if, as in Chomsky and Halle (1968), there is a fundamental choice between compound stress and phrasal stress, many apparent phrases are treated as compounds.

Common NEA pronunciations of the examples given above are *'motor ''cycle* and *'Water 'Management ''Board*. (The RP/GA patterning is also heard, however, which again supports the 'contending forces' hypothesis.) For the names of states, NEA quite invariably gives extra stress to the last syllable: *'Kano ''State*, etc. Jowitt (1991) argues that the preference for end-stress in such phrases often harmonizes with the tonal pattern of the particular State name, when this belongs originally to a relevant indigenous language, and the pronunciation of the State name is not anglicized. Thus in *Ekiti State*, [ɛkiti ″stet], *Ekiti*, a Yoruba word, has low pitch throughout and no syllable is stressed more than any neighbouring syllable.

In sentences, NEA again prefers end-stress, as in

'Revenue 'dwindled and there was 'nothing we could 'do a″bout it.

Here, RP and GA would give the greatest amount of stress to *do*, unless some other word preceding *do* were to be stressed for emphasis (*nothing*, for example).

There are some exceptions to the rule that says that in Nigerian English connected speech function words are not stressed and are pronounced on a low pitch. One is that *who* as a relative pronoun as well as an interrogative pronoun is given stress and pronounced on a high pitch, as in

The 'man 'who 'told you 'that is ″lying.

The pitch of *who* here is moreover higher than that of *man*. Another exception is that sentence-initial conjunctions such as *If* and *When* often have very high pitch (perhaps especially when used by women).

(b) Emphatic and contrastive stress

Discussion of sentence stress naturally leads to the subject of emphatic and contrastive stress. What is striking about this for our purposes is that it hardly features in Nigerian English speech. Where RP and GA may place the sentence stress on any syllable for purposes of emphasis and contrast, NEA does not do so. Thus the example with which this section began is likely to be rendered in NEA as

She 'speaks 'Hausa 'better than 'I ″can.

In NEA, phonological means will here not be used to show a contrast of *I* with *She*. Another example is part of a Biblical text which in RP and GA is likely to be rendered

″My 'ways are 'not ″your 'ways.

Both *My* and *your* are here both marked for emphatic or contrastive stress. NEA would ignore the possibility of indicating the contrast phonologically, and the utterance would instead have the usual end-stress:

My 'ways are 'not your ″ways.

Jibril (1982b) shows that, while an English person uttering the sentence 'I didn't say he was guilty, I said he might be' would show a contrast between 'was' and 'might' by giving strong stress to each word, a Nigerian would read it 'in a neutral fashion, leaving the task of emphasis to the lexical meanings of the words'. Jibril adds that, generally, 'many of the effects that are achieved in English only or largely through the use of intonation are achieved instead by syntactic and lexical means in Nigerian English'. Regrettably no substantial corpus of data to support this important assertion has yet been made available.

In a few cases NEA does achieve emphasis by phonological means, by greater stress though not by a shift of stress. The utterance of the sentence *Every student must attend*, as it is sometimes heard, might be rendered orthographically thus:

E-e-e-very student must attend.

Here, emphasis on *Every*, i.e. on its first syllable, is achieved by higher pitch, greater force, and prolongation. *All* is often emphasized in the same way.

(c) Strong and weak forms
In RP and GA function words have two different pronunciations, 'strong' (or 'stressed') and 'weak' (or 'unstressed'): for example, *from* ([from] – strong; [frəm] – weak), or *can* ([kæn] – strong; [kən] – weak). The weak form is the one more often used in connected speech, the strong form being used for emphasis or in certain syntactic positions; and the weak form has the typical properties of unstressed syllables, especially vowel reduction.

In NEA, however, strong forms are generally preferred. This has been demonstrated in a study of educated Yoruba speakers by Akinjobi (2009b). Her principal general finding is that for each word most of the informants produced a strong form and few ever produced a weak form. For *from*, 94% of the informants produced the strong [frɔm]; for *at*, *us*, and *some* the percentage producing a strong form was in the range 80-90; the weak forms of *for*, *was*, and *must* were never produced. A strong form of *the* ([ði] or [di]) was produced by more than 75% before vowels and consonants alike, the weak form, [ðə], being used by 24% before consonants and 23% before vowels.

Certain comments on Akinjobi's study are in order. One is that the fact that some of her informants did produce weak forms suggests, once again, that two standardizing forces are in contention in Nigerian English. Another is that the fact that her informants usually made function words strong does not necessarily mean that they were giving 'stress' to such words, because the absence of vowel reduction is a property of secondary stress as well as of primary stress. In other words, if Akinjobi's informants were stressing more words than would be the case in RP, they were not stressing them equally.

Other observers (Udofot 2003; Gut 2005) have also argued that in Nigerian English connected speech more syllables are 'stressed' than in RP, and their findings suggest that this is true even if only high-pitched syllables are considered.

One reason for the greater number of stressed syllables in Nigerian English is that personal pronouns are stressed, and so have high pitch, when they follow prepositions. In a classic account of strong and weak forms in native-speaker English, such as Cruttenden (2001), pronouns are weak in this position, as they are elsewhere, e.g.

He re'fuses to "speak to her.

In NEA, however, preposition-complementing personal pronouns are stressed, and end-stress is also given to the pronoun if final. The above sentence would in NEA be rendered:

He re'fuses to 'speak to "her.

In RP and GA, the stress on *her* would be assumed to be emphatic – he refuses to speak to her, but he does not refuse to speak to other people.

The hypothesis that there is a tendency to treat English as a tonal language would explain why in NEA the stressing of words on a low pitch is not allowed. An example is as follows:

My ways are not your ways, says the Lord.

This is the same Biblical text as presented earlier, but now with the 'narrator's comment' *says the Lord* added. In RP and GA, the last stressed syllable also marked by high pitch would be *your*; *says* and *Lord* are stressed, but on a low pitch. In NEA, *says* and *Lord* are also stressed, but on a high pitch, and *Lord* also carries end-stress.

A problem for the hypothesis just referred to concerns *yes-no* questions. In Nigerian English, as in native-speaker English, but not in Nigerian languages, such a question is signalled by a rising tone (LH) on the last content word, as in

Are you sick?

This may seem to contravene the rule, according to the hypothesis, that content words have an inherent high pitch.

Many of the remarks made in this section are also relevant to the subject of intonation in Nigerian English, which is discussed later.

(d) Rhythm

The study of rhythm in spoken English presupposes the study of stress in connected speech. The rhythm of spoken Nigerian English has not been much studied; Udofot (1997) made it the principal focus of research for the first time.

Mainly some remarks are needed here about an issue of continuing interest, namely stress-timing vs. syllable-timing. At one time it was assumed that languages fall into one or the other of two categories: 'stress-timed' or 'syllable-timed'. English (i.e. certain varieties of native-speaker English including RP) was classified as a stress-timed language because in connected speech greater prominence is given to certain syllables (which are thus relatively 'strong') relative to those on either side of them (which are thus relatively 'weak'); hence an utterance is composed of sequences, each sentence, or foot, being in turn constituted by a strong syllable followed by zero, one, or more weak syllables. In contrast, Nigerian languages were classified as being syllable-timed because, it was argued, all syllables in an utterance are equally stressed. Equality of force and of length was the major basis for this claim, pitch not being a factor. It was then claimed that speakers of certain non-native varieties of English who have a 'syllable-timed' first language seek to impose the syllable-timed rhythm of this first language on English. Where Nigerian English is concerned, this view is reflected in the suggestion made by Eka (1985, 1987): Nigerian English rhythm could be better described as 'inelastic-timed', since whereas in RP or GA a number of syllables are crammed into the 'space' between two peaks, with consequent vowel reduction in each syllable, in Nigerian English such reduction is not operated. But Akinjobi (2006) argues that this alternative label is just a 'terminological switch'

Research (Dauer 1983, as mentioned in 2.1.1; Fuchs, 2016) has suggested, however, that on the parameter of 'timing', varieties of English cannot be neatly categorized as either 'stress-timed' or 'syllable-timed'; rather, there is a tendency in one direction (or conversely in the other), so that, for example, Indian English or Nigerian English is further removed than British English from the 'stress-timed' polarity. Only with this qualification would it then be legitimate to say that spoken Nigerian English is syllable-timed.

This more qualified view is in effect developed by Udofot (2002, 2003). She shows that in Nigerian English, as in RP, peaks of prominence occur in connected speech, but that the weak syllables of RP speech are in Nigerian English made stronger, without being made as strong as the 'strong' ones: thus there is a tendency towards stress-timing. On the other hand, utterances in which the aim of the speaker seems to be to make the syllables more equally timed can be heard in the speech even of some (+) speakers. One example relevant to Udofot's analysis is:

The police have arrested the four of them.

Here, the tendency is commonly (–) manifested in the lack of vowel reduction in the syllables *po-*, *have*, *-ted*, *of*, *them*, possibly on *ar-*, so that these syllables, along with *–lice*, *-res-*, and *four* are 'stressed'. But it is a secondary degree of stress: *–lice*, *-res-*, and *four* still have greater prominence. Moreover, the tendency does not also produce secondary stress on *The* and *the*.

The right conclusion seems to be that in Nigerian English 'syllable-timing' and 'stress-timing' are not binary opposites but, as suggested above, form a continuum; moreover it seems that, again, contending forces are in operation, the continuing influence of the exonormative standard being manifested in the tendency towards stress-timing observable particularly in (+) speech. Further experimental evidence for this conclusion is provided by Gut (2005). Comparing groups of speakers of British English, Nigerian English, Hausa, Igbo, and Yoruba respectively, she showed that the proportion of the total duration of vocalic intervals (i.e. the distance between one consonant and another) to the total duration of speech was higher for Nigerian English than for British English, but lower than for the Nigerian languages.

2.3.2.3 Intonation

As used to distinguish intonation languages from tone languages, intonation can be defined as the fluctuation of pitch (sometimes called a 'tune') that marks the whole course of a linguistic utterance and has semantic implications. The intonation system of RP and GA has the following principal elements:

1. An 'intonation unit' (or I-unit, I-group, etc.) may coincide with a sentence or part of a sentence (a clause or a phrase).
2. Its core, or 'nucleus' (Wells 2006), is the syllable that has the greatest degree of prominence in the unit.
3. Moreover, while the unit as a whole is marked by fluctuation of pitch, the pitch of this nuclear syllable itself changes: it will be a fall (HL), or a rise (LH), or a fall-rise (HLH), etc., and each of these is often referred to as a 'tone'. (This may seem confusing, since in 'tone languages' – but not in English – tone serves to distinguish lexical meaning. Also see 2.1.1.)
4. A falling or a rising tone is unidirectional or simple; a fall-rise or a rise-fall, bidirectional or complex.

5. In native-speaker usage, intonation has a variety of functions and meanings: syntactic, discoursal, attitudinal.
6. Cruttenden (1997) distinguishes 'abstract' meanings from 'local' meanings; thus the abstract meaning of any kind of rise (i.e. a rise or a fall-rise) is 'non-finality'. With these local, contextualized meanings, intonation becomes part of pragmatics.

Very little of the system which has just been outlined is explicitly taught in Nigerian schools, although some secondary-school textbooks attempt to teach understanding of the simple nuclei (or tones) and their uses. In the Oral English paper of the West African School Certificate English Language examination, intonation is currently not represented at all. (The paper is largely devoted to tests of segmental sounds and word-level stress placement; emphatic stress takes up one section.)

Scholars at one time gave little attention to the intonation of Nigerian English. Stevenson (1974) was an early but brief and general study. Tiffen (1974) showed that the problem of 'intelligibility', of Nigerians to native speakers and vice versa, lay principally in the area of the suprasegmentals, including intonation. Banjo (1976) made the observation, much quoted by Nigerian scholars, that the appropriate use of stress and intonation is "the final hurdle, which a vast majority of speakers of English as a foreign language never manage to cross".

As with stress, more work has been done on intonation in Nigerian English since about the mid-1980s. Studies include Eka (1985), Amayo (1986), Ufomata (1990), Jowitt (2000a, 2007b), Udofot (2002), Gut (2005), Atoye (2005), and Akinjobi and Oladipupo (2005). A consensus of views as to the principal features of Nigerian English intonation can be extracted from these studies taken together, as follows:
1. The great majority of tones used by Nigerians are unidirectional or simple (are either falls or rises). (Unsurprisingly, these constitute nearly all the subject-matter of Amayo 1986.)
2. Correspondingly, bidirectional or complex tones are rather rarely used, and almost exclusively the one that is used is the fall-rise.
3. The tones of Nigerian English speech have syntactic and discoursal functions, but not attitudinal functions.
4. A falling tune is invariably used for statements, wh- questions, and commands; a rising tune for yes-no questions.
5. The level or mid-drop tone is infrequently used.

Arguably, these features constitute a Nigerian English intonation system (Jowitt 2000a). As explicitly pointed out by some scholars, it is limited compared to that of RP or GA (Ufomata 1990). Its details are substantiated, or modified, in the work of particular researchers.

First, more attention has been given to production than to perception and interpretation. Where the latter is concerned, i.e. perception and interpretation, a comparatively recent study is that of Atoye (2005). He investigates in particular the ability to distinguish unit boundaries and the effect on meaning of boundary shifts. His 120 undergraduate informants listened to five pairs of sentences that were lexically identical but differed in intonational structure, and they were asked, first, to indicate whether they thought there was any difference between the two sentences in each pair; secondly to interpret each sentence. Interestingly, while the overall score reached 85.7% for the first test, it was only 25.7% for the second, and for some of the sentences scored individually it fell very low. It was very low for the sentence *He doesn't beat his wife because he loves her*, i.e. uttered as one I-unit and thus implying that the reason for his not beating his wife was other than love. In RP the meaning here would be conveyed by a 'spread' fall-rise on *loves her*.

Some important studies of production include those of Eka (1985) and Udofot (2002). Here, a major topic of interest has been the frequency of tones. Eka, who obtained data from sixty undergraduate informants in two Nigerian universities, found that of a total of 4,190 tone tokens used by them, 93.3% were simple and only 6.6% were complex (compared to 22% of the tokens used by the native-speaker control group). Udofot studied the frequency of tones in two different types of production (spoken prose, spontaneous speech), using sixty informants grouped according to the three Nigerian English varieties identified by her and discussed in Chapter One. For spoken prose, the percentage of falls was always above 70%, and for Variety 1 it rose to 85%; while the highest percentage of rises for any variety was 11.5%. Some surprising figures are that for spontaneous production the percentage of rises was 30.4 for Variety 2 and 24.3 for Variety 1, which suggests that when speaking spontaneously Nigerians of lesser education use this tone (which in native-speaker speech can sound more tentative but also more interactive) than the better-educated do.

Although Udofot's study produces some rather surprising results for the rise, the ICE-Nigeria corpus suggests that a fall, \ is often preferred to this tone where in native-speaker varieties a rise would be likely to occur, notably in pre-final subordinates. This in 'broadcast talks'-1 (btal_01) we find several instances:

> ...according to historical ac\counts, King Solomon loved many foreign \women. The more they suc\ceed, the higher their testosterone. The last time I \checked, ... dating remains an expensive \game.

Eka in his more extensive study also found that the incidence of tones correlated with syntactic structures: thus falls prevailed in final structures, i.e. in main clauses or final subordinates; rises, and sometimes fall-rises, in pre-final subordinates.

Predictably, given their infrequency in Nigerian English, complex tones have been little studied. Fall-rises actually accounted for 42% of the tones used in pre-final subordinates in Eka's study (in, for example, *As soon as this exercise is over, I shall go home*); but in the same study a fall-rise in a final structure was extremely rare. In Udofot's study, the fact that the percentage of fall-rises was 9.1 for Variety 2, more than for speakers of either of the other two varieties, is hard to explain.

A special study of the fall-rise tone was made by Jowitt (2007b). It explored perception, interpretation, and production, and data were obtained from twenty informants who underwent certain tests. In the first, they merely had to repeat a native-speaker's utterances, each of which contained a fall-rise. The second consisted of six two-part exchanges, the first part being a question to which each informant had to provide a response, and in native-speaker usage the intonation of this would be likely to contain a spread fall-rise. For example:

A. What do you think of my suit? B. The \colour's all /right.

- where the implication of B's response is that in B's view the colour of the suit was all right but other aspects were not. The 'success' rate for the first test was 69%; but for the second there was no spontaneous production of the fall-rise. In the third test, informants were asked to build a specific implication (e.g. a warning, a reproach) into their responses to a series of utterances by using a fall-rise; but the preference for a fall was sometimes more than 90%. In the fourth test, they had to choose the 'right' interpretation of a series of utterances that employed a fall-rise; but when they chose the 'right' one it may have been that contextual factors determined the choice.

In general, Jowitt's study confirms Eka's findings. In particular, it shows that a one-syllable fall-rise rarely occurs in a final structure in Nigerian English. It is not altogether unknown, and a common example given by Jowitt is that, when a speaker at a public function in Nigeria seeks to secure the attention of the audience, he or she often calls into the microphone 'Halᵛlo!', and the audience often responds with an imitative 'ᵛHi!'. Possibly, however, the fall-rise is used each time for comic effect.

The attitudes associated with the use of the fall-rise in British English include scorn, self-pity and self-dramatization; and Jowitt remarks in the conclusion of his study that Nigerian English is perhaps better off 'without such excessive emotional baggage packed into its intonational forms'.

With regard generally to the expression of attitudes, and as asserted above, intonation is not used in Nigerian English for this purpose. Ufomata (1990) is surely right to assert:

> The intonation system of this accent is .... restricted, in the sense that it is hardly used to convey extremes of emotion as in native accents.

She suggests that this can be explained by the fact that

> ...the use of English is very often restricted to official and social occasions, while people tend to use their mother tongue for private and personal matters.

The 'is very often' here contains a now perhaps controversial qualification; it could be replaced with 'tends to be'.

For any variety the study of the attitudes associated with intonation patterns is not an easy task; but given that human beings naturally do express their attitudes in their use of language, the ways in which they are so expressed deserve more investigation. This is one direction in which research in Nigerian English in particular might move.

3 Morphosyntax

3.1 Preliminaries

3.1.1 The neglect of morphosyntax

Descriptive studies of the morphosyntax of Nigerian English have been rather on the sparse side. Banjo (1995) observed that, by the time he was writing, less attention had been given to it than to phonology and to lexis. The descriptive survey of Bamgbose (1971) provides phonological and lexical but virtually no grammatical examples. More of such examples appear in Kujore (1985), but he treats 'variations' of grammar along with those of lexis, and his approach is partly pedagogical and also to some extent prescriptive. Jowitt (1991) has one chapter on 'syntax and morphology', compared to two on phonology, and it is shorter than the chapter on 'lexis and style'. The survey by Alo and Mesthrie (2008) largely confines itself to morphosyntax, and its approach is entirely descriptive; nevertheless, its references are to works published not later than 1995. None of these studies seeks to answer the question whether morphosyntactic variation in Nigerian English is related to ethnicity.

Although the dearth of studies in this area continued well into the present century, more substantial studies have begun to appear, especially with ICE-Nigeria now providing data.

3.1.2 The question of morphosyntactic errors

Reasons for this neglect of morphosyntax are not hard to find. As the latter sections of Chapter One showed, Nigerian English has been a matter of debate among Nigerians since the 1960s, but a great number of Nigerian scholars (Adesanoye, Amadiaogbe, Eyisi, Fakoya, Oji, etc.) and other pundits (such as the late newspaper columnist Bayo Oguntunase) have constantly argued that much common usage in the area of morphosyntax consists of erroneous forms, with the corollary that these are unacceptable and should not be dignified with the label 'variant'. Such scholars and writers are usually hostile to the concept of 'Nigerian English' as such.

Perhaps even the majority of those who are generally favourable to the recognition of Nigerian English maintain that, where morphosyntatic features are different from those of the exonormative standard, they are unacceptable; unlike lexical Nigerianisms they should not, in their view, be considered as potential signs of healthy adaptation of the English language to the Nigerian environment.

https://doi.org/10.1515/9781501504600-003

Banjo (1996) has given his sanction to this general position: he argues that the grammar of his acrolectal, potentially endonormative 'Variety III' 'would differ hardly at all from standard English in its syntactic component'. This implies that there would be some differences between 'Variety III' and Standard (British) English, although Banjo does not give details. He adds that 'there are certain aspects of the grammar of English, as spoken internationally, which any diatopic variety [*e.g. Nigerian English*] interferes with at its peril', and presumably this is because in his view to do so would interfere with 'intelligibility', i.e. comprehensibility; but again he does not give examples. Jowitt (1991) suggests some reasons why this cautious position is adopted by Banjo and others, reasons which apply to other ESL varieties: deviant grammatical forms 'mean the breaking of rules for forming or combining whole classes or categories of words'; moreover, they 'rarely if at all feature in the difference between one Standard variety of English and another'.

The hostility to grammatical errors expressed by many Nigerian scholars is further manifested in a lack of interest in error analysis. Errors are highlighted chiefly with a view to the correction of them (as, for example, in Eyisi 2003), and there is little interest in describing and accounting for them. However, in Jowitt and Nnamonu (1985), fundamentally a prescriptive work, errors are specified according to the form of production of the error (omission, insertion, etc.), and in Jowitt (1991) they are categorized under the headings 'classification' (e.g. conversion from one part of speech to another, or making uncountable nouns countable); 'inflection' (e.g. omission of verbal −s or −d); 'selection' (e.g. the use of *had* instead of *have/has*); 'copying' (e.g. the use of two determiners in *...no any...*); 'ordering' (e.g. *other five* instead of *five other*); and 'restriction' (or 'avoidance', e.g. the non-use of tag questions other than *isn't it?*).

To explain the occurrence of errors, Jowitt (1991) makes use of interlanguage theory as developed by Selinker (1972); but little further work has been done along these lines. Jowitt also suggests a categorization of errors roughly according to 'users': thus there are 'idiosyncratic' and there are 'common' errors, the latter comprising those that are 'vulgar' (i.e. basilectal-mesolectal) and those that are 'institutionalized' (i.e. acrolectal), which would be candidates for inclusion in the specifications of 'Standard Nigerian English' (and would then cease to be categorized as errors). The example given by Jowitt is the use of *for* after *advocate* and *demand* used as verbs.

The idiosyncratic vs. common distinction corresponds to a 'random errors' vs. 'characteristic errors' distinction developed by Adekunle (1974) and later by Okoro (1986, 2004). Okoro's 'characteristic breaches of the code' (as in *Buy your stationeries here*), or 'characteristic errors', is one of his four constituents of Nigerian English. He also shows that he recognizes that it is the most controversial of them, by his review of a number of criteria that have been proposed by various scholars for regarding a feature as acceptable in Standard Nigerian English. He finds each of them in turn unsatisfactory: thus 'the consent of linguists' criterion is unsatisfactory because linguists have disagreed over, for example, the acceptability of *equipments*; while the criterion 'usage in formal education' would give sanction to the teacher's question 'Are you hearing me at the back?', which contains the 'fossilized error' of the use of *hear* in the progressive. Here, Okoro implicitly recognizes the danger of circularity in argument, which is present if a certain feature is regarded as an error because it is unacceptable and is then deemed unacceptable because it is an error. What is required is a justification of an error that is separate from the question of its social acceptability: and Okoro offers one. He produces three groups of ten sentences, each of which contains a Nigerianism, and suggests that while those in Group 1 (containing lexical non-Standard usages) are acceptable and those in Group 2 are definitely unacceptable, about those in Group 3 there ought to be some debate. His test example is *He horned to attract her attention*, with its conversion of *horn* from the noun to the verb class. Okoro points out that there is a long history in English of this type of conversion, recent examples in native-speaker usage being *dialogue* and *source*. The implication is that, on these grounds, this particular Nigerian English usage should be accepted.

Okoro expresses this position very cautiously, but the argument from history might of course be applied to justify many other Nigerian usages. What might be cited as an extreme example is found in Odumuh (1987). He regards the dropping of the final '–s' of the third person singular, present simple tense of verbs as among the 'typical', because widespread, features of Nigerian English, which seemingly in his view may therefore be regarded as 'standard'; and Odumuh indeed apparently gives it his approval by claiming that it demonstrates the continuance of a steady process of suffix-attrition which has been a feature of the history of English in the last 1,000 years.

Others who more recently have expressed what may be called 'advanced' views of this type with regard to grammatical errors include Lamidi (2007) and Mustapha (2011). Lamidi asserts, perhaps *pace* Banjo:

> When [deviant features] contravene the rules setting up a standard language, such that the meaning of the language is impaired or the language becomes unintelligible, they are unacceptable. If on the other hand, the intended audience understands perfectly what the speaker says, we may say that the deviation is acceptable.

Mustapha, in a strong defence of Nigerian English as 'a fully-fledged second language variety of English in every technical sense of it', deprecates a position that 'favours only the standard variety of a language' (where, presumably, 'standard' should be 'Standard'). Quoting with approval sociolinguists such as Coates (1993), he insists that 'non-standard' varieties have their own regular forms, including syntactic forms.

The position fundamentally adopted by Odumuh, Lamidi and Mustapha would nevertheless give sanction to a great number of non-Standard usages. In many cases they might not impede comprehensibility, even internationally; but both at home and abroad they are likely to meet with disapproval and perhaps with ridicule. It is not certain, moreover, that Nigerian advocates of this position adhere wholeheartedly to it. Mustapha later in his article makes use of the well-known competence-performance distinction to assert that 'competence mistakes (technically errors)... are to be excluded from the forms of Standard Nigerian English'. He does not discuss any examples; and his qualification of his own position suggests that anyone who is both a researcher in the field of Nigerian English studies and a teacher of English – a characterization of every Nigerian researcher in this field who is employed by a Nigerian university – is likely to be unable to escape from prescriptive concerns.

It seems likely that what are now regarded as errors in the area of morphosyntax will generally continue to be regarded by most Nigerian educationists as errors. Fundamentally this is because they are considered unacceptable; and they are considered unacceptable in English in Nigeria because they are unacceptable in Standard British English.

3.1.3 Morphosyntax and sub-varieties

Discussion of grammatical errors and whether or not they might feature in an endonormative standard inevitably leads to fresh consideration of the efforts to distinguish varieties of Nigerian English that were discussed in Chapter One. Scepticism was expressed there about the varieties and especially about their discreteness from one another. Okoro (2004) shares this scepticism. Limiting his remarks to only two putative varieties, he argues:

> Some people often talk of "Standard Nigerian English" and "Non-Standard Nigerian English", employing the terms as if they refer to two mutually exclusive varieties of English that co-exist in Nigeria, as in a diglossic situation. But in practical terms, this is certainly cannot be the case.

He adds:

> ...rather than talk about "Standard Nigerian English" and "Non-standard Nigerian English", it appears more practical... to talk about a single variety – Nigerian English – which contains *standard* and *non-standard* usages, these usages varying in their relative frequency of occurrence in the English of each Nigerian....

Schmied (1991) says virtually the same thing in his general African survey, also making a positive point about non-Standard usages:

> It is therefore safe to say that the basic grammatical system of Standard English is retained but certain additions, omissions or modifications are made, often in a very logical and sometimes even less irregular way than in Standard English.

This could be called a diffusionist hypothesis; and it seems to be the right position to take, entailing that the usage of a large number even of educated people contains a smaller or greater number of non-Standard forms. The corpus supplies several examples. One concerns the use of *majority*: in (distinctive) Nigerian English, unlike Standard English, it is often used without *the* or another determiner preceding it; and of 91 hits for the word in the corpus, 40, or nearly half, use it in this way, as in 'The large proportion ... indicates that majority can still be ... engaged in farming'. This comes from an academic social sciences text (ASsc_03), but the omission occurs in all kinds of texts. With such an example and others like it in view, it is not possible to say that feature X does – or alternatively does not – belong to Standard Nigerian English. Admittedly, other examples which have been cited as typical of Nigerian English usage do not show the same kind of even distribution. Thus for what in Standard English is deemed the tautologous collocation of *can/could* with *be able*, there are 12 hits in the corpus, compared to 90 in which *able* is preceded by an indicative form of *be* (*is/are*, etc.). Bamgbose (1998) says that expressions such as 'I cannot be able to go' are 'likely to be stigmatized as non-standard, since their occurrence in the acrolectal variety is virtually nil'; however, the evidence shows that their occurrence is more frequent than that.

Many of the non-Standard features of Nigerian English morphosyntactic usage are also found in other varieties of English in Africa and beyond. Schmied (1991) postulates fifteen such general 'African tendencies', divided into three groups of five (respectively concerned with verbs, the noun phrase, and larger syntactic structures). He also postulates four factors to account for them (general language-learning strategies, the influence of African languages, the salience for the learner of the written medium, and the influence of non-British models). He adds that 'partly at least English varieties all seem to develop in similar directions, as for instance in terms of simplification and regularization' (which belong to the first factor).

3.1.4 Nigerian English morphsyntax and eWAVE

An important data-base for studying the morphosyntax of Nigerian English and other varieties is provided by eWAVE (Kortmann and Lunkenheimer 2013). The informant for each variety gives a rating for each of 235 morphosyntactic features, ranging through 'A' ('feature is pervasive or obligatory'), 'B' ('feature is neither pervasive nor extremely rare'), and 'C' ('feature exists, but is extremely rare'), while additional possible ratings are 'D' ('attested absence of feature') and '?' ('no information on feature is available'). The informant for Nigerian English, Rotimi Taiwo, gives just fifteen 'A' ratings, but even so in some cases the judgment seems too generous, while on the other hand some features do not seem to merit a 'D' rating. Thus for feature 145, 'Use of *gotten* instead of *got*', 'A' is awarded; but the corpus suggests that the use of *gotten*, though widespread in Nigerian English, is by no means 'pervasive or obligatory'. (For this feature, also see page 100.) Likewise 'A' is awarded for 174, 'Deletion of auxiliary *be* before progressive', but this is rare or non-existent even in severely non-acroletcal usage. Comments on other ratings appear in the summary of non-Standard Nigerian English usages that follows.

3.2 Nigerian English non-Standard forms: a summary

The trend of the discussion above makes it seem justifiable to refer to the usages summarized below as 'non-Standard'. As in Chapter Two, an attempt is also made, and inevitably it is impressionistic, to contrast the usage of acrolectal with that of non-acrolectal speakers. The symbols (+) and (–) are respectively again used to distinguish these two 'levels', although it must be again pointed out that the use of the one or the other does not mean that the usage *generally* occurs at the level in question. The acronyms NigE and StEng are used to refer to Nigerian English and Standard English respectively; while the following acronyms stand for publications in which a large number of examples of non-Standard forms are given: A (Adegbite et al. 2014); B (Blench 2005); E (Eyisi 2003); J&N (Jowitt & Nnamonu 1985); K (Kujore 1985); O (Okoro 2011); S (Schmied 1991). (The number shown beside 'A', 'K', or 'O' indicates the page number in that book; the number beside 'J&N' or 'E' the error number in that book.) 'RT' stands for a rating given by Rotimi Taiwo in eWAVE.

3.2.1 Nouns

1. Some irregular plurals are made regular: *cattles, sheeps* (–).

2. Uncountable nouns are frequently made countable and are thus used in the plural, as are many collective nouns (+, –). In addition to *equipment*, dis-

cussed above, nouns in this category include *advice, agenda, beard, behaviour, blame, chalk, cutlery, elite, furniture, grass, issue, jewellery, machinery, offspring, property, slang, staff, wear* (J&N 2-45; E; S). In StEng, moreover, certain nouns have one sense, in which case they are countable and can be pluralized, and another sense, in which case they are uncountable and cannot be pluralized; NigE, like other ESL varieties, often uses the plural form with the 'uncountable' sense. Some examples are:

a) *Property* is uncountable in StEng when it means "things owned by someone". It is countable with other meanings, including "a building or buildings with the surrounding land". In NigE, the plural can also mean "things owned by someone" (J&N 43) (+,–).

b) *Speech* in StEng is countable with the meaning 'formal talk given to an audience', uncountable with the meaning 'the ability to speak', 'the language used in speaking'; but NigE often makes the word plural and so countable when the second sense is meant. A corpus example (from the spoken texts, com_04) is that someone asserts that students can speak English fluently but cannot write properly, and adds: 'if we are to capture the speeches of these students and analyse them you will see all kinds of errors'.

In contrast, StE *funds* with the meaning 'pecuniary resources' is often in NigE made singular and uncountable (+,–), perhaps because *money*, with which it is thus synonymous, is uncountable. Of 68 corpus hits for *fund*, most of which concern *fund* as a verb or as a noun in another StEng sense (i.e. "stock of money ... set apart for a purpose"), at least 6 show the NigE sense, for example (bnew_01): 'The officials of the Federal Capital Territory has [*sic*] been warned not to use public fund for Sallah or Christmas gift'.

3. *Pluralia tantum* nouns such as *pants, scissors, pyjamas, trousers* are made singular (*pant, scissor, pyjama, trouser*) when one pair only is meant (–). *Shoe* is often used when the plural is clearly meant (E 252). *Glasses* and *quarters* are also made singular when the meanings are "spectacles" and "living accommodation" respectively.

4. *Species*. In StEng this means "group" or "sort" and it has the same form in the singular and the plural, while *specie* meaning "coins, not paper money" occurs only in the register of banking; but in NigE *specie* is sometimes used as a countable noun with the first meaning (+; J&N 50). The corpus (ATec_2) has this solitary example (tagged as an error): '...the few publications available

describe the specie without highlighting the properties that may be of engineering importance...'.

5. StEng *grass roots* meaning "ordinary people" and often functioning adjectivally, is nearly always singular in NigE: 'Only a change in the administration can prevent a grassroot revolt' (K 47). One of the two corpus hits (in nov_18) shows a metaphorical extension in creative writing: 'He felt sure that he was alone, but suddenly and slowly, some grassroot fear took hold of him'.

6. When in StEng *rest* is a partitive noun meaning "remaining part" and is followed by *of the*, in NigE it is sometimes treated as an adjective, i.e. without *of the*: e.g. 'The rest students were let off' (J&N 162). A corpus example (ph_01) is: 'I've left the rest things for God'.

7. In StE, when a noun phrase of duration or measurement with the structure *cardinal number + plural noun* (e.g. *ten miles, two inches*) is used adjectivally, the noun becomes singular (e.g. *a ten-mile journey*); in NigE it often remains plural (e.g. *a ten-miles journey*; E 741) (+).

8. When in StE the numeral *one* is followed by *of* and a plural noun that denotes the group of which the one is part, NigE may make this noun singular (–), as in 'One of my friend'.

9. In certain idioms, the noun forms used are sometimes different from those of StEng (i.e. plural for singular, or vice versa) (+,–): *pull someone's legs*; *take the bull by the horn*; *at all cost*; *at loggerhead*; *have the gut*; *make amend*; *in pains* (i.e. suffering from pain); *in details*. In the idiom *run for dear life*, *life* is made plural if the subject of *run* is plural (and a possessive is often introduced before 'dear'). Understandably, given the relative rarity of idioms in English language use, there are few hits for these idioms in the corpus. Some examples are: *at all cost* (cr_19), 'You don't need to be tutored to implicate somebody at all cost', and *in pains* (sl_22), 'I write in pains; trusting God to help me'. In the idioms just mentioned the difference between the NigE form and the StE form is a matter of inflectional morphology. In many other idioms the difference is lexical, as is apparent from in table 4; the idioms are presented here (rather than in the next chapter) for convenience.

In a creative writing file of the corpus (nov_16), a female character prays that God will send her a husband, and adds: 'He may be poor, poorer than a church rat'.

Table 4: Nigerian English variants of Standard idioms

NigE variant	Standard form
the handwriting on the wall	the writing on the wall
cut your coat according to your size	cut your coat according to your cloth
birds of the same feather	birds of a feather
the taste of the pudding is in the eating	the proof of the pudding is in the eating
sleep like a log of wood	sleep like a log
a beggar has no choice	beggars can't be choosers
turn back the hand of the clock	turn the clock back
in the twinkle of an eye	in the twinkling of an eye
dance to the gallery	play to the gallery
from the frying pan to the fire	out of the frying pan into the fire
eat your cake and have it (too)	have your cake and eat it (BrEng)
join the bandwagon	climb/jump on the bandwagon
put up an appearance	put in an appearance
as poor as church rats	as poor as church mice
on ground	on the ground
every nook and corner	every nook and cranny
at par with (meaning 'as good, important, etc. as')	on a par with

On ground is a very common idiom, with no fewer than 56 hits in the corpus. Possibly just because of its very high frequency it has no mention in Igb and A, but it does appear, with lengthy comment, in O (231).

3.2.2 Adjectives

1. The base form of an adjective is sometimes used when comparison is intended, especially when indicated by the presence of *than* (J&N 78; Lamidi 2007) (+). A corpus example (from AHum_04) is: 'This is in realisation of the importance of capacities for planning and for management in distance learning than in the conventional face-to-face education' (+).

More is often introduced tautologically before the comparative adjectives *better, superior* (–). (RT gives only a 'C' rating for eWAVE feature 78, 'Double comparatives and superlatives'.)

Worse and *worst* are not distinguished, the second being used in the comparison of two items (–).

2. Adjectives are used as head nouns with a preceding definite article and a generic meaning, as in StEng, but with –*s* added to the adjective to show plurality: *the blinds* (–), *the faithfuls* (+). There is a lone corpus example of the latter (from bnew_22): 'the Oja Oba Central Mosque was filled to its capacity with Muslim faithfuls'. Some nationality adjectives that can be used nominally in the plural in StEng can be made singular also ('He is a British' – J&N 70) (+).

3. The –*d* of an –*ed* participle used adjectivally is often omitted (e.g. 'Road Close'; and J&N 62, 63). The motivation may be phonological.(+,–)

4. *Matured* is sometimes used adjectivally where StEng uses *mature* (e.g. 'He is a matured politician' (J&N 64) (+,–). Of fourteen corpus hits for *matured*, just one (from btal_10) seems to be used in this adjectival sense: 'corporate prayers are more effective than individual prayers especially if you are not a matured Christian'.

   Welcomed is sometimes used adjectivally (–) instead of *welcome*, e.g. 'You are highly welcomed'.

3.2.3 Determiners and pronouns

1. *Articles.* There is a tendency for nouns to be used without any preceding article, even when the noun is countable and singular (S) (+,–). A notable set of colloquial instances is when the noun follows a very common verb such as *find, get, give,* etc., for example: *find solution, get contract, give chance, have accident, have headache, make attempt, make mistake, make noise, offer/take bribe, tell lie* (Jowitt 1991; Lamidi 2007).

   When uncountable nouns are treated as countable (see above), the indefinite article may be introduced to show singularity, e.g. *an equipment, a staff*. It may likewise be used before a *pluralia tantum* noun, e.g. *a trouser*.

   The indefinite article is usually omitted before the collective but countable noun *series*, e.g.'He asked me series of questions' (J&N 49; E 69).

   The definite article is often omitted before geographical names where it is present in StEng, e.g. *He travelled to UK*. Conversely, it may be inserted where StEng would omit it, notably before the names of the States of Nigeria, e.g. *the Rivers State* (+).

   RT gives an 'A' rating in eWAVE to feature 62, 'Use of zero article where StE has definite article', and this seems justified. The eWAVE example from Malaysian English, 'Did you get mileage claim for that trip?' could have been taken from Nigerian English.

Some isolated cases are:

a) *The* is used before *society* (J&N 107).
b) As shown above, *the* is frequently not used before *majority of...*, e.g. 'Majority of his friends are women'.
c) *The* is not used before *late* meaning "recently deceased", e.g. 'Late Chief Okonyia was in the army' (E21).

2. *Demonstratives and possessives. This* may be used where concord demands *these*, e.g. 'This books are mine'; probably a phonological confusion (–; also see page 44).

A demonstrative may be followed by a possessive, e.g. 'I see a great future for this our country' (J&N 163; K 77; Lamidi 2007). RT gives an 'A' rating for eWAVE feature 59 ('Double determiners'), which seems somewhat generous.

(*All*) *these* is used with anaphoric reference when the antecedent is plural, e.g. 'His greed, his boastfulness, his lack of manners – all these made me dislike him' (J&N 153) (+).

Where the use of possessives in the environment *Every...*(possessive)... is concerned, NigE (+) prefers the cumbersome but 'correct' *his or her* to the 'incorrect' *their* which has become widespread in native-speaker usage, e.g. (from a letter to *The Nation* of 14.12.2016): 'Everyone dresses his or her best to various occasions according to his or her church programs, clubs, town groups and other social meetings'.

3. *Quantifiers. Few* is quite often used as if it has the same meaning as *a few*, i.e. without a negative connotation (+,–). Thus in the corpus there are 82 hits for *a few* and 69 for *few* without a preceding *a*; of instances of the latter, some are preceded by some other word (*the,very*, etc.) and some appear correctly in 'isolation'. But there are several cases where *a few* is clearly required instead of *few*, e.g. 'She spent few weeks in such hardship and later divorced' (nov_01); 'Few years ago, the cost of *Kampala* was affordable' (PSsc_14).

Much is used before plural countable nouns, e.g. 'much problems' (–). An anomalous comparative form of *much* was produced by a young female graduate who said 'Don't you know that you are mucher than us?' (the situation being that a group of 'girls' were struggling in a queue with a group of 'guys').

No is followed by *any* (+,–), e.g. 'There are no any decent eating-places in this town' (J&N 156). Possibly emphasis is intended, or possibly the StEng sequence *not any* is the motivation. In the corpus there are five occurrences, all in the 'conversations' category of the spoken texts, for example: 'there'll be no any usefulness of taking us to that kingdom of God'.

4. *Numbers.* A cardinal number word is often followed by brackets containing the same number in figures, e.g. 'Seven (7) epistles are generally accepted as coming from Paul': an example of the usage of a particular register (here finance) being

made general (+,–). The use of cardinals in dates, American-style, is discussed in section 4 below.

5. *Personal pronouns and determiners. She* and *he*, and *her* and *him* or *his* may be confused (especially by persons whose L1 has no grammatical gender; this applies to Igbo and Yoruba but not Hausa) (S). Femininity is attributed to a wider range of objects than in StEng, including various corporate entities to which members can be expected to feel loyalty or affection, such as an association, one's old school, etc.; for example, 'The Old Boys' Association calls on her members to attend the Annual General Meeting' (+,–). There appears to be one corpus example: 'Udoh ... mentions that the Ibibio State Union held her inaugural meeting in Ikot Ekpene ... in 1928' (ess_11). However, there are several hits for *she* or *her* where the antecedent is 'Nigeria'.

A possessive determiner + a pronominal *own* is used instead of a possessive pronoun, e.g. *my own* instead of *mine*, more often than in StEng (–). In StEng the .. *own* variant is possible for purposes of contrastive emphasis, which seems lacking in, for example, 'They broke the windows of every car, including my own'.

You people. This coinage serves as a plural form of *you*, used for addressing more than one person: 'We work day and night just to satisfy you people' (Lamidi 2007) (+,–). There are 28 hits in the corpus, for example (dem_16): 'the way we make our ewedu is different from the way you people make it'. Nigerian languages have separate singular and plural second person pronoun forms (Hausa: *ka/ki – ku*; Igbo: *i/ị – unu*; Yoruba: *o – ẹ;*), and this may have influenced the NigE usage, which overcomes the inherent ambiguity of *you*. Pidgin has the plural form *una*. *You people* is sometimes used in StEng, but as an expression of disapproval.

For the eWAVE feature 34, 'Forms or phrases for the second person plural pronoun other than *you*', RT rightly gives a 'B' rating, undoubtedly with *you people* in mind.

Pronoun copying: A pronoun may be used as a 'copy' of a subject noun phrase, e.g. 'My brother he works for a mining company' (J&N165; S) (–). Such copying is a syntactic rule in Hausa (*Dan uwana ya na aiki..*, literally 'My brother he works...'). Its presence in the English of those whose L1 is not Hausa may have another motivation (e.g. focusing of the copied noun phrase).

Relative pronouns: Copying is also a commonly occurring feature of relative clause formation, as these examples make clear (+,–):

> He gave me some yams, *which* I put *them* in the boot of my car. (J&N 174) People *who their* power is great should use it wisely. (J&N 176)

It seems that while in StEng the 'relative' element and the 'pronoun'/'determiner' element are fused, in NigE they are separated – as they are in Nigerian languages. An interesting example of the same kind of separation is where *as* functions as a relative pronoun, as in: '[There] is a fear of ESL varieties emerging as separate languages *as it* has happened to the Romance languages' (from a published academic article). A somewhat opaque corpus example (ess_10) is: 'These caliber of workers need challenging job other than a daily routine work as it is appropriate to the principal's schedule of duty'.

Of which (sometimes *in which*) is widely used as a relativizer, with the preposition playing no clear syntactic role (–). This is an extract from a conversation between two university students overheard by a researcher:

A. Who is your supervisor?
B. Professor Umoru, of which he told me that he liked my project topic.

The mother tongue of B was Yoruba, and B suggested to the researcher that his *of which* was Yoruba-influenced (*Professor Umoru, ti o* [contracted in speech to *t'o*] *so wipe...*, where *ti*, normally translated *who/which*, with a preceding noun as the antecedent, is translated as *of which*). The corpus (sl_02) has these two striking examples in one sentence of a student's informal letter: 'I am very sorry for delaying the reply to your letter of which I know you have forgiven me, it is due to some circumstances beyond my control of which I know you will understand what I am really trying to say'.

There is a widespread preference for *that* instead of *who* as a subject relative pronoun, as pointed out by Gut and Coronel (2012) (+,–). Possibly this is because *who* chiefly functions as an interrogative; but, more importantly, *that* seems to be regarded as a general relativizer, thus corresponding to MT forms (Hau. *da*, Igb. *nke*, Yor. *ti*), and often used where StEng would use *which*.

Pronoun reduplication. The interrogative pronouns *who* and *what* are sometimes reduplicated, to show plurality (+,–): 'Come and tell us *who and who* to expect in this progamme' (Jowitt 1991). The corpus has this unclear example (from con_03): 'who and who are you beating you'.

Ourselves, yourselves, themselves. The NigE tendency to use these plural reflexive pronouns as reciprocals has often been mentioned in the literature, for example: 'Unselfishness means that we should love ourselves' (J&N 171) (+,–).

Such. As a pronoun, this is often used in post-verbal, i.e. object position: 'It was a most horrible accident. I have never seen such before'. Although treated in J&N as an error (179), it could be regarded as simply an extension of the formal use of the pronoun in subject position, as in 'Such is the fate of all mankind'. (Also see *as such*, Chapter Four.)

3.2.4 Verbs

1. *Verb morphology*. The base form of the verb may be treated as an all-purpose form (–) (S). On the other hand, the past simple tense form may be used instead of the base form after *did* in interrogative and negative structures (e.g. 'Did he taught them well?'); and sometimes if the verb is past and it has a *to* + verb complement, this second verb will be likewise inflected (e.g. 'They wanted to travelled'). Surprisingly, RT in eWAVE gives only a 'D' rating for 'Double marking of past tense' (feature 133).

Certain irregular verbs tend to be made regular (–), as this table shows:

Table 5: Irregular verbs made regular in Nigerian English

Base	past simple/past participle	
	NigE	StEng
(1) cast, cost, split, spread, etc.	casted, costed, splitted, spreaded, etc.	cast, cost, split, spread, etc.
(2) bind, grind	binded, grinded	bound, ground

Some other verbs of type (1), however, such as *let* and *shut*, are not regularized. The corpus has a lone example of *grinded*: 'This seeds were grinded using mortar and pestle' (ANsc_07).

Choose may have the past participle *choosen*.

Loose (regular) and *lose* (irregular) are confused, so that *loosed* is used in place of *lost* (–). (*Lost*, moreover, is often used in place of the noun *loss*.)

Of the parts of *be*, *been* and *being* are each sometimes used in place of the other, i.e. producing (1) *has/have/had being*, (2) *am/is/are/was/were been*, (3) preposition + *been*, (4) *been* as the main verb of a non-finite clause. The vast majority of the corpus hits show correct use of each, but there some instances of the confusion, found mostly in the categories representing students' writing or informal writing. They include: 'our two days interaction seemed to have bridged the gaps... of our imagined relationship that should have being in the longer time' (sl_33); 'After the war Okunade been vengeful joined the Army' (ex_50); 'the conceptual theories were criticized for not been adequate enough' (ess_02).

2. In ... *not only...* constructions with a simple lexical verb, NigE normally (and no doubt in obedience to grammatical logic) introduces auxiliary *do* before *not* while StEng permits the simple verb after *only*, e.g. 'The coming of GSM... created a huge industry that did not only employ millions...., it also heralded... the golden age of advertising in Nigeria' (from a newspaper report) (+).

3. *Tense and aspect.* The StEng sequence of tenses rules are often not followed in subordinate clauses (+,–), and perhaps NigE seeks to operate a different set of rules: thus in indirect or reported speech, the tense used will often be the same as that which would be used in the corresponding direct speech form. RT gives an eWAVE 'D' rating for 'Loosening of sequence of tenses rule' (feature 113), but it really deserves at least 'B'. Recent, corpus-based studies of tense and aspect in NigE are Gut and Fuchs (2013), Fuchs and Gut (2015), and Werner and Fuchs (2016), the latter showing the relative infrequency of the present perfect in NigE.

Although the uses of the present perfect generally match those of StEng, the present simple may be used instead of the present perfect before *since*, e.g. 'I am in his village since last year' (–).

Where the past perfect is concerned, very common (+,–) is (1) the use of this 'tense' where StEng would use the past simple, and vice versa; and (2) the use of it where StEng would use the present perfect, and vice versa. A possible corpus example of (1) is: 'Modernism... embraces disruption, rejection or moving beyond simple realism in literature and art. This is what set modernists apart from 19th century artists, who *had tended* to believe in progress' (AHum_02). An example of (2) is: 'The products offer low toxicity, low evaporation rates, low emissions and rapid biodegradability... The health and nutritional benefit of vegetable oil... *had been reported* since the oil is metabolized in the body to release monolaurin' (ANsc_07). It is hard to avoid the conclusion that the uses of the past perfect are not adequately learned. Unlike the present perfect, this 'tense' (i.e. this combination of tense and aspect) is not represented in the verb systems of indigenous languages.

4. In reported questions, the word order of direct questions is often maintained, e.g. 'I cannot tell you what is the matter' (S).

5. The 'modal past' tends not to be used in the clause following '...wish...' or 'It is (high) time...', the present simple tense being preferred, e.g. 'I wish he is here' (K 80), 'It's high time you stop cheating' (E 506). A corpus example (parl_05) is '... it is high time we look into this case' (+,–).

6. *Stative verbs.* Some stative verbs are made dynamic, such as *have* (meaning "possess"), *hear*, and *understand*, e.g. 'I am having a lot of money' (+,–). The tendency is also present in other African varieties (S) and in South Asian varieties (Melchers and Shaw 2013).

7. *Voice.* The active voice is used more often than the passive; and where StEng would use the passive, NigE tends to use the active with a non-specific subject pronoun *they* (–). Lamidi (2007) gives as examples 'They have stolen my pen' and 'They have arrested him'. Transfer here is obvious: 'He has been arrested' corresponds to *Won ti mu u* in Yoruba, *Sun kama shi* in Hausa, each being a literal translation of 'They have arrested him'.

8. *Tag questions and echo questions.* As in other ESL varieties including Indian English and Singaporean English (Trudgill and Hannah 2008), *isn't it?* is used as an invariant, all-purpose, agreement-seeking tag (+,–); and it corresponds to invariant L1 forms (Hau. *Ko (ba haka ba*?), Igb. *Ọ bụ kwa ya*?, Yor. *Abi*?) and also to the Pidgin *No bi so*?. There is also an invariant echo question, 'Is that so?' (sometimes 'Really?').

9. *Verb complementation.* Where after certain verbs (*give*, *bring*, etc.) StEng has a choice between the pattern (i) *indirect object + direct object* and (ii) *direct object + to-* or *for*-prepositional phrase, NigE (–) may produce the pattern *prepositional phrase + direct object*, as in 'You will buy for us water'.

Disappoint and *enjoy* are sometimes made intransitive, and more often so than in StEng, as in 'She always likes to disappoint'; 'Bola has been enjoying since her husband went to the US' (Igboanusi 2002). *Mention* is often made intransitive in the colloquial expression of politeness 'Don't mention' (J 210; Igb 182; A 68). *Block* is an interesting example of a verb which can be ergative in NigE, as in: 'The water has blocked' (meaning that it has turned to ice) (–).

After *enable*, the pattern is quite often *object + bare infinitive*, e.g. 'This loan will enable me pay the bride-price' (J&N 468). The corpus here yields interesting results. Of approximately 132 hits for *enable* in its different verbal forms, 90 are instances of the structure *enable NP (to) V*, i.e. *enable* followed by an object, then by a *to-* or a bare infinitive. The '*to*' type accounts for 54 of the instances (60%), the 'bare' type for 36 (40%). The data here suggest that the 'A' rating that RT gives in eWAVE to 'Deletion of *to* before infinitives' (feature 208) is too generous.

In contrast, after *make* the pattern is normally *object + to-infinitive*, e.g. 'They made me to pay the bride-price'.

Borrow, which is often used with the meaning of *lend* (–), is complemented in the same way as *lend*, e.g. 'I want you to borrow me some money'.

An –*ing* participle may follow *refuse* and also *be about* when used to express a near-future event, as in 'He was about entering the hotel' (J&N 427) (–).

Succeed is sometimes followed by the *to-infinitive*.

An infinitive often follows *be used to, look forward to*, e.g. 'He is used to eat three times a day' (–).

10. *Prepositional verbs*. A number of verbs are made phrasal or prepositional in NigE (+,–): *behove on, comprise of, contemplate on, cope up, discuss about, emphasize on, fashion out, lend out, list out, raise up, stress on, voice out*; while *advocate, demand, order, request* are all followed by *for*. Some examples are: 'The examination comprises of a written test and an oral interview' (O 116); 'He was trying to fashion out the modalities of the programme' (A 45); 'They advocated for the abolition of the death penalty' (J&N 371). *Return* is often followed by *back;* Segun Omolayo uses this tautology as his first example when advertising his book on English errors (Omolayo 2017) in a Channels Television interview on February 6, 2018.

Conversely, some verbs are sometimes made non-prepositional (+,–): *condole, operate, provide, reply, side, supply*, as in 'She always sides her children against their father' (E 544).

Some verbs are prepositional in both StEng and NigE, but the preposition may differ. Since a lexical choice is involved, some examples appear in the next chapter.

In NigE, *find out*, followed by *that*, is quite often used in the sense of *find that* (i.e. discover by studying, thinking, etc.) (+).

11. *Modal auxiliaries*. Of the modals, *can-could, may-might, will-would* and *shall-should* form present tense-past tense pairs. In NigE, the present tense form is often used in subordinate clauses where the StEng sequence of tenses rules would predict the past, for the reason given in 4.4: thus 'She asked the teacher if she may go for a break' (E 498) (+,–).

The tautologous *must have to* occurs in non-acrolectal usage; as pointed out earlier, *can be able to* occurs at all levels, as does *can be possible*.

Non-modal *need to* is used more often than modal *need*, but sometimes the non-modal and modal forms are combined: e.g., 'He needs not to return the money' (+,–).

In StEng, *used to* has past-time reference only; NigE attempts a present-tense form, *use to* (–), without inflection for the third-person singular: 'He has stopped smoking, but he still use to drink too much' (J&N 240).

In time clauses with some kind of future time reference, NigE uses the structure *must* or *might* + perfect infinitive (+,–), as in 'After he must have come back, I will give him the money' (J&N 237); 'Make sure you submit your scripts after you might have finished writing' (E 540). A corpus example (from PNsc_11) is '… these pipelines are not replaced by the said oil/gas companies after they must have served their durability'. StEng would use the present simple or the present perfect: 'After he comes back…', '…after you have finished writing', etc. J (120) has a lengthy discussion of the NigE structure.

Would is widely used (+,–): (1) where the reference is to future time and native-speaker varieties prefer *will*; (2) with a habitual meaning where native-speaker varieties prefer the present simple tense of the lexical verb. RT gives a 'D' rating to the relevant eWAVE feature (119), but 'A' seems merited because of its widespread use in either sense. There are numerous examples in the corpus, and sometimes it seems that underlying the decision to use *would* instead of *will* is an assumption that the two words are in free variation. Thus in 'business letters' (bl_08) the writer poses the question 'What is our dream Nigeria?', and gives no fewer than twenty answers. Each is a sentence following the pattern 'Some say that it is a Nigeria where X will Y'; however, in just one case *would* is used in place of *will*: 'Some say that it is a Nigeria where sick people would be picked by equipped ambulances and more lives saved'.

Shall is discussed in Chapter Four.

12. *Miscellaneous.* Some other NigE verbal variations are as follows:
   a) *Hold.* In StEng, this verb is usually transitive but it may be intransitive, with the meaning "endure" (as in W.B.Yeats' line, utilized by Chinua Achebe for the title of his first and most famous novel, 'Things fall apart, the centre cannot hold'). NigE additionally makes it intransitive with the meaning "take place", e.g. 'I shall be disappointed if the meeting does not hold' (J&N 220) (+,–); 'The meeting will hold at 4 o'clock' (B 23).
   b) *Sleep*: NigE uses the present perfect, as in 'He has slept', with an inchoative meaning, i.e. "He has fallen asleep, and is therefore now sleeping", where StEng would say 'He is sleeping' with the meaning "He has already fallen asleep". The NigE usage shows L1 influence (cf. Yor. *O ti sun*, 'He has slept').
   c) *Suppose*: Normally passive in StEng, it is sometimes made active: 'You suppose to write your registration number' (J&N 221) (–). A corpus example is: '… these are the things a standardized test suppose to meet' (from les_08).

13. It is not easy to explain *be rest assured*, as in 'You can be rest assured that I will never tell anyone' (E 643) (+,–). Syntactically the position of 'rest' after 'be' suggests that 'rest' is assumed to be functioning adjectivally, even though it is followed by a participle also functioning adjectivally. Clearly the usage represents a coalescence of 'be assured' and 'rest assured'.

3.2.5 Adverbs, prepositions, conjunctions

1. *Adverbs*. *Even* is sometimes placed at the beginning of a sentence with the sentence as its focus; StEng would place it before the verb (+,–). An example is: 'Eze insulted his father. Even, he said he would never come home again' (J&N 339). Special NigE uses of *even* and *still* are discussed by Fuchs, Gut and Soneye (2013).

Among is used as an adverb, e.g. 'They went to the stadium, but I was not among' (J&N 294) (–); and *after* is more often used as an adverb, simply meaning "later" or "afterwards", than it is in StEng.

There is a confusion of *some time* and *some time* (+,–), the plural often being used in the adverbial phrase of duration *for some times* (StEng *for some time*). *Sometimes*, with the meaning 'at an unspecified time' (where the Standard meaning is "occasionally") is often used when Standard would use *some time*, as in 'He promised to see me sometimes in August' (A 96).

Other common adverbial phrases are: *not quite long* (i.e. "not long afterwards"), as in 'The Guest of Honour arrived at the event and not quite long, the programme started' (A 74)(–); *most times* (i.e. "usually"): thus in an article by Kolawole (2004) we find 'Most times, students are penalized for wrong spelling due to no fault of theirs' (+,–); *next tomorrow* (i.e. "the day after tomorrow", as in the example 'We are visiting him next tomorrow'; A 73), and *last week Wednesday* (i.e. "last Wednesday", an example from E being 'I came to your office last week Wednesday') (+,–). *At my front* and *at my back* are used for *in front of me* and *behind me* (–), respectively, clearly reflecting L1 usage (e.g. Igbo *n'ihu m*, Yoruba *n'iwaju mi*, "at my front"; Igbo *n'azụ m*; Yoruba *l'ehin mi*, "at my back"); an example (E 909) is: 'The beautiful lady was standing at his front'.

2. *Prepositions*. An extensive study of prepositional usage, related to sociolinguistic variables, is Jibril (1991). It uses as examples both prepositions as obligatory complements of phrasal and prepositional verbs, which have been discussed above (4.12), and prepositions initiating prepositional phrases. Since the choice of a preposition can be regarded as a lexical matter, examples are given in the next chapter.

NigE sometimes combines two prepositions in *since on...* and *until on...*, e.g. 'Do not pay him until on Wednesday' (J&N 306) (–). The logic seems to be that it is necessary to indicate both a point of time (with *on*) and a period of time, extending either from the point (therefore *since*) or up to the point (therefore *until*).

Sequel to (+) is used in sentence-initial position with the meaning of StEng 'After..' or 'Following', e.g. 'Sequel to this announcement, people rushed out of the hall' (K 80). Similar in structure and syntactic positioning is *Consequent upon...*(+), with the meaning 'As a result of....'.

3. *Conjunctions. Although* initiating a clause of concession is often followed by *but* or *yet* at the beginning of the main clause (+,–): 'Although the wall was high, yet the prisoner managed to escape' (J&N 348).

At the beginning of a 'Type I' conditional clause, where among other options StEng permits *In case..* and also the tentative *Should...*, NigE (–) combines the two: 'Should in case you see him, please tell him to come quickly' (J&N 344). In a 'Type III' conditional structure, the 'counter-factual' type, StEng uses the past perfect and therefore *had* in the conditional clause (at least according to the pre-scriptive rules), but may invert this with the subject. NigE sometimes produces a variation of the inverted option, by beginning the subordinate clause with *Had it been (that)* (–) ...., e.g. 'Had it been you informed me earlier, I would have included your name' (J&N 345). The form is common enough at lower levels and among those with Igbo as L1, 'Had it been that ...' translating Igbo *Ọ bụrụ na...*

A clause of reason is sometimes introduced by *being that* (which also occurs in some native-speaker usage) or by *for the fact that* (+,–), sometimes sentence-initially, as in the somewhat opaque corpus example (from PTec_02): 'For the fact that we have many ethnic groups, there are more we can talk about ourselves'. *For the fact that* functions in other ways, too: thus in the corpus example (from nov_14) 'If not for the fact that my parents have been living in Lagos for a long time, we would have had to go to our village for the wedding', it seems to be used as part of a strategy for avoiding the 'canonical' structure of the subordinate clause of a 'Type III' conditional.

Or, which in StEng usually marks the beginning of the second of two coordi-nate clauses, may be used to open a conversational turn, but with the first clause left implied (–). A situation is that A buys a phone card for B and gives it to B, who does not at once proceed to 'scratch' it to find the PIN number; A says: 'Or I should scratch it for you?'.

3.2.6 Punctuation and spelling

The syntactic importance of punctuation makes this a suitable point to mention a few common differences from StEng in this area. Among common spelling errors, some probably have a phonological motivation and have been mentioned in Chapter Two; a few others are mentioned below.

1. As generally in the English-speaking world, *its* (possessive) and *it's* (= *it is*) are sometimes confused (+,–).

2. A comma is sometimes inserted after *although* when no kind of parenthe-sis follows or after *though* when it is not parenthetic (+,–), for example: 'Although, he declined making any additional disclosure, our correspondent

learned from an informed source that...' (*New Age* newspaper, 29/10/2004). Moreover, *-though* or *Though* with a comma following is pronounced with a fall-rise tone. Only one instance appears in the written part of the corpus, (where there are 74 hits for *although*): 'Although, buying ... from friends and loved ones... has helped her wardrobe a lot, the current situation...' (PSsc_14).

3. In writing both formal and informal, *am* is used as the supposed contraction of *I am*, i.e. *I'm*, when clearly the colloquial StEng kind of omission of subject before verb is not intended. The corpus actually has altogether 1,656 hits for *I'm*, but they all occur in spoken texts, and it is not clear whether the speaker intended *I'm* ([aim]) or *am* ([am]). At the same time, there are 571 hits for *am*, of which the great majority show it occurring in the sequence *I am* in both spoken and written texts. But in the written texts there are also several hits for *am* where it clearly represents the contraction *I'm*. One of the most notable examples is a string of instances in bl_15, where a postgraduate student writes to a professor seeking advice about where to do postdoctoral research: 'Am Dr ___ from Nigeria. Am a linguist in Linguistics... Am currently a senior lecturer... Am wondering if there will be opportunity for me to....' Another example comes from nov_09: ' "Well, well! Am delighted to meet you at last" '.

4. The abbreviation *e.t.c.* is commonly used instead of *etc.* (+,–).

5. The semicolon is sometimes used where a colon is required (+,–).

6. Spelling errors (–) include *dinning* (for *dining*), *interprete*, *non-challant*, *strainous*.

3.3 Nigerian English morphosyntax in selected texts

The previous section has showed the range and variety of non-Standard grammatical forms that are common in Nigerian English at various levels. Chapter Five shows that some of them have for long been in use. They can be illustrated from texts written during the whole historical period since Nigerians began writing English, and the sample texts set out in Chapter Seven can serve this purpose rather well. From the grammatical point of view they range from texts in which no non-Standard forms are observable to others which contain a considerable number of such forms. All of them belong to the category of Nigerian English, in the sense that none is a Pidgin English text; on the other hand, Pidgin is used in what is largely a Nigerian English text by some authors, for reasons that will be made clear at the appropriate point. The Antera Duke passage, (1), is the only one that can generally be said to belong to the category of 'broken' English.

A rather arbitrary decision has been made to classify the texts into three groups: (A) those in which no non-Standard morphosyntactic usages are detectable; (B) those in which just one or two such usages are detectable; (C) those in which a number of such usages in excess of two are detectable. A few remaining texts of a special character are discussed in (D). Each text is given a mnemonic name which also appears at the head of it in Chapter Seven.

A. No non-Standard forms detectable
The texts in this category are: Soyinka (3); Enahoro (12); Taxi-driver (18); Okonkwo (20); Afikpo (31); Achebe (34); and perhaps Maitama (23). A second group is made up of Equiano (2), Omo Ijesha (6), Ekiti (8), Johnson (19), and Odutola (26).

Soyinka (3) contains no non-Standard forms, but in the third line from the bottom 'the Biafran secession' would on pragmatic grounds be preferable to 'Biafran secessions', since there was just one such attempted secession.

The **Achebe (34)** passage, (34), which comes from one of his earlier novels, deserves special comment. The narrator's language is entirely Standard; however, for the sake of both realism and humour, Achebe in his fiction makes persons of low income or limited education speak Pidgin: thus the cook in this passage says 'Put poison for master?'. (The 'Nevertheless!' that follows presumably means an emphatic 'Never!', and is an example of the admixture of 'broken', not of Pidgin.) His employer, the supposedly poisoned Minister, who early in the passage uses Standard English, switches to Pidgin to address the cook. Achebe's practice has been adopted by a countless number of fiction-writers, and necessarily so if the variety of language found among Nigerians of different classes is to be captured.

Maitama (23) contains no non-Standard forms, but a certain awkwardness, of a syntactic sort, appears at the end of the second sentence ('and which Nigerians').

Apart from **Afikpo (31)**, which is mainly made up of resolutions written in 1950, the texts so far mentioned are all contemporary, i.e. they date from the post-indepenence era. Also in category A, however, are some texts written or published much earlier and calling for some comment: Equiano (2), Omo Ijesha (6), Weekly Record (11), Johnson (19), Odutola (26), and Ekiti (8), which were written in 1789, 1894, 1904, 1897/1921, 1938, and 1946 respectively.

Ekiti (8) contains no non-Standard forms, but at the end of the first paragraph StEng would perhaps prefer 'all hope seems...' to 'all hopes seem..'.

In **Odutola (26)**, 'Changing' is placed at the front of its sentence, probably for focus, although the sentence reads awkwardly.

In Equiano (2), Omo Ijesha (6), Weekly Record (11), and Johnson (19) we find the highly complex style, arising out of much syntactic subordination, that was the norm of literary usage in the English-speaking world in the eighteenth and nineteenth centuries. In **Equiano (2)** it is also a sentimental style, again reflecting the fashion of the time. Interestingly, at the beginning of this passage the author twice uses the 'T' second-person singular pronoun, *thou*, but soon switches to 'Y' forms (*you*, *your*); by the late eighteenth century in Standard English the 'T' forms had become restricted to rhetorical or poetical usage.

In **Weekly Record (11)**, the few infelicities are not grammatical, but stylistic or lexical (e.g. concerning choice of prepositions).

In **Johnson (19)** we find the 'although' at the beginning of its clause balanced by 'yet' at the beginning of the main clause, a feature of the style referred to which is still popular among Nigerians (and is arguably not an error, in spite of its inclusion in 5.3 above).

B. One, or two non-Standard forms detectable

The texts in this category are: Osho Davies (7); Osundare (16); Dare (17); Hagher (21); Ajayi (22); Tafawa Balewa (27); Ebonyi (28); Ehusani (29); Alkali (35); Aliyu (37); Atta (38); Christmas prayer (40); Banwell (41); and Congratulations (42).

Osho Davies (7). At the beginning of the second sentence, 'many a time' has been collocated with 'How', where in StEng 'How many times' would be expected. The idiom with which the passage ends is typically Nigerian in form, with 'good' used instead of 'sauce' and with the introduction of 'also'.

Osundare (16). 'Time there was when..' probably represents the author's desire to vary the hackneyed 'Time was when...'. In the last line, the indefinite article is twice missing.

Dare (17). In the fifth paragraph, 'may' appears (twice) where StEng would use 'might', according to the sequence of tenses rules.

Hagher (17). There is a failure of concord in '... form ... were'; perhaps the choice of 'were' was motivated by the preceding 'dances'.

Ajayi (22). StEng might insert the indefinite article before 'growth-oriented economy'.

Tafawa Balewa (27). An error of spelling appears in the third line; otherwise the only expression of doubtful acceptability is 'wish for no heads to roll in the gutters' (where the idiom *heads will roll* is colourfully blended with the idiomatic *the gutter*, made plural).

Ebonyi (28). The only non-Standard feature, and a common error (see 1.6 above), is *specie*.

Ehusani (29). The only non-Standard feature, and a common error is the use of *crave* as a noun (see 1.1 above).

Alkali (35). Perhaps the only oddity, and perhaps lexical, is 'boredom to escape'.

Aliyu (37). The one departure from StEng is Dija's "Neither do I"; the pro-form demanded by the syntactic context is "..... have I".

Atta (38). StEng would probably prefer 'of' instead of 'for' after 'ashamed, but the main interest of this passage is the use of 'her' in the last line, the antecedent of which is 'the Cathedral': feminine gender has thus been attributed not only to a revered institution (here obviously the Church) but to manifestations of it (her?), such as a building.

Christmas prayer (40). The use of 'shall' where StEng is much more likely to use 'will' is a strong 'Nigerian' indicator, and is arguably a lexico-semantic matter. The only example of non-Standard morphosyntax is the plural of 'in returns'.

Banwell (41). The remarks just made about 'shall' apply here too. A clearly non-Standard feature is '2 minutes opportunity' (see 1.9).

Congratulations (42). The most obvious non-Standard form is 'it's', used in place of 'its'.

C. More than two non-Standard forms detectable

The texts in this category are: Crowther (4); Nanna (5); Ifeanyi (9); Boniface (10); Health care (13); Army convicts (14); Banks (15); Lenses (24); Aro (25); Tafsir (30); Onitsha (33).

Syntactically, **Crowther (4)** is notable for several instances of lack of sentence separation, which creates certain difficulties for overall interpretation, although otherwise the text is quite impeccably 'Standard'.

Nanna (5) approaches 'broken' English especially in its indifference to past-tense forms of verbs. 'Shamed' and 'present' are other morphological deviations. Comprehensibility breaks down towards the end of the second paragraph.

Ifeanyi (9). Part of the interest of this passage is that it contains several non-Standard features, but is written by someone who has reached a high level of education. Some of the non-Standard forms, such as 'joyed' and 'patience-tasking' perhaps spring from a creative desire to stretch the limits of what is acceptable. The 'Had it been...' construction at the end of the third paragraph was noted in 5.3 above.

Boniface (10). Generally well-written, this section of a letter has a few non-Standard features such as the indefinite article used before 'study leave'. The use of 'to' in the complementation of 'made' in the last sentence of the first paragraph is a common error (see 4.10). In the same sentence, 'that is' suggests a reluctance to use a participial clause simply beginning with 'immersed'.

Health care (13). In the first sentence, '...lack... have' shows a failure of concord. 'Backgrounds' is expected after '..of diverse...' instead of the singular 'background'. The omission of 'the' before 'then' in the third paragraph suggests a reluctance to produce a seeming oddity. In the last line, the past perfect seems to have been avoided; and 'on ground' is a common error.

Army convicts (14). 'Seven years jail term' exhibits the common error of using a plural instead of a singular noun after a numeral in adjectival expressions that was noted in the comments on Banwell (41) above. The indefinite article has been omitted before it, and also before 'unconditional pardon'. 'Matured' in the third paragraph is a common error (see above, 2.2.4). On the other hand, the Standard use of 'in' and not 'to' after 'resulted' (second paragraph) illustrates the important point that the appearance of a common error can never be predicted with certainty.

Banks (15). The numerous non-Standard grammatical features include 'gain saying', and using 'to manage' as a complement of 'inefficiency'. The syntax of the third paragraph is difficult to sort out; and the non-Standard use of *adduce* (a transitive verb in StEng) makes this paragraph still less comprehensible.

Lenses (24). This passage is quite characteristic of much students' writing in containing numerous errors in a small space. Notably, 'converged' in the second line can be construed either as a participle in a passive construction (but the verb *converge* does not lend itself to passivization), or as the past tense of an active verb (but the syntactic context demands the present). 'Have' in the third line is a typical example of failure of concord.

Aro (25). This passage contains too many errors to be mentioned, and exemplifies the defectiveness of some academic writing in the twenty-first century. A notable common error is the use of 'been' instead of 'being' (see above, 'Summary').

Tafsir (30). In this generally well-written passage we find as a very common error the omission of 'the' before 'majority'. In addition, 'had been' in the second paragraph is probably an example of the past perfect being used instead of the past simple tense; and 'fifth' is left singular. 'Language' is used after 'Arabic' (as it normally is in Nigerian English where in StEng the language-denoting adjective has a nominal function). 'Ought to' would in StEng probably be 'needed to'.

Onitsha (33). Overall, the interest of the passage is that, although it is a sample of the sub-genre known as Onitsha market literature, which has attracted attention in part because of its non-Standard language aspects (see Chapter Five), its grammar is not particularly deficient. In fact, the writer shows a considerable knowledge of quite advanced grammatical structures, though he has bungled the conditional sentence beginning 'Were it to be that...' Otherwise the principal errors are plurals instead of singulars, and vice versa; and 'came' used instead of 'come'.

D. Other texts

Antera Duke (1); Tutuola (32); Saro-Wiwa (36); Pepeiye (39).

Antera Duke (1). As pointed out above, this belongs to the category of 'broken English', not Pidgin; Banjo (1996) cites it as an example of 'demotic' English. In particular, the lack of punctuation makes its syntactic divisions unclear; and only base forms of verbs are used.

Tutuola (32). When Tutuola began publishing his novels in the 1950s they attracted attention partly because of Tutuola's sub-Standard language. As in the case of Onitsha (33), it can be argued that what is more striking is the extent to which they are written in StEng. Thus in the long second sentence of this passage, Tutuola uses a remarkable series of 'Type II' conditional structures (only overdoing things in the last line: StEng would prefer 'left' to 'would leave'). A notable error is the use of 'jealous' as a verb (4.2 above).

Saro-Wiwa (33). In a preface to the novel from which this extract comes the author says this:

> Sozaboy's language is what I call 'rotten English', a mixture of Nigerian pidgin English, broken English and occasional flashes of good, even idiomatic English.... To its speakers, it has the advantage of having no rules and no syntax. It thrives on lawlessness, and is part of the dislocated and discordant society in which Sozaboy must live, move and have not his being.

In fact, we find in the extract itself plenty of rules, plenty of syntax, but also some notable deviations from StEng including the use of 'glad' as a verb; repetition ('small small'); the lack of the possessive marker -'s ('your mama chop'); and the general use of the base form of any verb. In Saro-Wiwa's note, the ironical 'not' of the last few words is a parody of a Biblical text.

Pepeiye (39). The special interest of this extract from a cartoon text is that in her monologues Miss Pepeiye mixes Pidgin with StEng. The "translation" of the first line is: "Imagine – if they say it is an animal with horns that will kill somebody, is it an animal like a snail?" Her 'Chei!' towards the end is an interjection of surprise often used in Nigerian English speech and is of Igbo origin (although her name suggests that Miss Pepeiye is a Yoruba). She is a young lady of quite a high level of education (as suggested by her Latin 'Infra dignitatem!'), but as pointed out in Chapter One, and in Chapter Four, many younger Nigerians, especially Southerners, use Pidgin as a linguistic strategy for identification with the masses. Her StEng is slightly defective (e.g., 'see' instead of 'saw'; the omission of 'a' before 'motor cycle').

3.4 American influences on Nigerian English grammar

As emphasized by Trudgill and Hannah (2008), there are relatively few differences in grammar and spelling between BrEng and AmEng, and those that exist do not impair mutual understanding. It may be emphasized, too, that distinctively American grammatical forms are increasingly used in BrEng.

It is not surprising, then, that little American influence on the grammar of NigE can be detected. Some studies of American influence have been made by

Nigerian scholars (e.g. Awonusi 1994), but they have largely concentrated on lexis and spelling. A few relevant observations are as follows:

1. In the area of pluralization of nouns normally uncountable, a well-known difference between the British and American varieties is that in the latter *accommodation* is pluralized; NigE, although it pluralizes several other such nouns, does not show a particular tendency to pluralize this one also.

2. For the utterance of dates, NigE very often follows the American model in using cardinal, not ordinal numbers. Often *the* is inserted before the number, on the British model, as shown in this paradigm:

Table 6: The utterance of dates in Nigerian English

Date	AmEng	BrEng	NigE
January 5/ January 5th	"January five"	"January the fifth"	"January the five"

3. Where verbal morphology is concerned, the AmEng tendency to shift nouns to the verb class (e.g. *to author*) is also found in NigE; but it would be difficult to show that this is generally due to American influence, especially since some of the Nigerian neologisms, such as *to horn* (meaning "to sound one's horn", noted by Walsh 1967, and referred to above), are not also American ones and they predate the period of more intensive personal contact between Nigerians and Americans.

4. NigE tends to regularize irregular verbs, as noted above; hence it more often forms the past simple tense and past participle of verbs such as *dream, learn, spill* and *spell* by adding *–ed*, after the American model, instead of *–t* after the British model.

5. The corpus suggests that preferences among educated Nigerians for either BrE *got* or AmEng *gotten* as the past participle of *get* are very evenly divided. This is suggested by the number of times each form is used in the corpus immediately after some form of *have* (i.e. producing an perfect-aspect verb group): *got* occurs 22 times, *gotten* 21 times.

6. Werner and Fuchs (2016) show that NigE frequently uses the 'American' *just + past simple* structure (e.g. 'He just arrived') where British English uses *just + present perfect* ('He has just arrived'); but it is not certain that American influence is the cause.

7. The author's informal eliciting of the responses of a class of undergraduates indicated that of the following alternative ways of forming the *yes-no* interrogative of *have*: (1) Have you any money? (2) Have you got any money?

(3) Do you have any money?, the great majority preferred (3), which was originally the American form (though now also common in BrE); hardly any student chose (1), and none chose (2) (the colloquial BrEng form).

8. After the verbs *go* and *come* AmEng, but not BrEng or NigE, may use another verb immediately (e.g. 'Go ask him'). (Here an interesting point of pragmatics is that in NigE the bare, blunt imperative *Go and...* is often used by public figures when they are answering questions in interviews and perhaps feel on the defensive.)

9. In subordinate *that*-clauses where AmEng uses the 'mandative' subjunctive, NigE like BrEng prefers a structure using an auxiliary, e.g. 'It is essential that this mission should/does not fail'; the AmEng 'It is essential that this mission not fail' is unlikely to occur in NigE.

10. *Shall* is said to be rare in AmEng, but some uses of it flourish in NigE even more than in BrEng (see Chapter Four).

11. Where prepositions after verbs are concerned, NigE sometimes follows the American rather than the British model (e.g. *protest something* may be used instead of *protest against/at something*).

3.5 The grammar of Nigerian Pidgin (NP)

It is worth including in this chapter some remarks on the grammar of Nigerian Pidgin, partly because of a continuing widespread assumption that Nigerian English equals 'Pidgin English', or at least that 'Pidgin English' is a variety, a sub-Standard variety, of Nigerian English.

A number of scholars have studied various aspects of NP including its grammatical features, or have made these part of a broader study (Mafeni 1971, Agheyisi 1971, Elugbe and Omamor 1991, Deuber 2005, Faraclas 2008), and they concur in regarding NP as a distinct language, with its own grammar, not as a debased or sub-standard form of English. It is for this reason that they object to the designation 'Pidgin English'; but at the same time they distinguish it as '*Nigerian* Pidgin' because other varieties of Pidgin are found in West Africa. They point out that NP has its native speakers, especially in the Sapele and Warri areas of Delta State, and that its speakers in general are not just to be counted among people with little or no formal education. Nor must it be confused with 'broken English', which is in fact the severely sub-Standard English often spoken by people to whom that kind of description applies.

There are continuing theoretical problems in discussing the relationship of NP to English, one of which is that, as Elugbe and Omamor readily admit, 'NP draws a good percentage of its vocabulary from English'. Against this must be set the fact that 'the sentences of NP cannot possibly be accounted for in terms of the grammar of English'.

General categories can of course be applied to the description of the grammar of NP, some salient features of which are now presented. The orthography used is largely that of Elugbe and Omamor (1991).

Nouns and articles. A noun does not change its form, so that *plet* in *Plet no de fɔ makɛt* can have either singular or plural reference ("There is no plate/There are no plates in the market"). Singular number can be indicated by *won* functioning like an indefinite article and coming before the noun; plural number by *dem* coming after it. The definite article is *di*.

Personal pronouns. These tables show the subject, object, and possessive forms of the personal pronouns:

Table 7: Personal pronouns in Nigerian Pidgin

Subject:				*Object:*				*Possessive:*		
	sg	pl			sg	pl			sg	pl
1	a	wi	1	mi	wi/ɔs	1	mai	awa
2	yu	una	2	yu	una	2	yɔ	una
3	i	dɛm	3	am	dɛm	3	in	dɛm

The third-person singular possessive *in* (or *im*) is also used (1) as the subject in a subordinate clause when the subject of this and the subject of the main clause are identical, e.g. *i se in no laik di man*, "He said that he does not like the man"; (2) to show a 'genitival' relationship, e.g. *di dɔg in noz*, "the dog's nose" (just like *his* in Early Modern English).

Verbs. Like nouns, verbs are not inflected. A number of verbs are 'adjectival verbs' (Faraclas 2008), e.g. *A go hɔt di wɔta* ("I will heat the water").

An important common verb is *de*. It functions as (1) an existential: *Mɔni no de* ("There is no money"); (2) a locative: *I no de diɛ* ("He/She is not there"); (3) an auxiliary, with two different aspectual meanings, continuous and habitual: *A de rɔn* ("I am running"/"I habitually run"). However, *de* does not altogether correspond to English 'be', because Pidgin also has *bi*, which corresponds to the equative or copular 'be' of English, as in *I bi ticha* ("He/She is a teacher").

Various preverbal auxiliaries are used in an elaborate tense and aspect system, as shown here with *kɔm* serving for the paradigm:

present or past continuous/habitual: *a de kɔm* ("I am/was coming, habitually come/came")

past simple: *a kɔm* (for a single event)
perfect simple: *a dɔn kɔm* ("I have come")
perfect continuous/habitual: *a dɔn de kɔm* ("I have been coming')
future simple: *a go kɔm* ("I shall come")
future continuous/habitual: *a go de kɔm* ("I shall be coming")
future perfect: *a go dɔn kɔm* ("I shall have come")

Past time can also be indicated by an adverbial (e.g. *yɛstade*), or by the use of another auxiliary, *bin*, which can have a past perfect meaning, as in *Di taim yu rich ma ples, a bin dɔn go taun* ("When you reached my place, I had already gone to town") (Faraclas 2008).

In addition, there are a number of 'preverbal modality markers' (Faraclas 2008): *fit, mɔs, wan, trai*, as in *A fit wɔk* ("I am fit to/am able to work"). Useful here too is *fɔ*, which roughly corresponds to 'ought to', but can have future or past time reference, e.g. *Dɛm fɔ frai di planten* ("They should fry/should have fried the plantain").

Negation is expressed by *no* preceding the verb or the first of any auxiliaries, e.g. *a no go kɔm*; but *nɛva* is used to express a stronger negative, and *a nɛva kɔm* is the negative of *a dɔn kɔm*. Yes-no questions are expressed intonationally, the last word of the corresponding statement being given a rising tone. Wh- questions are formed with wh- words such as *wɛtin?* ('what?').

Additional verbal phenomena pointed out by Faraclas (2008) include 'post-verbal auxiliaries', such as *finish*, as in *a go dɔn chɔp finish* ("I will have finished eating"); and 'serial verbs', i.e. a verb such as *kari* in *Kari di buk kɔm* ("Bring the book"), where the second verb follows immediately after the object of *kari*.

Comparison. Pas ('pass') is used after an adjective or a verb to express comparison, e.g. *Ma haus fain pas yɔ on* ("My house is better than yours"); *A waka pas yu* ("I walked more than you did").

Other notable features. Na is a much-used 'highlighter' (Faraclas), placed at the beginning of a sentence and emphasizing or focusing the syntagm following it, e.g. *Na mi tɛl am* ("I am the one who told him"). When a verb is so highlighted, the verb is reduplicated, e.g. *Na bai i bai di moto* ("What he did was buy the car").

Sɛf is another highlighter, emphasizing the syntagm preceding it, e.g. *dis una rɛd moto sɛf* ("even this your red car") (Elugbe and Omamor). *We* is an all-purpose relativizer, e.g. *Di pipul we no kɔm...* ("The people who didn't come..."). *Se* functions as a complementizer in noun clauses, e.g. *Wai i bi se na yu dɛm sɛn?* ("Why is it that you are the one they sent?").

Pidgin and non-Standard Nigerian English (NSNE) compared

At the beginning of this section it was pointed out that there is a widespread perception of Nigerian Pidgin (NP) as a debased variety of English. It is moreover often assumed that 'broken', or severely non-Standard Nigerian English is English that has been heavily influenced by Pidgin.

Are there in fact any similarities between NP and NSNE? On the side of answering this question in the positive, a comparison of the Nigerian English errors tabulated earlier in this chapter with the forms of NP just presented will show that:

1. in NP there is no indefinite article, which corresponds to the tendency in NSNE not to use it;
2. in NP verbs are not inflected, which corresponds to the tendency in NSNE to use only the base form of a verb;
3. there is a tendency in both NP and NSNE to use a possessive determiner + *own* (or *on* in NP) where StEng uses a possessive pronoun;
4. in NP, *pas* is alone used to express comparison, which corresponds to the NSNE tendency to use only *than* for this purpose and not to inflect the relevant adjectives or adverbs;
5. the use of *we* as a general relativizer in NP corresponds to the general use of *that* in NSNE.

Against these arguments should be set the following:

1. NSNE does not use *de*, or other NP auxiliaries such as *go*, *dɔn*, *bin*, and *fɔ*;
2. the highlighter *na* is not used in NSNE (although 'self sometimes is, corresponding to NP *sɛf*);
3. despite the tendency mentioned in 2 above, verb forms other than the base, and the auxiliaries *be*, *have*, and *do*, are used in NSNE. Thus Jacob, who has not been to secondary school, hears a knock at the door and says 'Someone was knocking at the door'. His tense is wrong, but he has produced a well-formed sentence in Standard English.

On balance, it seems fair to say that Pidgin has had some influence on the forms of NSNE, as indigenous languages have. The indigenous languages have also influenced Pidgin, however. An example is the general relativizer *we* in Pidgin: its Hausa, Igbo and Yoruba correlates are mentioned in 3.8 of the Summary above.

A note on Chief Zebrudaya's English

This chapter ends with a glance at a home-grown variety of English that has been familiar to Nigerians for several decades and has been analysed by Elugbe and

Mgbemena (2007). It can be called Chief Zebrudaya's English, the Chief being the comic 'hero' of *Masquerade*, a Nigerian TV 'soap' of the 1980s, in which he featured along with other characters – his wife Ovuleria, their houseboy Gringory, and his friend Jegede. A range of different kinds of English is represented in their talk: Jegede's is ludicrously bombastic (hence a Nigerian kind of Indian babu), while Ovuleria and Gringory speak NP; but the English of the Chief himself is *sui generis*, as this excerpt shows:

> Ovuleria shut up your mouth. I say shut up your mouth with immediate effect... What are you know about church? Alright, okay, *odimma*. If me, who are layman, are prayer prayer, what he the preacher will do? He who have go Bible college to learn how to prayer prayer, what will he be do? Mr Preacher, the time you were in the college of Bible was you saw me?

With its non-Standard use of verb forms, bits of Igbo, echoes of very formal English ('with immediate effect' was a phrase often used by past military regimes), this is emphatically not Pidgin. Nor, argue Elugbe and Mgbemena, should it be confused with 'broken' English. It is, rather, 'deliberately offensive' – which surely means, not that the Chief deliberately seeks to offend, but that the creator of the series, Chika Okpalla, intended to do so. Or rather, to make his fellow-Nigerians laugh; and the very fact that they have done so, over the years, suggests that, while in Nigeria an abundance of non- or less-Standard English is spoken and written, there is also a widespread awareness of what counts as 'good' English and what does not.

4 Lexis and Discourse

4.1 Preliminaries

The lexis of Nigerian English has been an abiding source of interest, to specialists and non-specialists alike. It has for long been recognized that the variety contains a number of 'new' words, and that it gives meanings to existing words that are different from those of other varieties. The New Englishes movement beginning in the 1970s brought about renewed interest in the subject. It was pointed out that in Nigeria too the English language was being adapted to serve domestic communicative needs; and the adaptation was found to be particularly evident in the realm of lexis and discourse, which was natural, given that the lexis of a language comprises the real-world referents which a culture uses to make sense of itself.

Examples of such distinctive lexis are provided in early article-length surveys of Nigerian English such as Bamgbose (1971) and Jibril (1982a). As time went on, the number of examples requiring mention and discussion increased, which encouraged the compilation of alphabetically-arranged lexicons, glossaries, and mini-dictionaries. At first, these formed part of works that also investigated other areas of language, notably Kujore (1985), Odumuh (1987), and Jowitt (1991); even so, in each case the number of lexical items inventoried and to some extent commented on runs into hundreds. Attempts were eventually made to produce full-scale dictionaries, with increased numbers of headwords, namely those of Igboanusi (2002a), Blench (2005), Okoro (2011), and Adegbite et al. (2014). The number of entries in the latter is well over one thousand. None of all the dictionary-type works mentioned can claim to be exhaustive, and some are stronger than others in particular areas: Igboanusi in loan-words, Blench in names of flora and fauna. Kperogi (2015) gives fresh book-length attention to Nigerian English as a whole, albeit from a journalist's point of view, but his chief interest is in lexis, with numerous items featuring in the book, along with extensive comments. Bamiro (2015) gives a list of some 200 'new ethnolexemes': new because they have come into use or have been identified since most of the works mentioned above were published.

Alongside these works of general scope, a limited number of published works have had as their focus a particular area of lexis, such as kinship terms and modes of address (Akere 1982, Ofulue 2011) and archaisms (Jowitt 2014); and in some cases the focus is on one particular expression, such as *OK* (Adegbija and Bello 2001), *sentimental* (Jowitt 2000b), and *as in* (Ogoanah 2011). Asomugha (1981) has as its subtitle 'a dictionary of slangs and unconventional English', and students' slang is also the subject of Longe (1999). Idioms, as distinct from general lexis, are

https://doi.org/10.1515/9781501504600-004

the subject of Adegbija (2003); he provides a list of 102 items that manifest 'idiomatic variation'. Regrettably, the relationship between formal style and informal style in Nigerian usage has been little studied, although 'bookish' English (Ubahakwe 1974) was one relatively early study. Another focus of interest has been Nigerian English lexis as it features in Nigerian literature (Taiwo 1979; Bamiro 1991; Igboanusi 2002b). There is also a large, ever-growing number of studies of the language of Nigerian literary works, with a theoretical background being provided by stylistics (including feminist and postcolonial stylistics) or more recently pragmatics, but with no particular prominence given to Nigerian English as narrowly defined. Arguably this shows English in Nigeria 'coming of age', with not so much interest being shown in what makes it different from English elsewhere. The same could be said of the currently popular studies of the use of English in Nigeria in particular registers. Those concerned include advertisements, newspaper headlines, politics, and text messaging.

4.2 Categories of Nigerian English lexis

The number of distinctively Nigerian English expressions being so extensive, there is a natural desire to group them under different categories. The categorization usually reflects the processes by which the expressions have become part of usage. Adegbija (1989) identified five categories: 'transfer', 'analogy', 'acronyms', 'semantic shift or extension', and 'coinages and neologisms'. A few of these also appear in the longer list of ten categories proposed by Bamiro (1994), and he also includes 'reduplication/ redundancy', 'ellipsis', 'conversion', 'clipping', and 'underdifferentiation'. To his own original list Adegbija (2004) adds 'hybridization' and 'affixation'.

Jowitt (2014) reviews these categories and attempts some rationalization: 'affixation', for example, can clearly be treated under 'coinage'. He then proposes a fresh 'working' list. All the expressions are characterized broadly as 'neologisms', and as in Crystal (1997) they are divided into 'major' and 'minor' categories. The MAJOR categories are labelled (1) coinage, (2) extension, and (3) transfer. They are rightly termed 'major' because a very large percentage of the total number of expressions identified by the compilers of the dictionaries and other works referred to above can be assigned to one of these three.

Each major category has sub-divisions. Thus coinage, (1), comprises both (a) 'newly coined words', formed sometimes by affixation, such as *decampee* (meaning someone who leaves one political party for another), and (b) 'new collocations' (a category that does not feature in other lists), such as *area boys* (an expression that has come into use in the present century, meaning 'youthful male urban miscreants'). Extension, (2), comprises the familiar (a) 'extension of sense', such as *take in* meaning 'become pregnant', but also (b) 'extension of use', where an expression with a certain meaning is found elsewhere but is more frequently used in Nigeria (sometimes to the point of becoming a cliché), such as *hoodlums* (sometimes used as a synonym for *area boys*). Transfer, (3), includes (a) loan-words, i.e. 'loaned' or 'borrowed' from indigenous Nigerian languages – Igboanusi's dictionary contains a notably large number of these – and also (b) 'translation' from these languages; and translation may take the form of either direct translation, i.e. the result may be a calque (e.g. *long-leg*, perhaps originally from Yoruba *ẹsẹ gigun* and meaning 'useful connection with influential people'); or 'loan-rendition', such as '*Sorry*' used as an expression of sympathy (for bereavement, sickness, etc.) and clearly corresponding to a similarly brief, formulaic expression that is found in every mother tongue and is used in the same kind of context.

MINOR categories include ellipsis (e.g. *gauge* used as a verb with no object following); pleonasm or redundancy (e.g. *jeans trousers*, where other varieties would use *jeans* alone); conversion (e.g. *horn* used as a verb); acronymization (e.g. *NDA*, the Nigeria Defence Academy); reduplication (e.g. *now-now*); clipping (e.g. *main camp* for 'main campus'); back-formation (e.g. *barb* as a verb). This categorization is adopted here, with a few additions under 'minor categories': blending, which includes Adegbija's 'hybridization'; archaisms; generic trade names; and prepositional usage.

The categories and their relationships to one another are illustrated in the following diagram:

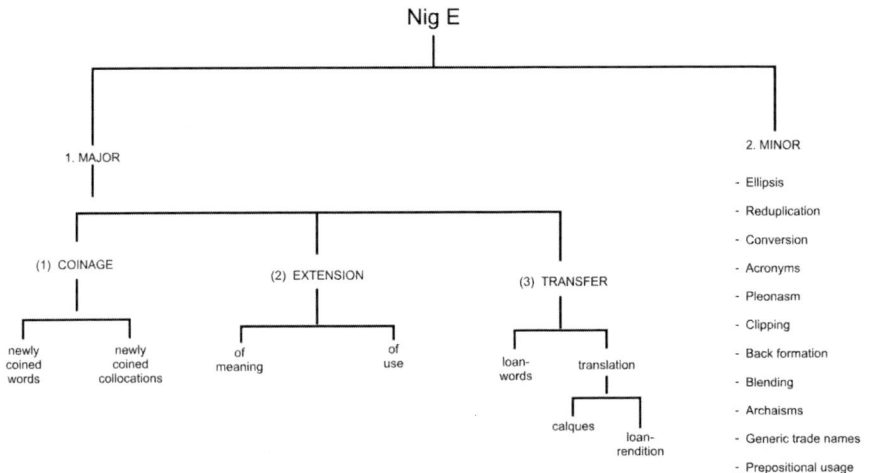

Figure 4: Categories of Nigerian English lexis

Further items follow, with some comment. As in Chapter 3, one or more examples-in-context are given in many cases, and these are taken from the corpus or, more often, from earlier collections of Nigerian English lexical items, indicated as follows: A (Adegbite et al. 2014); B (Blench 2005); E (Eyisi 2003); Igb (Igboanusi 2002); J (Jowitt 1991); J&N (Jowitt & Nnamonu 1985); K (Kujore 1985); O (Okoro 2011). (The number shown beside 'A', 'B', 'Igb' 'K', or 'O' indicates the page number in that book; the number beside 'J&N' or 'E' the error number in that book.) The items listed here are only a selection from a much greater number. The reader interested in appreciating the range and variety of Nigerian English lexis is referred to those earlier publications.

As in earlier chapters, the symbols (+) and (−) are sometimes used to suggest that the expression being described is more typical of acrolectal or of non-acrolectal usage respectively. It is in fact harder to suggest these attributions for lexis than for phonology and morphosyntax, because a very great number of Nigerian English lexical expressions are generally used by Nigerians of whatever 'level'.

4.2.1 Major categories

4.2.1.1 Coinages

(a) New words
been-to. Used as a noun, and meaning "someone who has travelled overseas" (Bamgbose 1971), often with superior attitudes that render the person unpopular. It was once a classic, much-cited Nigerian English expression; but today many younger Nigerians are unfamiliar with it, undoubtedly because travelling outside the country is no longer the novelty it once was.

corper. A noun meaning "a member of the National Youth Service Corps", i.e. a graduate of a higher institution undergoing a one-year period of national service (J 171; Igb 85; O 126; A 36). The word was coined when the NYSC was established in the 1970s.

cultism. Used to refer to the practices of secret societies in higher institutions that centre on a 'cult' and are often violent. 'The government seeks an end to cultism in varsities' (A 37).

deanage. Used in university circles to mean "office of dean" (of a faculty).

decampee. Mentioned above; an example is 'APP aspirant woos decampees back to party' (Igb 92). Other examples of nouns with *−ee* are *arrangee* (defined by Asomugha somewhat obscurely as 'a person involved in .. an arrangement to do something usually believed to be sinister'); *retiree* (although the OALD indicates that this also features in American English); and *invitee* (although the evidence of the OED suggests that this too may not be a Nigerian coinage).

disvirgin. A verb, meaning "disvirgin a woman is to stop or remove her condition of being a virgin" (O 154). It could serve as an example of the use of 'sexist ethnolexemes which deliberately dismiss, negatively define, and deprecate the female Other in the Nigerian context' (Bamiro 2015).

emphasy. Sometimes used for StEng *emphasis*, perhaps on the analogy of *ecstasy* (and so a Freudian slip?).

followership. Coined as an obvious counterpart to 'leadership', where other varieties would use 'following'. 'Good leadership attracts good followership' (A 47).

four-one-nine ('4-1-9'). As a noun, widely used to mean any kind of fraudster, as in 'He is a 4-1-9', but originally meaning someone involved in Advance Fee Fraud, sanctions against which were laid down in a military decree of the 1990s that bore the number 419. It is apparently regarded by Igb (117) as a synonym for 'dupe', but 'dupe' as a noun in this sense is also a Nigerianism (i.e. in NigE a dupe is someone who dupes, while in BrE it is a victim of someone who dupes).

ice-block. Ice-cube.

insultive. An adjectival coinage, as is *tensive* (synonymous with the adjective *tense*) (+). 'I take strong exception to your insultive remarks' (O 281). Other such coinages noted by E are *churchous* (i.e. attached to things of the Church), *plumpy*, and *trickish* (–).

knockout. Firework or banger. Children and teenagers let off knockouts during festive seasons. 'It's New Year again! The sound of knockout and "Happy New Year" fills the air' (A 59).

moreso (+, –). Presumably this developed from *...(all) the more so...* K (56) and some regard it as equivalent to *especially*, but frequently today it is a sentence-initial connective, with the meaning "Furthermore", "In addition" (in contrast to the Standard "the same, but to a greater degree"; and possibly it arises out of a confusion with 'Moreover'). There are six hits in the corpus, including (sl_13): 'I know they will not be happy about the arrangement, moreso the expenses of the wedding will be basically on both of us'.

offhead. A much-discussed example, perhaps used where other varieties would use *offhand*, with the meaning 'without being able to check something or think about it' (OALD); but the principal Nigerian English meaning is "using only the memory'", as in 'I read the poem offhead' (A 75). In its structure *offhead* is perhaps influenced by the idiom *be off one's head*.

outrightly (+,–). Obviously formed by affixing –*ly* to *outright* regarded as an adjective. *Fastly* (–) can be explained in the same way, but it is more stigmatized than *outrightly*. 'They outrightly objected to it' (B 19).

pokenose. An intransitive verb, meaning "poke one's nose (into).." (–). J, Igb, and A all mention it and give examples ('Slaves, to whom the normal cooking was left, were not allowed to poke-nose' – J 226.) There is no example in the corpus.

practicalize: "put into practice". The sole corpus example (from dem_17) is: 'now let's come and *practicalize* our C-cup'.

send-forth. The OALD defines *send-off* as "an occasion when people come together to say goodbye to someone who is leaving". With this meaning it commonly occurs in NigE in the expression *send-off party*, which is often held in honour of someone who is leaving one job to take up a new one somewhere else (Igb 247). However, the coinage *send-forth* has increasingly come into use instead. A suggest that it is a euphemism, used because *send-off* sounds pejorative (as if to say, presumably, that everyone is glad to say goodbye to the person being honoured).

smoothen. Adegbija (2004) uses this – perhaps deliberately – in his own writing. The corpus has this example (from dem_08): 'it is very important that you smoothen it properly'.

upliftment. Obviously formed by analogy with other words containing the nominalizing affix–*ment*. An example is: 'The new regime has demonstrated that it is committed towards the upliftment of the standard of living of all Nigerians' (Igb 287). Another, less common Nigerianism is *preachment*: thus a senior journalist writes in a leading newspaper: 'They knew and God knows, that we are tired of high-minded but patently empty preachments from the high throne of public officers.'

youngman. It is often thus written in NigEng, as a true compound; likewise *blackman, whiteman* (J 266).

(b) New collocations
African time. 'Colloquially used as a jocular reference to unpunctuality' (Igb 35).

bag a degree. The verb, which has the informal meaning 'obtain' in the register of sport in other varieties, is regularly collocated with 'degree' in NigE, and is otherwise seldom used (J; A). 'He recently bagged a PhD for [sc. *from*] the university' (A 24).

beer parlour. Equivalent to BrEng *pub* or *public house*, it is the normal expression used to refer to a place where people meet and sit to drink beer (J 160; Igb 59).

brown envelope. This means not so much the envelope itself as the money that is put inside it and offered as a gratification (A 29); hence an example of metonymy, or of euphemism.

cash madam. 'A large-scale woman trader, generally in the South' (A 32).

chanced, be. NigE collocates *be* with *chanced*, thus coining a passive form of the verb *chance* with the meaning "have the chance", as in 'I wanted to see you, but I was not chanced' (J&N 251; -). With the same meaning is '...I was not opportuned' (J&N 258). The corpus has one example (sl_15): 'I have not been chanced to go to her house'.

chewing stick. A piece of wood that is moistened and chewed at one end and is used (by someone lacking a toothbrush, sometimes in preference to it) to clean the teeth (O 103).

colonial masters. A kind of euphemism used to refer to the British in their pre-1960 role as the sovereign power in Nigeria (Igb 80; +,–).

do one's freedom. An apprenticeship remains the normal method for a young person in Nigeria to learn a trade such as tailoring, carpentry, or motor mechanics. The end of the process is marked by a ceremony at which a certificate is awarded and there is some merry-making. This is to 'do one's freedom' (–). (J 182; Igb 118; A 48.)

entertain fears. The two words are frequently collocated in popular usage in Nigeria, where in other varieties 'be afraid' or 'feel afraid' would be more usual; an example of a certain tendency to use more formal expressions in informal contexts and therefore of what Ubahakwe (1974) called 'bookish' English. (J 177; Igb 105; A 43.)

exercise patience. The same kind of observation just made about *entertain fears* could be made about this collocation, which really means no more than "be patient".

fail woefully. It has for long been commonly used in the educational context to mean that the performance in a test or examination has been disappointing (–); 'Many of you failed woefully in my course' (Igb 110).

Ghana-must-go. A large canvas bag (the expression often being used elliptically for '....bag'). It dates from the early 1980s when Nigeria began deporting the large number of Ghanaians who had come to Nigeria in search of jobs. A Ghana-must-go bag at first thus meant the type of large bag in which the Ghanaians carried their belongings home. (A 49.)

God so good. Used clause-initially as a kind of adverbial to mean "fortunately" (J 185; +,–).

good enough. Often used clause-initially with the same meaning as *God so good* (+,–) 'Burglers broke into my house yesterday. Good enough there wasn't much for them to steal' (Igb 130).

idol worshippers. This has for long been in use to refer, sometimes derogatorily, to people who practise 'traditional' religion and have not accepted Christianity or Islam (J 195; Igb 144).

last price. In the context of buying and selling, which in the open-air market in Nigeria involves haggling, 'last price' is said by the seller to indicate the price below which he or she will not go. Alternatively, and let us suppose the price demanded is N200, the seller is likely to say 'Two hundred naira last'. (J 201; Igb 165; A 60.)

last two weeks. Last is commonly placed before a time phrase where other varieties would place *ago* after it (+,–). *Ago* is underused in Nigerian English.

lie carelessly. The carelessness referred to is the unintended exposure of one's private parts, when sleeping, for example. A similar example is *sit carelessly* (A 31).

'*Likewise myself.*' The two words would rarely be used together in other varieties, but this collocation is quite common in NigE (-), with the meaning expressed in other varieties as 'So do I', 'So am I', etc. 'Additive' *so...* phrases of this sort are rarely used. (J 204; A 62.)

medicated glasses. The two words are thus collocated when the glasses are prescribed by an optician (in contrast to sunglasses). (J 209; Igb 181; A 67-8.)

meet ... absence. 'I met his absence' is a well-known Nigerianism, corresponding to 'I found him absent' in other varieties (–). 'I came to your office and met your absence' (Igb 181).

motor boy. A boy or young man who accompanies and assists the driver of a bus or lorry.

motor park. This is another much-cited Nigerianism, referring to an area situated within or on the outskirts of a large town, where long-distance taxis and buses pick up passengers intending to travel to other towns. The nearest BrEng equivalent is 'bus station'. (J 211-2; A 70.)

naming ceremony. The expression is rightly often cited as an example of the adaptation of English to local culture. At such a ceremony a new-born child is formally given a name by its parents, and the occasion is accompanied with merry-making and, sometimes, donations of money (B 18).

of recent. Equivalent to StEng *recently*, *lately*, *of late*, this is a well-known and very widespread NigE coinage (+,–). The corpus has this example (from ANsc_01): 'Of recent, several studies have shown that ... the effects ... appear to be species-specific'.

(not) on seat. Usually in the negative form, this has become a kind of classic Nigerianism, meaning "not at his/her duty-post". An example given by Bamgbose (1971) is 'The director is not on seat'.

pad. The collocation of *pad* as a verb in its different forms (e.g. *padding*) with *budget* suddenly became common in public discourse in 2015 because of alleged attempts by members of the country's House of Representatives to inflate the national budget for dishonest reasons.

pepper soup. A watery soup prepared with meat or fish and much pepper, usually not served as part of a main meal (J 224; Igb 219; A 80).

rig out. It means "use dubious means to eliminate an opponent from an electoral contest". Sometimes it has the form *outrig*.

roam the streets. Commonly used where other varieties might use a variety of other expressions such as 'wander about', 'hang around', etc., and suggestive of joblessness or idleness. (J 232; Igb 240; A 89).

scale through. Commonly used to mean "succeed", undoubtedly equivalent to the *sail through* of other varieties, and probably resulting from the common use there of *scale* to mean the overcoming of difficulties. 'The examination was difficult but I managed to scale through' (A 91).

second burial. A notable example of the adaptation of English to express aspects of traditional culture. In some societies in the South a second burial takes place some time after the first, and is a more public and elaborate, even joyous affair (B 23).

'Shine your eyes.' Maybe of Pidgin origin and meaning "look closely", it became a highly popular expression when, some years ago, NAFDAC (see below, acronyms) embarked on a campaign to encourage Nigerians to look closely at medical products to know whether they were genuine or not (A 93).

speak through the nose. An idiom, and A 74 give the meaning as "speak indistinctly"; "mumble". A secondary meaning is "try to speak like a white man" (probably, therefore, to speak indistinctly because one is trying unsuccessfully to speak like a white man).

spray money. An idiom meaning "give money, especially by placing currency notes on musicians' or dancers' foreheads to show appreciation or encouragement" (A 97); a good example of the adaptation of the English language to express Nigerian cultural practices. In a Central Bank of Nigeria advertisement entitled 'Keep the Naira Clean', one of the pieces of advice given to citizens is 'Do not spray the Naira'.

talk less (of). NigE (–) uses this as a kind of compound preposition where other varieties would say 'not to talk of' or 'let alone'. Examples are: 'The boy cannot write a single sentence, talk less of a letter' (E 1027); 'He cannot buy a bicycle, talk less of a car' (A 61).

the type of... NigE often says 'See the type of your car' where other varieties would say 'There's a car just like yours'. (J 252.)

upper. Collocated with names of days of the week to mean not the next day so named, but the one following it, e.g. *upper Monday*; other varieties would say 'the Monday after next' (which is, of course, more verbose) (J 253; A 105).

white garment. Often also collocated with *church*. A *white-garment church* refers to a Christian sect whose adherents are noted for their wearing of white robes, such as the Cherubim and Seraphim.

woman wrapper. This interesting collocation makes use of Standard *woman* and an apparent Nigerian coinage, *wrapper*, which means a large piece of cloth that is tied around the waist and stretches to the feet and is worn informally inside the house. The collocation itself means a man who is subservient to or is easily manipulated by a woman, usually his wife. Igb (300) correctly explains it thus; in A it is wrongly defined as 'womanizer'.

4.2.1.2 Extension

(a) Extension of sense
In some ways 'shift' is a more suitable word here than 'extension', since sometimes the sense of the Nigerian English word is both restricted and extended in relation to the sense it has in other varieties.

academics. The frequent meaning in NigE is "academic matters", in contrast to the "academic persons" of BrEng (J&N 468).

admire. NigE extends the dictionary meaning given in the OALD as "look at something [*or somebody*] and think it [*he, she*] is attractive" to mean "look at with lustful intent". When a man says 'I admire her', the meaning he intends and is understood by other Nigerians to mean is thus different from its meaning in the British or American context.

alphabet, alphabets. Especially (–), *alphabet* is treated as a countable noun, not as a collective noun, and means "letter of the alphabet"; *letter* is seldom used in Nigeria to mean "letter of the alphabet" (J&N 469).

applicant. An applicant in Nigeria is, primarily, someone who is unemployed and is applying for jobs (–) (B 2). The implication is that he or she has applied for several jobs, so far without success; nevertheless the word perhaps has more positive connotations than *unemployed*. The extensive note in Jowitt (156) suggests that in the Nigerian public consciousness applicants almost form a social group – one person is a civil servant, another is a teacher, another is an applicant, etc.

appreciate. Although there are no hits in the written corpus reflecting it, a Nigerian extension of the meaning of this word has come into wide use in recent years (+, –). In other varieties, the meaning is psychological and could be paraphrased as 'feel appreciation', as in 'His talents are not fully appreciated in that company' (OALD). In Nigeria, however, the extended meaning is 'demonstrate' (by word or action) as well as 'feel' appreciation. Thus someone chairing a meeting will often say: 'I would like to appreciate the presence of X', and the very words express the appreciation. In appropriate contexts *appreciate* in this sense may be a euphemism, i.e. the intended meaning is "show appreciation in the form of a monetary gift"; by a further extension, the 'gift' may actually be understood, by both parties, as a bribe.

A (21) give a classroom context: a teacher may ask the class to express admiration for the performance of a particular pupil by saying: 'Her answer is correct; appreciate her' – and the other pupils will then clap. O (41) shows that, though transitive, the verb is often used without an object in Nigeria, e.g. 'Thank you very much – I appreciate'.

as such. NigE shifts the dictionary meaning so that it becomes equivalent to 'therefore', as in the corpus example (from sl_15): 'I now have your e-mail address and as such as I can get in touch with you any time I wish'.

attachment. There are two main extensions of meaning in NigE, as shown in A 22: 1. An attachment may be a place in a bus, especially a 'luxury' bus for which a lower fare is charged, which is sometimes the space to the right of the driver that can be used as a seat, or is merely standing room; *on attachment* can be used with this sense in, e.g., 'He travelled to Lagos on attachment'. 2. The word can also mean a wig made of straight hair which some women fit to their heads to make them look modern and Western. The hair may be synthetic, or it may be real, originating from outside the country.

axis. Commonly used (+) to mean nothing more than "location, "geographical area", as in 'People in that axis [i.e. *part of the city in question*] are grumbling because they have not had light for many days'.

back. Especially (–), it often means "carry someone on one's back". 'Your child is crying, can't you back her?' (A 23).

Belgian/Belgium. A 'Belgian car' or 'Belgium car' means that is secondhand, though in good condition, and also imported (B 3; +, –). The usage started several years ago when a consignment of cars was shipped into Nigeria from Antwerp in Belgium. *Tokunbo*, from Yoruba (see page 128) has the same meaning.

bounce. Bouncing is frequently collocated with *baby boy* (sometimes *girl*), and the collocation is a stock expression used to announce a baby's birth, with the implication that the baby is strong and healthy. *Bounce* also means "walk with strong, springy, confident steps".

branch. Bamgbose (1971) defines the extended meaning as "call (on one's way to another place)" as in 'I am going to branch at my uncle's house'; it is an example of NigE usage that was noted very early in the development of Nigerian English studies.

burst out. The most common NigE meaning is 'suddenly emerge at a main road from an access road'. 'We were driving along the main road, and suddenly a truck burst out from nowhere' (A 30).

'*Can I...?*' This is often heard as part of the utterance 'Can I bring it?', and the typical context is that in a bar or restaurant a customer expresses interest in a certain drink, and the waiter asks this question to find out whether the customer wishes him or her to bring it. Pragmatically the waiter places himself/herself at the disposal of the customer. BrEng would use 'Shall I..?'.

carpet; *rug.* In Nigeria, a *carpet* is what other varieties call 'linoleum' or lino', i.e. the plastic material with a shiny surface used to cover a floor (A 31). In the USA or the UK, a carpet is made of thick fibre, is more expensive, and is often 'fitted', i.e. made to cover the entire space between the walls of a room. Nigerian English calls this a *rug*, and it also uses the word as a verb, meaning 'cover the entire floor space of a room with a rug'.

carry over, carry-over. The verb is commonly used in higher institutions with the extended meaning 'repeat a course of study that one has failed' (A 31). The corresponding noun is *carry-over*.

chance. Extended to refer to a seat in a bus or taxi that is yet to be filled, and so equivalent to the uncountable use of 'room' in other varieties (J 166). Also an example of loan translation, since *chance* clearly corresponds to Hau. *dama*, Yor. *aiye*, Igb. *efe*.

conclusively. Often used sentence-initially, especially by students, to mean nothing more than "Finally", "In conclusion" (E 212; O 117). An example, perhaps, of a complete shift of meaning.

condemned. Often used adjectivally to mean "utterly beyond repair", as in 'We can't use any of these photocopying machines – they are all condemned' (O 118; -)

conducive. Widely used without complementation and with the apparently extended general meaning "beneficial", "congenial", e.g. 'The climate of Plateau State is very conducive' (J 170). In other varieties, *conducive* is complemented with a *to* prepositional phrase and has the more limited meaning "contributing beneficially to (the particular thing named)".

continue. J (171) uses examples such as 'continue knocking' to show that NigE uses *continue* + verb+*ing* in the same sense as *keep (on)* + verb+*ing*, with the general meaning "do something repeatedly".

dowry. Often used as a synonym for *bride-price*, and so meaning the money paid by a man to the family of his intended bride (B 8); the payment is normal in Nigerian cultures. The meaning is sanctioned by the OALD, which nevertheless first gives the completely opposite meaning, i.e. money paid by a woman or her family to her husband.

draw. Used as a noun and collocated with 'soup', it refers to the mucilaginous substance produced by the vegetables okra and ogbono when being cooked, so that *draw soup* can be paraphrased as 'soup that draws' (B 8). Sometimes by ellipsis it is used on its own (as the names of other soups are).

dress. It may have the intransitive meaning "move", "shift", as when a bus conductor says to a passenger to 'Please dress'(A 40; -). Also found in Pidgin, and ultimately derived from the military register.

drop. 1. Of the many Standard meanings of the verb, NigE extends "stop so that somebody can get out of a car" by making it intransitive, as in 'We are dropping here' (B 8). 2. In the same transport register, NigE uses *drop* as a noun with the meaning "a single straight trip in which the passenger takes a taxicab and pays for the other passengers the driver would have carried" (A 40); i.e. the passenger charters the taxi.

elderly. J (176) argues that the word may be used by a speaker to refer to someone else who may be senior to the speaker in age but may not necessarily be very advanced in age – someone occupying the post of elder in a church, for example (–).

equally. Extended to mean "also", "likewise", as in 'My father is very caring in his own way, and I pray that God equally give me such a husband' (O 175).

escort. While in NigE this may have the Standard dictionary meanings, it also as a verb has the extended meaning "see someone off without the implication of providing protection", as in 'Let me escort you' (J 177) and 'Bola escorted her visitor to the end of the street before turning back' (O 176).

far-fetched. NigE consistently uses this to mean "hard to explain", while in other varieties it means "hard to believe" and so "strange", "weird", etc.

flash. It is commonly used as an intransitive verb meaning "call someone but terminate the call after a few rings in the hope that the person will call back" (Kperogi). It came to be thus used with the onset of the mobile phone revolution in Nigeria early in the present century. Kperogi adds that a Nigerian using the word might be seriously misunderstood in the USA or the UK, where in popular usage it has a very different, sexual meaning.

fried egg. Generally in Nigeria 'fried egg' means that the yolk and the white of an egg are mixed together before being fried; equivalent therefore to the *omelette* of other varieties (O 211).

gallon. Extended to refer to a plastic container of a certain size, perhaps originally one that could contain a gallon of some liquid (B 10).

gallop. Often, as a noun, used to refer to a bump or a pot-hole in a road that may cause a car to bounce up and down, which suggests the galloping of a horse (B 10).

garage. Along with the usual dictionary meanings, it often has the same meaning as the *motor park* of Nigerian English (B 10).

gauge. The verb is often used intransitively as well as transitively, as in 'The oil does not gauge', i.e. the oil does not come up to the required level (O 220).

George. Patterned cloth worn by women, especially Igbo women. It is said that the original patterning featured the British King George V, who died in 1936 (B 11). Sometimes Igbonized to *Joji*.

gist. Used as a noun and also as a verb, especially (–), to mean "chat", "tell someone the news or the gossip" (A 49).

go-slow. A classic Nigerianism, extended to the register of road transport to mean "traffic-jam" or even "gridlock" (if that is the point that the 'going-slow' has reached; A 50).

hiss. J 193 explains that in NigE to hiss means to produce a sound 'by protruding the lips and drawing air inwards noisily', which expresses disapproval or derision. No Standard dictionary word conveys this meaning. An example given by Jowitt from John Munonye's novel *Obi* is: 'His countenance fell and he hissed mournfully'.

inclusive. Apart from its dictionary meaning, this is used almost universally in NigE where other varieties would use *included* (J 196). A literary example comes from the novelist Isidore Okpehwo's *The Victim*, where a certain character says 'My greetings to every single thing in this house, soup-pot inclusive'.

join. In the register of transport it often means 'go by...', as in 'join taxi'. It thus has virtually the same meaning as *climb* (q.v.); however, *join* is used when the movement to enter the vehicle does not involve 'climbing' (A 57, B 14).

laps. In NigE this plural form has the same meaning as the singular *lap* in other varieties; it is thus virtually equivalent to *thighs* (B 15, J 201).

leather bag. Especially (–), it refers to a polythene bag, which has become a familiar sight throughout the world in the past fifty years (A 61, B 15).

lesson. Often used to mean "private tuition" (A 61).

light. Another classic Nigerianism, it often has the extended meaning "light supplied by electricity", or, by further extension, "power supplied by electricity" (hence, e.g., for heating as well as lighting) (Igb 169).

local. The extended meaning in NigE is "narrow", "backward", "unenlightened", and the word is often thus used by town-dwellers to describe someone who lives in or exhibits the outlook of people living in a rural area (–) (A 62; J 205).

machine. Its most popular meaning in NigE is "motorcycle", which suggests semantic restriction rather than extension (A 65; Igb 173).

manage. NigE uses and develops the several dictionary meanings, both transitive and intransitive, as follows (J 208): 1. In 'We are managing what we have', the sense is that of using limited resources in a rational way (rather than merely organizing or controlling them). 2. In 'I managed the car as far as Enugu' the sense is that of driving the car in spite of what was wrong with it; in other varieties the same sense would be given by 'I managed to drive the car as far as Enugu'. 3. In 'We are just managing', with the verb used intransitively, the sense contrasts with that of feeling comfortable or enjoying life, implying that one can survive, if only just, on the available resources. Interestingly, in Hausa the word *maneji*, a loan-rendition from English, means a place situated in a bus behind the driver's seat that is not really meant as a passenger's seat, but which one might just 'manage' as a seat, for lack of an alternative, and without feeling comfortable.

marry. NigE uses the present or past progressive active to mean "has/had a wife", as in 'He is marrying two wives' (A 67; J 209). This can be heard quite often because polygamy is widely practised in Nigeria. A connotation is that it is assumed that a wife is the husband's property. (On the basis of the same assumptions, NigE would not permit the use of *marry* with a female subject, e.g. 'She is marrying a man from Ekiti State', which could only mean that she is about to get married to him.) This use of *marry*, as of the L1 word that it translates (Yor. *f̣ẹ*, Igb.*nụ*), reflects male-centred assumptions of traditional culture.

midnight. Especially (–), NigE has the expression 'in the midnight', which in other varieties would be 'in the middle of the night' (J 210).

mind. *Mind* as a verb in NigE often means "take seriously what someone has said", which seems to be an extension beyond the numerous dictionary meanings. It is used thus in the common expression of advice 'Don't mind him/her' (A 69).

must. In Standard usage, when the meaning is dynamic (Palmer 1990), *must* expresses an obligation which is felt or is shared by the speaker. In NigE, an extension often occurs in conditional clauses (+): thus a certain public figure was said 'to require an urgent kidney transplant, if his life must be spared'. In other varieties, 'was to' would be preferred to 'must' here, the idea being that of a future plan originating with some unspecified authority.

pack. Dictionaries give many meanings of *pack* as a verb and many more where *pack* is the first element of a phrasal verb. Some of these are also common in NigE, but NigE has certain extensions, notably where *pack* means "leave one's abode" and is perhaps ellipticial for *pack one's belongings* (in order to effect one's departure). It is then often followed by *out*, *out of*, or *into*, as in the clichéd 'He told her to pack out of the matrimonial home' (Igb 180; J 209). By extension, *pack* may mean "steal" ('The house girl packed all my jewellery') or "collect" ('The tipper lorries packed sand from our farmland') (A 78).

pick. 1. *Pick* is used in place of the phrasal verb *pick up* when the meaning is "go somewhere in your car and collect someone who is waiting for you".

2. An extended meaning is "answer" in the context of mobile phone use, as in 'I called you but you did not pick'; perhaps here too *pick* is elliptical for *pick up* in the literal sense (since it is normal for one to pick up a mobile phone before answering it). 3. *Pick* is collocated with *race* with the meaning "start" (as in Standard *pick a quarrel*) (A 81; J 224).

put on. Commonly used to express a state, not an action, and equivalent to 'wear', as in 'She is putting on lace' (Igb 230).

room, the. 'He/She is in the room' is a common way of saying that the person concerned is in his/her (own) room, meaning the room in a house that is regarded as specially his or hers (J 232).

rush. At non-acrolectal levels, *rush* is used in 'The water is not rushing' where other varieties would use *flow*.

scandalize. In Nig E, it means "bring scandal to" (as in 'You have scandalized my name!'), not 'offend', 'outrage' as in other varieties (+).

sentiment, sentimental. In NigE, *sentiment* is often synonymous not just with 'emotion' (as in other varieties) but also with 'strong emotion', and *sentimental* likewise may mean not just "emotional" but "strongly emotional" (+). In other varieties, the adjective is used in certain contexts and often with disapproval (e.g. 'a sentimental love story'). In NigE both *sentiment* and *sentimental* are mostly also used with disapproval, but the contexts are different: often they are discussions about politics or religion. In his lengthy discussion Kperogi says that in Nigeria the noun means "prejudice that is activated by visceral, unreasoning, primordial loyalties". In an article which presents the results of a test of the acceptability of different meanings of the adjective to ten non-Nigerians and fifty-two Nigerians, Jowitt (2000b) gives as an example: 'Many Nigerians are very sentimental, and that is why they would like to replace English as the official language with a Nigerian language'. Significantly, while 71.2% of the Nigerians found this usage acceptable, none of the non-Nigerians did so.

settle. This has been much commented on as meaning "bribe", or "use money to render a potential opponent innocuous". In the early 1990s, in an era of military rule, a leading member of a new junta addressed senior officers with the words 'We will not be spendthrifts and will not "settle" anybody'. A (93) also point out that the meaning is sometimes "pay the money for someone's apprenticeship".

severally. In NigE this commonly means "several times", not "separately" as in other varieties, and it is not confined to formal or legal usage (+). 'I have gone to him severally but did not see him' (E 821).

shock. Especially (–), it may mean "give a physical shock" (A 93).

slap. It is extended to mean "inflict any kind of blow with the hand"; it is therefore used where other varieties would use *punch*.

soup. Generally in NigE this refers to a thick, oil-based concoction that accompanies the starchy principal component of a main meal. Soups are named and distinguished from one another by the principal vegetable used in the preparation: egusi soup, ogbono soup, bitterleaf soup, and so on; and they also contain meat or fish. In the UK or the USA *soup* has a different meaning, as the light first course of a main meal. (J 242.)

tea. As J (246) points out, *tea* is extended in NigE to refer to any hot beverage, usually with milk in it (–). To be quite sure that the word is understood in the most common British or American sense, a speaker needs to say 'Lipton', which was once the most common brand of tea in this sense available in Nigeria. In addition, *tea* in NigE can refer to a light meal consisting of tea (in the extended sense) and bread, and so corresponds to the 'afternoon tea' of BrEng (–).

to and fro. Used in the register of travelling with the meaning "moving in a certain direction and back again", as in 'The journey costs N10,000 to and fro'. (Igb 276.)

waterproof. A word that is commonly extended to denote the type of cellophane bag used for packaging small quantities of salt, sugar, groundnuts, etc. (A 108).

working-class. J (261) points out that 'working-class' in NigE refers to anybody who is in regular, paid employment, often in an office, in teaching, etc., and therefore has a white-collar job. This is the meaning present when a 'personal ad' in a newspaper says: 'X is looking for a mature and working-class lady between 28 and 32 for a relationship'. In contrast, in the UK and the USA, where social classes are more clearly defined than in Africa, to be 'working-class' means that one does not belong to the middle class, and often has a blue-collar job.

(b) Extension of use
A considerable number of these items have not been described in any published work before.

devoted. NigE frequently uses this word where other varieties would use 'devout', as in 'a devout Christian', 'a devout Muslim'.

dubious character. The two words are thus commonly collocated to refer to someone of doubtful character or who acts in a suspicious manner. (J 176.)

enter. An example of a word more typical of formal usage being widely used in informal contexts (+,–) (J 177). In cities such as Lagos, bus conductors will shout out to intending passengers 'Enter with your change!' (Igboanusi's example, which means that passengers may only travel if they have the exact money to pay the fare).

entire. As shown by the example 'the entire members' (A 43; B 9), this word is used with plural countable nouns as well as with singular countable or uncountable nouns.

glaring. The expression 'It is glaring that...' often appears in academic writing where in other varieties 'It is striking that..' or 'It is obvious that...' would be used.

help. NigE extends the use as follows (A 53, Igb 137, J 190). 1. In 'Help me carry this water' the meaning is not that the addressee should carry the water jointly with the speaker, but should carry it alone, in that way helping the speaker. 2. In 'Help me with your biro' the meaning is "Help me by lending me your biro".

lack home training. 'He lacks home training' is a popular way of saying what in other varieties might be expressed as 'He hasn't been well brought up'.

majestically. It is frequently used in a collocation with *walk*, the meaning of which is "walk in an imposing manner, seeking to draw attention to oneself".

opine. Widely used in academic discourse, much more so than in other varieties, which would be more likely to use other verbs such as 'remark', 'observe', 'maintain', 'assert', etc. (+).

overgrow. As in 'They have overgrown their clothes' with the meaning "become too big for", NigE uses this where BrEng has *outgrow*; AmEng also appears to allow *overgrow*.

proffer. Also widely used in formal writing, meaning "suggest", "propose", and often collocated with 'solutions' (+).

slump. Where the meaning is "physically fall", NigE consistently uses *slump* without a complementary prepositional phrase (+,–). The meaning is "fall down as a result of losing consciousness", as in the newspaper headline 'Two slump during pensioners' protest...' (*The Nation*, 4.8.2016). Other varieties would use *collapse* or perhaps *faint*.

snatch. In other varieties, the meaning, given in the OELD as "take something by force rudely" is very vivid and physical, as well as disapproving. In NigE, the word is commonly used less literally, as when a man loses a girlfriend to another man, who is then said to have 'snatched' her, or when people in a certain university department say of another department to which their colleague Mr X has moved: 'They have snatched him from us'.

'*...you understand?*' This is commonly appended to a statement, e.g. 'Fresh estimates will have to be prepared, you understand?' (+,−). With a falling intonation pattern it thus functions like the type of falling tag question that in native-speaker varieties 'appeals for agreement' (Wells 2006), and so perhaps should not be construed as a question at all.

whisk (off, away). Used almost automatically to refer to the action of someone being forcibly taken away, especially by the police, as in J 257 and Igb 297, and: 'Some [students] had their digital cameras seized; others were whisked away' (*The Nation*, 4.8.2016).

4.2.1.3 Transfer

(a) Loan-words

The most easily recognized kind of 'loan'-word is one that primarily features in an 'indigenous' language, but is also freely and frequently used alongside the 'host' words of English discourse. Under this definition loan-words are found in nearly every English variety. In Nigerian English the distinction between loan-words and host-words is actually more complex because of the presence in the linguistic spectrum of Pidgin, the lexis of which is drawn largely from English. Hence, while certain words used in Nigerian English are of Pidgin origin, they may not be easily recognizable as such.

Loan-words can be grouped under the following headings: (i) cuisine and drink; (ii) dress; (iii) transport; (iv) traditional titles; (v) traditional festivals, customs, etc.; (vi) Islam; (vii) others. Several notable examples follow. A further group, (viii), is made up of interjections and particles; examples will appear later in the chapter.

(i) **Cuisine and drink**. Names of soups: *okro, okra* (prepared from the seed-pods of a type of hibiscus; it features in the OED, but the linguistic origin of the word is given there only as 'West African'); *egusi* (Yor., from a type of melon seed); *ora/oha, utazi, onugbo* (Igbo, from different types of leaves); *ogbono* (Igbo, from the seed of a type of mango tree); *edikang ikong* (Efik-Ibibio, made from various leaves and including various types of sea-food). Names of the flour and/or the starchy mass prepared with the flour and water which is accompanied by a soup to constitute a main meal: *elubọ* (Yor.), flour derived from yam and made into *amala*; *gari/garri* (Hau.), the cassava-derived flour used to prepare *ẹba* (Yor., Igb.); *akpu* (Igb.)/*lafun* (Yor.)/*fufu* (of unknown origin), also a cassava-derivative. Other food items: *akara* (Yor.)/*kosai* or more often *kwosai* (Hau.), fried bean-cakes; *akamu* (Igbo)/*koko* (Hau.)/*ogi* (Yor.), guinea-corn gruel, often translated as *pap*; *kuli-kuli* (Hau. groundnut cakes); *kunu* (Hau., gruel made of guinea-corn or millet and flavoured with tamarind); *moin-moin* (Yor.)/*mai-mai* (Igb.), made of ground beans, a light meal; *ngwongwo* (Igb.), but more generally known as 'pepper soup', i.e. a water-based peppery soup prepared with fish or meat and served as an appetizer; *suya* (Hau., strips of grilled meat); *tuwo* (Hau.), a general word used to refer to the 'starchy mass' of a main meal, often collocated with another word, e.g. *shinkafa* (Hau., 'rice').

These and their corresponding names are known throughout the country. Many others have a more local currency, such as the Yoruba soups *ewedu* and *gbegiri*; *banga*, a soup made from palm-fruit, an Urhobo speciality; *brabisko*, a kind of cous-cous, a Kanuri speciality; *isi-ewu*, 'goat-head', an Igbo dish made from parts of the head of a goat and other ingredients; *gwete*, a watery stew prepared with various vegetables, popular in Plateau State. Drink items include: *ogogoro* (Yor.)/*kai-kai* (Igb. etc.), local gin; *burukutu*/*pito* or *fito* (Hau.), beer made from guinea-corn or millet in the North; *fura da nono* (Hau.), balls of millet soaked in the milk of Fulani cows; *zoborodo*/*zobo* (Hau.), a soft drink, prepared from *yakuwa* (red sorrel) and red in colour.

(ii) **Dress**. Some of many items include: *adire* (Yor.; also known as 'Kampala' and 'tie-dye'), a type of cloth with a pattern formed through soaking and drying; *agbada* (Yor.)/*babariga* (Hau. – variously spelled), a 'big flowing gown' (Igboanusi 2002a), actually in its complete form consisting of trousers, shirt, and gown; *akwete*, a type of thick colourful cloth from Rivers State with geometrical designs; *ankara*, wax printed cloth; *aṣo-ebi* (Yor.), cloth of the same design worn by many people on a special occasion; *aṣo-oke* (Yor.), expensive woven cloth; *buba* (Yor.), a loose-fitting upper garment with sleeves reaching to the elbows, worn by women over *iro* (tied cloth) or by men over trousers; *gẹle* (Yor.), cloth of stiff material folded to form a woman's expansive headgear; *okrika*, secondhand goods; *shadda* (Hau.), guinea brocade.

(iii) **Transport**. *bolekaja* (a rickety bus of an earlier period, usually crammed with passengers); *danfo* (a smaller bus); *molue* (a large bus formerly much in use in Lagos, now being replaced, so that the word is not as much in use as previously). These are all from Yoruba. From Hausa or Igbo comes *gongoro*/*gwongworo*, referring to a long-distance truck with upper body-work made of wood). *Kabu-kabu* (Yor.) means a private car used as a taxi and not registered as such.

Two other notable examples are 1. *achaba*/*okada*, both meaning 'commercial motorcycle', which was once ubiquitous in Nigerian cities but has now largely been replaced by the *keke* (q.v.); *achaba*, from Hausa, is the word generally used in the North, *okada*, from Edo (according to Igboanusi 2002a) in the South. 2. *keke*: In Nigerian cities since the early 2000s, the commercial tricycle, carrying two or three passengers in a compartment behind the driver and somewhat resembling the rickshaw of Asian cities, has steadily become the most popular form of cheap transport. The word is borrowed from Hausa and Yoruba, and originally meant 'bicycle' in those languages. At first the new tricycle was known as *keke-NAPEP* (NAPEP standing for 'National Association for the Prevention and Eradication of Poverty', the body which was responsible for its introduction).

(iv) **Traditional titles**. There is a rich profusion of traditional titles in Nigeria, featuring both in indigenous languages and in English discourse. Many are held by local 'kings'. *Oba* (Yor., Bini) and to some extent *obi* and *eze* (Igb.) have a generic denotation, as does *emir*, denoting a Muslim ruler in the North, of Arabic origin, and more widely used than *sarki*, which is the Hausa equivalent. A selection of particular titles is as follows: the Alaafin of Oyo; the Alake of Abeokuta; the Amanyanabo of Bonny; the Emir of Bauchi; the Emir of Ilorin; the Emir of Kano; the Emir of Zazzau; the Etsu Nupe; the Gbom Gwong Jos; the Lamido of Adamawa; the Obi of Onitsha; the Obong of Calabar; the Ohinoyi of Ebira; the Olu of Warri; the Oni of Ife; the Shehu of Bornu; the Sultan of Sokoto; the Tor Tiv. Those who bear these titles exercise limited authority over a certain geographical area, and each has around him a number of subordinates also holding titles and sometimes acting as king-makers.

(v) **Traditional festivals, customs, institutions, etc.** There is a potentially huge number of words in these registers, and it is particularly difficult to decide which among them really count as loan-words. The following are a few examples: *atilogwu* (Igb.), a vigorous, acrobatic dance performed in concert by several young people; *babalawo* (Yor.), 'a traditional healer or diviner (Igboanusi 2002a); *bori* (Hau.), a pre-Islamic cult of spirit possession; *dibia* (Igb.), one who has roughly the same functions as the Yoruba *babalawo*; *Eyo* (Yor.), a masquerade performed annually in Lagos; *igba-nkwu* (Igb.), the first stage in the traditional Igbo marriage rites; *ikenga* (Igb.), a carved wooden figure symbolizing strength and achievement; *magun* (Yor.), a spell cast on a woman by her husband when he develops suspicions of infidelity on her part; *mmanwu* (Igb.), a masquerade, or one taking part in it; *ogboni* (Yor.), a secret fraternity.

(vi) **Islam**. A number of words pertaining to the Islamic faith and ultimately mainly of Arabic origin feature in the English discourse of Nigerians, and not only of Nigerian Muslims. They include: *alhaji*, denoting a man who has performed a pilgrimage to Mecca, with *hajiya* (Hau.) or *alhaja* (Yor.) denoting a woman, all these words also being used as titles; *fidau*, denoting a special prayer to commemorate the deceased; *Id*, denoting a major festival, especially the *Id-el-Kibir* and the *Id-el-Fitri*; *haj*, denoting the greater pilgrimage; *jummat*, as in 'jummat prayer', referring to the Friday afternoon prayer in a mosque; *malam*, 'teacher', 'scholar', also used as a title; *Ramadan*, the name of the holy fasting month; *salla* (Hau.), meaning either one of the five obligatory daily prayer times or one of the major festivals; *sharia/shari'a*, the system of Islamic law; *tafsir*, exegesis of Scripture. Other expressions include names of Sufi orders (e.g. *Tijjaniyya*, variously spelled) and of sects (e.g. *Izala*), and *Boko Haram* (Hau.), literally 'Western education is evil', the name of the violent insurgent movement of the early twenty-first century.

(vii) **Others.** Some other examples include: *ajebota/ajebo* (Yor.), literally 'an eater-of-butter', someone belonging to the bourgeoisie, who is well-off enough to eat butter (in contrast to *ajepako*, a lower-class person who 'eats wood'; both words really belong to slang); *Aladura* (Yor., 'one-with-prayer'), the name of a Christian sect; *almajiri* (Hau., ultimately from Arabic), meaning originally a pupil in a Quranic school, but more popularly a young person begging on the streets of Northern cities; *ayo* (Yor. corresponding to Hau. *dara*), a competitive game rather like Ludo, played with small stones; *dash*, from Pidgin and ultimately from Portuguese, meaning 'give'; *mudu* (Hau.), denoting a bowl used in markets to measure quantities; *mumu* (Pidgin), 'a fool'; *owambe* (Yor.), a party for drinking and general merry-making; *sabon-gari* (Hau.), denoting the 'strangers' quarters' of Northern Muslim cities occupied by non-Muslims; *tokunbo* (Yor.), literally meaning 'coming from overseas', and used to refer to imported secondhand goods; *wahala* (Hau., 'trouble'); *wayo* (Hau., 'cleverness', 'deceit'); *yanga/inyanga* or *shakara* (Pidgin), showing-off.

(b) Translation
Both 'loan translation' (or calques) and 'loan-rendition' are included here, since it is not easy to distinguish the one from the other, and clear cases of loan-rendition are rather few.

bush-meat. The meat of various animals, such as antelope, bush-cow, grass-cutter, etc., that typically are killed by hunters in their habitats in rural areas (A 30). The cured meat is offered for sale at local markets or at the roadside. MTs which are the obvious sources include Igbo (*anu ohia*) and Yoruba (*eran igbe*), each expression here literally meaning "meat –bush".

climb. The fundamental meaning is "lift one foot higher than the other in order to move upwards", but the word is commonly used when the purpose is to enter or get seated on a commercial vehicle; common collocations are therefore *climb keke, climb okada, climb machine,* and sometimes *climb bus* (but *enter bus* is also used). MT sources of *climb* include Hausa (*hau*) and Yoruba (*gun*).

correct, not. Used at non-acrolectal levels, 'His/her head is not correct' is a common way of saying that the person is behaving foolishly (J 171; A 36). The expression seems to be a direct translation from MTs (cf. Yor. *Ori rẹ ko pẹ*).

forget. NigE will say 'I forgot my key inside the house' where other varieties would say 'I left my key inside the house' (meaning, of course, that I forgot to take it with me). The use of *forget* in such a context is a translation of, e.g. Hau. *manta*, Yor. *gbabe* (thus, Yor. *Mo gbabe kọkọrọ mi s'inu ile*, 'I forgot key-my to-inside house') (O 209).

home people. 'How are your home people?' commonly occurs in the exchange of greetings and is a way of asking about the extended family living in 'the village' (A 53).

itch, scratch. Mother-tongue transfer probably accounts for certain NigE uses of (and confusions in the use of) these verbs, as in 'My skin is scratching me' or 'My skin is itching me' (BrEng and AmEng 'My skin is itching'); cf. Yor. *Ara mi nyu mi*; Igb. *Anya na-akọ m ọkọ*, literally 'My eye is itching me'.

like this/that. 'Go like this/that', a way of saying 'Take this/that way', translates Yoruba *Lọ bayi*.

refuse. NigE may say 'The car refuses to start' where other varieties would say 'The car won't start'. *Refuses* here is a direct translation from mother tongues such as Hausa and Yoruba (e.g. Hau. *ki* in *Motata ta ki ta tashi*, literally 'My car she refuses she starts').

satisfied, be. 'I am satisfied' is a way of saying that one has had enough to eat, and while an extension of the dictionary meaning of *satisfied* it also clearly renders various MT expressions used in the same context (Hau. *Na koshi*, Yor. *Mo ti yio*, etc., literally 'I have satisfied') (J 233; A 90).

share. In the register associated with playing games of cards (such as the popular WOT), it is used, with the meaning "distribute", where other varieties would use *deal*. A clear example of mother-tongue transfer (cf. Igbo. *ke*, Yor. *pin*). (J 237.)

'*Sorry*.' A classic Nigerianism expressing sympathy, it corresponds to *(Ẹ)pẹlẹ* (Yor.), *Sannu* (Hau.), *Ndo* (Igb.), etc. Like that of other loan translations or renditions, its meaning is also an example of extension of sense. Mentioned in Kirk-Greene (1971).

transport money. Money used to pay the fare for a journey; cf. Hau. *kudin mota*, Igb. *ego moto* (literally 'money-motor'). Also a 'new' collocation (actually now quite an old one).

try. The verb frequently has the extended meaning "do fairly well", as in 'He has tried' (meaning, for example, that he has written a far from perfect but still commendable essay). 'She is trying' means that she is making commendable efforts to succeed. Used in this way, without any complementation, the verb seems to show mother-tongue transfer: cf. Hau. *Ta na kokari*, Igb. *O na-anwa*, Yor. *O ngbe iyanju* (each meaning "She is trying"). (J 251; A 104.)

use. In 'He used five days in Lagos' (other varieties would say *spent*) the verb is clearly translated from certain mother tongues. Thus in the Yoruba equivalent, *O lo ọjọ marun l'Eko*, the verb is *lo* and in other contexts would be translated 'use'. (J 253; A 106.)

wash. May have the extended meaning "celebrate" the acquisition of something new, such as a car; a translation from MTs (notably from Yoruba *wẹ*, which generally means "put water on something"). 'When are we washing your new car?' (A 108).

4.2.2 Minor categories

4.2.2.1 Ellipsis
Types of ellipsis are: (a) the omission of the head of a phrase, leaving behind a qualifier, or sometimes the qualifier is omitted; (b) the omission of verbal complements. Some common examples of (a) are: *broken* ('... English'); *canvas* ('... shoes'); *carol* ('... service'); *collection* ('...of photographs'); *daily-paid* ('...worker(s)'); *foam* ('...mattress'); *Irish* ('...potatoes'); *low-cost* ('... Housing Estate'); *passport* ('...photograph'); *tape* ('.'...-recorder'); *tipper* ('... lorry'). Examples of the omission of the qualifier are *blade* ('razor ...'); and *the cell*, as in 'He is in the cell', which is elliptical for 'He is in the prison-cell'; BrEng would say 'He is in prison'. Some examples-in-context include: 'They live at low-cost in Ngodo Afikpo' (O 321); 'Bring me one passport' (B 20); 'The suspect was put in the cell without trial' (A 32).

Examples of (b) are: *brush* ('.... one's teeth', as in, for example, 'I have not brushed yet'); *deliver* ('...a baby', and it is the mother, not anyone else, who does the delivering); *disturb* ('... somebody/anybody', as in 'Do not disturb'); *give up* ('... the ghost', thus meaning 'die'); *mean* (as in 'It doesn't mean', i.e. '....anything'); *mention* ('... it', as in the polite formula 'Don't mention', equivalent to 'Don't mention it' in other varieties); *reach* ('... one's destination', as in 'They are on their way to Kano, but they have not reached yet'); *receive* ('...one's pay, salary, etc.'); *swallow* ('....'solid food such as pounded yam). Some examples-in-context are: 'My wife has delivered a baby boy' (A 39); 'No, I don't want jollof rice, I want to swallow' (B 25).

4.2.2.2 Redundancy
Common further examples (mostly -) are: *adequate enough*; *bed-sheet*; *church service*; *frown one's face*; *get up from bed*; *honey-bee*; *pussy-cat*; *rose flower*; *should in case*; *still yet*; *torchlight*; *wave one's hand*; *white colour*. *Sabbatical leave* is common in academic discourse. Common at all levels is the redundant *year* in

expressions in which *anniversary* is also used, such as *first year anniversary*; 'The couple will soon celebrate their 10th year wedding anniversary' (O 37).

4.2.2.3 Conversion
Several examples are found in NigE of conversion from one word-class to another (i.e. a word that initially belongs to one class is made to function also as a member of another). They mostly show conversion to the verb class, although *crave* and *strive* are examples of verb-to-noun conversion (+). Some cases clearly suggest transfer from L1: thus 'The food doesn't ready' parallels Yor. *Ounje naa ko ti jina* (literally 'Food-that not has ready'), where *jina* is a verb.

Examples of conversion to a verb (mainly -) appear in the table below:

Table 8: Conversions to the verb class

Word	Example
horn	Horn before you overtake this vehicle (A 54).
jealous	She jealoused her sister (J&N 254).
less	Could you please less the price? (E 539)
message	I messaged him to my brother (E 167; meaning "I sent him with a message...")
off	She offed the light (i.e. turned it off). (Igb 198)
ready	The food doesn't ready.
senior	Hassan seniors Murtala.
tantamount	His action tantamounts to theft.
worth	My car doesn't worth much.

As increasingly in native-speaker usage, *disrespect* is used as a verb as well as a noun (+). A corpus example (from nov_01, slightly edited) is: "Am I a liar? Is it what you teach her? Disrespecting people older than her...?".

4.2.2.4 Acronymisation
A few of the acronyms commonly used at the time of the writing of this book are as follows, with their expansions:

ABU: Ahmadu Bello University (the premier university in the North, at Zaria)

APC: All Progressives Congress (one of the two main parties in recent elections)

ASUU: Academic Staff Union of Universities (the university lecturers' trade union)

CAN:	Christian Association of Nigeria
CBN:	Central Bank of Nigeria
ECWA:	Evangelical Churches of West Africa
EFCC:	Economic and Financial Crimes Commission
FCT:	Federal Capital Territory (i.e. Abuja and its environs)
FRSC:	Federal Road Safety Corps
INEC:	Independent National Electoral Commission (the body responsible for the conduct of elections at national level, which since independence has gone under various names)
JAMB:	Joint Admissions and Matriculation Boad (a body that conducts entrance exams into higher institutions)
JNI:	Jama'atu Nasril Islam ('Society for the Support of Islam', the umbrella Muslim body)
LASU:	Lagos State University
LGA:	Local Government Authority
NAFDAC:	National Agency for Food and Drugs Administration and Control
NTA:	Nigerian Television Authority
NYSC:	National Youth Service Corps
OFR:	Order of the Federal Republic (one of various national honours)
PDP:	People's Democratic Party (one of the two main parties in recent elections)
PHCN:	Power Holding Company of Nigeria (the body responsible for the distribution of electricity, which replaced the National Electric Power Authority, NEPA)
SAN:	Senior Advocate of Nigeria
WAEC:	West African Examinations Council

In some cases the letters composing the acronym are pronounced separately, e.g. NTA, [en.ti.'e], the last receiving end-stress; where possible they are pronounced as one word, e.g. ASUU. ['asju]. Nigerians used to say humorously about the now-defunct Nigerian Electric Power Authority, NEPA (['nepa]), with its poor record for supplying electricity, that 'NEPA' stood for 'Never Expect Power Always'.

Certain political figures of recent history are also often referred to by a three-letter acronym: thus 'IBB' (Ibrahim Gbadamosi Babangida, military Head of State from 1985 to 1993), 'OBJ' (Olusegun Obasanjo, President from 1999 to 2007).

4.2.2.5 Reduplication
This is common in non-acrolectal NigE as it is in Nigerian Pidgin and in Nigerian languages, and it is employed mainly for emphasis. Some common examples are

fine-fine; *now-now*; *sharp-sharp* (meaning 'without delay'); *well-well. Who and who* (+), used to introduce an indirect question when the speaker assumes that more than one person is to be referred to, was mentioned on page 86; *what and what* (B 28) is similar.

A very common example is the reduplication of a number. This occurs in the context of market transactions, where a customer may for example enquire about the cost of tomatoes, arranged in sets, and the vendor replies 'Hundred hundred naira', meaning 'One hundred naira per set' (–).

4.2.2.6 Clipping

Examples include *agric* (for 'agriculture'); *main camp* (for 'main campus'); *perm sec* (for 'permanent secretary'); *guber* (for 'gubernatorial', an adjective which, along with 'governor' from which it is derived, features prominently in political discussion). *Acada* (LLH), for 'academics', is used as a noun or an adjective, and especially in students' slang, to refer to academic people or to academic studies. *Cele* ([sɛlɛ, HH]) is short for 'celestial' and in turn for 'Celestial Church of Christ', a Christian sect.

4.2.2.7 Back-formation

There are not many examples of this. *Barb*, a verb meaning "cut" and collocated with *hair* (–), was discussed in Chapter One; for example, 'Tony has gone to barb his hair' (E 465), with the curative meaning that Tony got someone (the barber) to cut his hair for him. There are no examples in the corpus; yet colloquially the usage is very widespread, and it receives a mention in most of the main dictionary-type works and collections of errors. The nominal *barbing* is also much used. The example that appears in B 21, 'Viable small businesses.... are mostly in such trades as hair dressing and barbing salons', is taken from *The Guardian*, one of Nigeria's most highly reputed newspapers.

Otherwise the most common example is *opportune* (–), as in 'I wanted to see you, but I was not opportuned' (J&N 258), which is presumably formed from *opportunity*. Another example, used in university environments, is *convocate* (O 124).

4.2.2.8 Blending

An example first mentioned by Jibril (1982a) is *bukateria*, meaning 'a cheap eating-place'. It humorously blends the Hausa *buka*, which itself means 'cheap eating-place', with the *-teria* of *cafeteria*. It has been much cited as a Nigerianism, but is probably a nonce word of the 1980s. Another example is the collocation *kiakia bus*, where *kiakia* is the Yoruba word for 'quickly', although the expression seems also to have fallen out of use. Others are *politricks*, a humorously contemptuous way of referring to politics and its practitioners; and *pastorpreneur*, a probably satirical way of referring to the kind of Christian pastor who heads a church and seems to run it as a business.

4.2.2.9 Archaisms

Jowitt (2014) provides a lone study of archaisms in NigE. A small number of words deemed 'archaic' or 'old-fashioned' or 'formal' in Standard dictionaries remain quite commonly in use in Nigeria (+). Thus *nay* is used as a connective, meaning "What now follows strengthens what has just been said", as in: 'It is with a great sense of shock ... that I received the sad news of the passing on of the great Igbo, nay Nigerian cum African icon' (from a letter in *The Guardian* newspaper of 12.4.2013 reacting to the then recent death of Chinua Achebe). Of 15 written corpus hits for *nay*, three exhibit this usage, the other twelve all being 'Standard' examples where *nay* is used for 'no' in debates. Other examples of NigE archaisms are *except* used as a conjunction and meaning "unless"; *gainsay*; *jest* (in the collocation *make jest of...*); *lest*; *tarry*; *thrice*; *yesteryear*; *yonder*.

The most common example, however, is *shall*. NigE frequently uses this with first persons, perhaps observing an old British grammarians' rule more strictly than it is observed today in Britain itself. A corollary of the rule is, or was, that with second or third persons *shall* has a strongly imperative meaning, and thus remains common enough in legal documents everywhere. It often has this meaning in NigE, and is so used in 112 of 286 written corpus hits for *shall*. A non-corpus example from outside the legal context – but perhaps influenced by it – is a notice displayed in a business centre in Jos that reads 'If girls do not dress decently, they shall be called prostitutes'. (It is difficult to decide whether this amounts to a prediction or a threat.) There are five corpus hits, however, where *shall* is used with second or third persons and clearly does not express any kind of imperative, as in '... this discourse shall argue instead that modernism is an imaginative response to the impossibility of being original' (from 'academic/ humanities, AHum_02).

4.2.2.10 Generic trade names

There are several cases of a trade name being used in Nigeria (especially -) to refer to all commercial brands of a product. They include: *Lipton* (all types of tea; Igb 110); *Maclean* (do. toothpaste, Igb 174); *Maggi* (do. stock-cube – B 16); *Omo* (do. washing powder); *Quaker Oats* (do. porridge oats); *Shelltox* (do. aerosol insecticide).

4.2.2.11 Prepositional usage

Jibril (1982a) claims that 'the point of greatest divergence in Nigerian English from World English.... is prepositional usage'. This is debatable; but there are numerous examples of such divergence, including those where NigE chooses a preposition different from that used in other varieties. The examples given here are arranged in two groups according to the syntax: (a) verb + preposition; (b) preposition + noun phrase (i.e. preposition as head of a prepositional phrase).

Examples of (a): *dabble into* ('... in'); *deal on* ('... in') *die from* ('... of'); *invest on* ('... in'); *result to* ('...in'). Examples of (b) are: *at the alert* ('on...'); *on the long run* ('in...'); *on the head/face/leg*, etc. ('in...').

Some examples-in-context are: 'He deals on motor parts' (A 39); 'Their disagreement resulted to an open quarrel' (K 67); 'They tried so hard, but lost the match on the long run' (A 76).

NigE prepositional usage has also featured in Chapter Three, as an aspect of the complementation of verbs.

4.3 Further aspects of NigE lexis

The above survey shows several cases of overlap between one category and another. There are also certain further aspects of lexical usage which cannot be easily fitted into any of the existing categories, or in which various categories are represented. They include (1) idioms, proverbs, and clichés; (2) slang; and (3) occupational usage.

4.3.1 Idioms, proverbs, clichés

4.3.1.1 Idioms

NigE (a) often varies the form of existing English idioms; but (b) it also changes the meaning of existing idioms; and (c) it has also created idioms of its own.

Examples of (a) appear in Chapter Three. Examples of (b) are: *see red*, "suffer punishment" (A 92), but meaning "get angry" in other varieties; *knock people's heads together*, "cause people to quarrel", but meaning "cause people to stop quarrelling" in other varieties.

Examples of (c) are: *see pepper* ("suffer punishment" – like *see red*); *show someone pepper* ("punish", or the common "deal with"); *look for/find someone's trouble* ("try to annoy"); *put sand in someone's garri* ("spoil things for someone"). Perhaps the most well known example is '*More grease to your elbow!*'(K 47), which expresses encouragement, rather like 'Keep at it!', and is obviously based on the idea expressed in 'elbow grease'.

4.3.1.2 Proverbs

Indigenous languages are rich in proverbs, and they are widely used in NigE too. There are two broad categories. First, many proverbs also feature in other varieties (although many found there do not feature in NigE), sometimes with some variation in form. Secondly, some proverbs are peculiar to NigE (although some feature in other West African varieties). In the first category are: *Behind every successful man there is a woman*; *Blood is thicker than water*; *Half (a) loaf is better than none*; *(What is) sauce/good for the goose is (also) sauce/good for the gander*; *A word is enough for the wise*. In the second category, proverbs of Nigerian origin (sometimes translated from mother tongues) include: *The downfall of a man is not the end of his life*; *Money is hard to get but easy to spend*; *Monkey (de) work, baboon (de) chop* (from Pidgin, literally 'A monkey works, a baboon eats', A 69), meaning that poor people labour but rich people enjoy the fruits of their labour); *Nobody is above mistake*; *Water don pass garri* (from Pidgin, literally 'Water has passed garri' and metaphorically meaning "The problem is beyond a solution"); *When two elephants fight, the grass suffers*.

4.3.1.3 Clichés

A number of examples of 'extension of use', including some of those listed above, come in the category of clichés: expressions which (in the opinion of some observers) are tiresomely overused (Jowitt and Nnamonu 1985). Current examples of clichéd words are: *challenges*; *governance* (used where other varieties would use 'government' meaning "the activity of governing'"); *issues*; *source* (as a verb, really just meaning "obtain"); *X-ray* (used as a verb meaning "examine"). Longer expressions often contain some attractive oddity of lexis or syntax, such as: *alma mater; and so on and so forth; does/did not augur well; be that as it may; beef up security; your busy/tight schedule; cannot be overemphasized; crystal-clear; to crown it all; day in, day out; every Tom, Dick, and Harry; there is no gainsaying (the fact) that; go a-borrowing; go down memory lane; kith and kin; last but not (the) least; the last straw that broke the camel's back; leave no stone unturned; to mention but a few; overheat the polity; run for dear life; spread like a bush fire in the harmattan; the wee hours (of the morning); what have you*. Many of these are regarded as clichés in other varieties too.

4.3.2 Slang

Slang is defined by McArthur (1995) as a set of "colloquial words and phrases generally considered distinct from and socially lower than the standard language". It is often "the usage of the young, the alienated, and those who see themselves as distinct from the rest of society". Arguably, any language that has a rich corpus of slang expressions alongside its general vocabulary is a vibrant language. The history of English has many examples of expressions that were once regarded as slang but were later accepted in the mainstream language.

NigE slang is of special interest because, as pointed out in the Introduction, the population contains a high percentage of young people, and ever-increasing numbers of them now undergo tertiary-level education. They make use of a variety of linguistic resources: mother tongues, but also, for inter-ethnic communication, Standard English and Pidgin. Into what is fundamentally Standard English or Pidgin they bring many slang expressions, usually well aware that such expressions are 'socially lower' than Standard English (as Pidgin generally is).

Thus there has evolved in Nigeria, as in other parts of Africa, an urban youth language. As pointed out in Chapter One, it has been described by Akinremi (2015) and by Akinremi and Dajang (2015), and they label it the 'Nigerian Pidgin-based youth variety'. Since the lexis of Pidgin itself largely comes from English, it can arguably be regarded as a sub-variety either of Pidgin or of Nigerian English. Here it will continue to be referred to as 'slang'.

Many NigE slang expressions have a short life, while others have more staying power, and some, like *gist*, described earlier, are perhaps colloquial rather than slang. Those which have been continuously in use since the 1970s (at least) and are mentioned in Asomugha (1981) or in Longe (1999) include: *expo* ("illegal items or items brought into an examination hall", or "leaked examination questions" – Adegbite et al.); *face-me-I-face-you* (used adjectivally, referring to rented rooms on either side of a corridor in a building, with their doors facing each other); *fashy, to* ("ignore"); *gragra* ("empty pretentious talk"); *Jambite* ("a student at a university who has passed the Joint Admissions and Matriculation Board exams"); *JJC* ('Johnny Just Come', a young man new to city life); *Kirikiri* (sometimes "prison'" in general, but referring in particular to a maximum security prison in Lagos); *mama-put* (a roadside eating-place, typically run by a middle-aged woman); *miss road* ("hold a wrong opinion"); *No show!* ("there was no success"); *rain-coat* ("condom"); *shunt* ("move to a better place in a queue"); *TDB* ('till daybreak', often used of students who read through the night when preparing for exams, but it may refer to sexual activity lasting the whole night); *tune* (with a male subject, "talk to a girl, with a sexual purpose in mind"); *wack* ("eat"). Some slang expressions of the 1970s that now seem to be obsolete are *cockroach*, meaning "stay awake at night to read for exams" (rather like *TDB*); and *abandoned properties*, meaning young women whom men no longer find sexually attractive. (The original meaning of this, common in political discourse in the early 1970s, was houses abandoned during the Civil War by Igbos fleeing from cities such as Port Harcourt.)

NigE slang expressions that have been 'invented' more recently and are currently (in 2016) in use include: *chill*, "relax"; *flex*, "enjoy" (thus students may greet each other with 'How flexing?', meaning "How are you enjoying life?"; and one of the telecommunications companies advertises a 'flex bundle', offering customers various services for 'enjoyment'); *fone* ([fo.nɛ], LH), clearly related to 'phonetics' and meaning "a posh, British- or American-type accent"; *form*, a clipping from *formal* used as an intransitive verb meaning "put on superior airs", but sometimes made transitive, with the same meaning, and collocated with *levels*, as in 'He likes to form levels'; *giraffe*, as a verb, meaning "stretch one's neck in an examination hall to read one's neighbour's script", i.e. cheat; *hammer*, "make a lot of money fast"; *hetch/haitch* ([hetʃ]), (i.e. 'H', standing for 'hunger/hungry', as in the Pidgin-based 'Ai de H', "I am hungry"); *jack*, "read", "study" (and a *jack-lord* means "book-worm"); *ogbeni*, "friend", "colleague"; *para*, *rake*, "get angry easily", "over-react"; *tight*, "good", "beautiful", as in 'That lecturer is tight' (i.e. does his/her job well); *wash*, which in addition to its verbal meaning "celebrate" (see above) may as a noun mean "lie", as in the Pidgin '*Na wash*', an alternative, more slangy version of the Pidgin 'Na lie'; *yarn*, used as a verb meaning "tell a story". '*No long thing*!' means "Do not procrastinate!". *Chow* ([tʃaʊ]) means "eat"; *bar* (? spelling) is one of several words meaning "money", others including *cheese*, *paper*, *raba*. *Straf* (? spelling) is one of several words meaning "have sex", others including *browse, chrome, log in, nack, scarra*, along with the long-established *bang*, which also features in other varieties.

Another more recent coinage is *Naija* (LH), usually meaning "Nigerian" or "Nigerian". According to the BBC's Nigerian-born correspondent Peter Okwoche, quoted by Bilkisu Labaran in a BBC Internet News Report dated 1.10.2012: 'The word was coined by the country's youth as a way of distancing themselves from the old guard who they blame on Nigeria's woes'. The Pidgin 'Na Naija wi de!' (literally, "In Nigeria we are") is a stoical way of saying something like 'This is the kind of country we live in'. Oribhabor (2010) uses the word to mean Pidgin itself.

Does the use of slang differ according to gender? Ademola-Adeoye (2004) investigates whether male and female students at the University of Lagos differ in their use of slang expressions, and finds that they are quite similar. However, she also finds that males use mainly demeaning expressions to refer to females, while the expressions used by females to refer to males are mostly complimentary.

4.3.3 Occupational usage

In Nigeria, as elsewhere, special English usages develop in connection with different occupations. The expressions peculiar to the discourse of, or to discourse with motor mechanics are a salient example because of the ubiquitousness of the motor vehicle in modern society. Common examples are: *boris* ("bearings";

J 160); *kick* ("start", originally used only of a motor-cycle but later of a car as well; the meaning of *kick-starter* is similarly extended - O 295); *over-floating* ('flooding', i.e. of the carburettor and presumably confused with *overflowing*). Fakoya (2004) briefly discusses them from his prescriptivist point of view. He points out, on the one hand, that a car-owner (often but not always better educated than the mechanic) needs to use such expressions in order to get problems solved quickly; on the other, that many Nigerians would be amazed to learn that they do not belong to Standard English (and would, presumably, then avoid them).

4.4 Further aspects of Nigerian English discourse

Linguists use the word 'discourse' in different ways, but always under consideration are texts that are longer than sentences. Conversation therefore provides data for analysis, and conversation analysis is a sub-discipline of its own. Many examples of NigE usage already presented in this chapter normally feature in such longer contexts, especially conversation, and in some cases the context has been specified in some detail (e.g. illustrating the NigE 'Can I...?').

This remaining section of Chapter Four focuses on certain other kinds of NigE lexical usage which can be considered as aspects of discourse, including interjections and discourse particles; kinship terms, modes of address, and greetings; politeness; formal style and informal style; and religiosity.

4.4.1 Interjections and discourse particles

In spoken NigE discourse a large number of interjections are used, perhaps more so than in other varieties. They may express one person's reaction (often an emotional reaction) to what has been said by another, or one person's wish to elicit a reaction from another.

The source of many of the interjections and also of certain much-used discourse particles is an indigenous language; hence many of them come in the category of loan-words. They contribute powerfully to the distinctiveness of NigE discourse. They are nevertheless used more at non-acrolectal than at acrolectal levels. With tones indicated, some examples are as follows:

a-a ([a.a] or [ʔaʔa]; HH). Perhaps of Yoruba origin, but widely used, especially in the South; expreses strong surprise.

a-a ([a.a] or [ʔaʔa]; HL). Used in South, as the equivalent of 'no' (as in 'A. Have you eaten yet? B. A-a.').

..*abi*? (LH, from Yoruba, commonly used in the South), ..*ko*? (H, from Hausa, used in the North). Often used in utterance-final position as an alternative to the generalized '...isn't it?' which corresponds to the tag questions of Standard varieties ('... can't she?', '... didn't they?' etc.). An alternative to ..*ko*? is ...*ba*?, both of these being elliptical for Hau. ...*ko ba haka ba*? ('...is that not so?').

aayyaa (HL.HL or LL.HL). Widely used in the North as an expression of sympathy.

e-hee ([ɛ.hɛɛ]; L.HL). Used in the South; expresses strong agreement.

ee? ([ɛɛ]; LH; very protracted). Used in the South as the equivalent of 'Really?', 'Is that so?' (or sometimes 'Is that?'); and all these expressions (i.e. 'loaned' or 'English') are used where other varieties would use echo questions ('Did she?', 'Will they?', etc.).

ewo! ([ewo]; HH or HM). From Igbo, and features almost exclusively in the English discourse of L1 Igbo speakers. An expression of strong dismay.

haba! (HL). From Hausa; expresses strong surprise, often also meaning 'Don't say so!'.

ii. (HH). From Hausa; 'yes'.

kai! (HL). From Hausa; expresses strong surprise. Igbo *chei*! (HL) may be a variant.

oo. (HH). Widespread in the South; 'yes'.

oo. (HL; very protracted.) Widespread in the South, expressing strong sympathy.

ooo. (LHL; very protracted). Widespread in the South as an expression of mock scorn, meaning 'Didn't I tell you so?'. A rare example of the use of the rise-fall tone in NigE.

Some 'loaned' particles that are enclitic on utterances also feature in NigE discourse:

-*o*. (H, or M after H.) Of Yoruba origin and widely used in the South to down-tone a command or a warning (as in 'Take time-o' or 'Rain is coming-o'), or to reinforce an expression of friendship, such as when calling someone's name ('Maureen-o!').

sha. ([ʃa]; H). Of Yoruba origin, but it is widely used, especially in the South, and has for long featured in Pidgin and in NigE slang. It might be translated as 'in fact', or 'nevertheless': *sha* is often concessive, or reinforces a concessive idea. An example is that, with rumours that lecturers are on strike, two students are debating whether or not to go to the university campus:

A. I will not go. It will just be a waste of time.
B. I have many assignments to write. But me, I will go sha. ('Sha' here reinforces 'But'.)

A number of other 'interjective', highly expressive utterances that occur in NigE discourse are 'English', such as: 'Can you imagine?' (or 'Imagine!'), 'God forbid!', 'God punish you!'. They feature at all levels. In 'Igbo English' a common expression is 'Wonderful!' (J 260; Igb 300), clearly a translation of Igb. *O di egwu* (lit. 'It is a-thing-of-wonder'). Surprise or admiration is here often expressed; alternatively, grief or disgust.

4.4 2 Kinship terms, modes of address, and greetings

4.4.2.1 Kinship terms
A substantial general study of these terms in NigE, with good references, is Ofulue (2011). As in other ESL varieties, kinship terms such as *brother* and *sister* have a wider denotation than in native-speaker varieties. Thus *brother* can refer to any male collateral within the extended family, a clear example of loan-translation from mother tongues. The qualifications *senior* and *junior* are used with each word as required, where native-speaker varieties would use 'older' and 'younger'. *Uncle* and *aunty* or *auntie* (in one of these forms, hence not *aunt*) denotes an older collateral relative within the extended family but also a friend of one's parent(s); here NigE and native-speaker varieties are closer in line. *Daddy* or *Mummy* is often also used to refer, respectfully but also affectionately, to an older person outside the family whom one knows well.

Brother or *sister* may also denote a fellow-member of certain organizations, especially Christian churches. It may also be used to refer to someone of the same ethnic group as oneself, or even to a fellow-Nigerian in general (especially when used outside the country). Another expression referring to someone else of the same ethnic group is 'my tribal brother/sister' or 'my tribal boy/girl' (–).

When people come together for a public occasion such as a wedding or a launching, an older person is often appointed as *father/mother of the day*. *Royal fathers/mothers* is used to refer to any holders of traditional titles who may be present on such occasions.

4.4.2.2 Modes of address
Kinship terms also of course serve as modes of address, and in general these have a greater currency in Nigerian society, with the importance that it attaches to public demonstrations of respect, than they have in the Western world. '*Daddy*'

and '*Mummy*' are used not only by small children when speaking to their parents, but also when they have become adults. '*Dad*' is also used by an adult; '*Mum*' perhaps less so. '*Mommy*' or '*Mom*' is used only by those influenced by AmEng usage. ''*Papa*' (HL)/'*Pa'pa* (LH) /'*Ba 'ba*' (LH) and '*Ma'ma*' (LH) are also used. '*Sir*' is generally used to address any male older than the speaker, even sometimes when the addressee is one's father or 'senior brother'. '*Ma*' or '*Madam*' is likewise used to address a woman. '*Uncle*'/'*aunty*' is also used to address an older person, sometimes implying an attempt at greater intimacy than is implied by '*Sir*'/'*Ma*'.

Modes of address corresponding to titles are much used. The most common are '*Mr*', '*Mrs*', and '*Miss*', and they are used in Nigeria much as elsewhere. A Muslim man is often addressed as '*Malam*', or as '*Alhaji*' if he is older or clearly deserving of greater respect; *Hajiya/Alhaja* (Yor.) is the equivalent for addressing an older woman. '*Mr*' or '*Mrs*' or '*Malam*' may be prefixed to an addressee's first name, e.g. '*Mr Ben*', '*Malam Dauda*', sometimes when a student wishes to address a slightly older student (who is therefore entitled to respect) and they are on quite cordial terms. An ironical form of address is '*Mr Man*'. Young men sometimes address each other as '*O' boy*' (? – the 'O'' is possibly short for 'Old'), sometimes as '*bros*' ('brother', presumably an echo of '*Bros.*' as used in the title of some commercial companies. Young women can address each other as '*babe*'.

Akere (1982) gives an extensive list of titles and occupations and their corresponding modes of address. Thus '*Prof*' is generally used to address a professor, '*Engineer*' to address an engineer, etc. *Your Royal Majesty* may be used to address a king (i.e. an oba, obi, etc.).

4.4.2.3 Greetings
As is well known, Nigerian society also attaches much importance to greetings. In NigE discourse '*Good morning*', '*Good afternoon*', etc., and also '*Good day*' are the most common; '*Hello*' is less often used; '*Hi*' is used among students. The much-cited '*Well done*' is used to address someone engaged in work, and is an example of loan-rendition, corresponding to Hau. *Sannu da aiki*, Yor. *Ẹku iṣẹ* (literally, 'Greetings for work'), etc. Indigenous-language greetings themselves quite often feature in NigE discourse, such as Hau. *Ranka ya daɗe!*, (literally 'May your life be long'), traditionally used to address a chief. '*Yawwa!*'(roughly 'Of course!'), also from Hausa, may be a reply to a greeting, or an expression of approval.

4.4.3 Politeness

Politeness is an important topic in the wide field of pragmatics, and it is not possible to offer more than a few observations about its expression in Nigerian English.

Strangely, although interest in pragmatics has grown in Nigeria, no really comprehensive study of politeness in Nigerian English has been carried out. Adegbija (1989) and Ofulue (2011) are two good studies.

In Nigeria, today as in the past, great value is placed on politeness in social relations. In particular, a social inferior is expected to show deference to a superior, with proper linguistic correlates, more perhaps than is the case in other cultures; thus the use of titles, discussed in the previous section, is *de rigueur*, and in conversation younger persons will sometimes introduce a title such as 'Prof' or 'Sir' more than once in one sentence. In conversing with elders, too, younger persons must not use slang expressions, and many of the discourse particles listed above, such as *–o* and *sha*, with their connotations of informality, are also avoided; naturally, also, taboo words must not be used. Such words generally remain taboo in Nigeria, no matter the relationship between participants in a discourse.

The relationship between a superior and an inferior is conditioned by age, family tie (itself related to age), organizational rank, even sex (a woman is expected to defer to her husband). In some Nigerian languages, notably Yoruba, deference finds grammatical expression in the pronoun system (as in various non-Nigerian languages). Thus the Yoruba second person plural forms *ẹ/yin* are used in speaking to a superior. This of course cannot be reflected in English discourse; however, in Yoruba the third person plural form *wọn* is used for speaking *about* a superior, and 'transfer' may be reflected in English, in the use of *they*. This conversation was once recorded between A and B, who was the younger brother of A's friend Bayo:

A. Where is Bayo?
B. They have gone to school.

As in every human society, politeness also characterizes relations between persons who can regard themselves as being approximately social peers. The conventions of the expression of politeness nevertheless differ, and those in Nigeria differ in several ways from those of other English-speaking societies. One example lies in ways of expressing an order or a request. In the UK or the USA the use of the unqualified imperative for this purpose would be unusual and considered impolite, an offence against the Maxim of Tact (Leech 1983); but in Nigeria it is entirely acceptable when a superior addresses an inferior. Moreover, in the UK or the USA, politeness requires the use of elaborate formulae such as 'Would you mind...?', 'I'd appreciate it if you would...'; in Nigeria these are likely to be regarded, except among the highly educated, as affected and rather ridiculous; simpler mitigations such as 'Please...' or 'Kindly...' are used. At the same time, 'please' is widely used, seemingly not only to mitigate the boldness of an order or a request but also just to reinforce the social bond that is established by any kind of utterance: thus 'Sorry, please' (as an expression of sympathy) is not rare, especially when said to someone who has given vent to anger (which may not necessarily have been directed at the sympathizer).

Commonly heard in Nigeria is an utterance beginning "Let me...", as in "Let me see the secretary ". "Let me..." is pragmatically the statement of an intention, corresponding to "I'm going to..." or "I'll..." in other varieties. Though formally imperative, it actually expresses politeness: the speaker is employing the Maxim of Tact (with its 'benefit to the hearer') by suggesting that the performance of the action (e.g. seeing the secretary) depends on the wishes not of the speaker, but of the hearer.

Among various other NigE politeness phenomena is that a polite warning can be expressed simply by the utterance of a noun phrase referring to an object in the situational context about which action needs to be taken, for example: "Your hand". This might be said by someone warning someone else to move his or her hand – if not, it might be caught in the car door) (–).

4.4.4 Formal and informal style

On the parameter of formality it is common practice to talk of two varieties of English style, 'formal' and 'informal'. Joos (1962), however, famously identified five 'clocks' of style, forming a continuum from the highly informal to the highly formal. With this qualification in mind, it is legitimate to continue to speak of a 'formal' style contrasting with an 'informal' style. Infelicity arises when some expressions that belong to the one appear in what is fundamentally the other. Thus, (A), a fundamentally informal style might contain inappropriately formal expressions; conversely, (B), a largely formal style might contain informal expressions.

The judgment as to what here counts as 'appropriate' or 'inappropriate', and indeed what is 'formal' and 'informal' is naturally subjective, even when made by highly experienced users of the language. Thus the poet and academic Niyi Osundare deplores 'variety under-differentiation', the outcome of which is that consistency of style is not maintained (Osundare 2014). He regards the 'excessive formality' type, i.e. (A) above, as being the more common, and he echoes Ubahakwe, who in articles of the 1970s (1974, 1979) examined 'bookish' English. An example is: 'Permit me, beloved dad, to wish you a most momentous and exhilarating 80th birthday'. An example from Jowitt (1991) is 'How are you? I hope you are in good health. For your information, I arrived home on the 18th of March.' Creative writing teems with examples. In Liwhu Betiang's *Beneath the Rubble*, published by Kraft Books in 2009, the central character has an encounter with juju which is described as follows (p.35):

...he wanted to lie on his bed and rest. A cold scaly object met his skin and he heard
something like a human cry of pain. On close examination, he discovered it was a crab,
big and black, sitting on his bed. Angry, he grabbed his bed sheet and flung the offensive
crustacean hard against the adjacent wall.

The converse type of stylistic inconsistency, i.e. (B), the use of informal expressions in a more formal style, may actually now be more common. Generally in English a formal style, one that eschews subjectivity and figurative language, is required in writing for academic, administrative, legal and other official purposes. An unprecedented number of Nigerians are today engaged in activities that call for such writing. The language used, however, would strike many discerning readers as being too informal, too colourful. An example from an English examination script given by Osundare and presumably relating to the fiction of Chinua Achebe is: 'Mr Brown is the right kind of guy for the proselytisation of the new religion in Umuofia'. An official report written some years ago on the state of affairs in a failing bank says: 'Substandard assets were only 5%, doubtful were 29%, and lost were 66% of total classified assets, as the bank nose-dived into financial chasm'. An editorial in *The Nation* newspaper of 18.8.2016 that discusses the prospects of getting returned to Nigeria the 'Abacha loot' (huge sums salted away by former military dictator Sani Abacha in the 1990s) concludes: 'We therefore demand that this fund in Switzerland and all others criminally held in Britain, USA and other European countries should be released pronto'.

An example of informality in a formal setting of spoken discourse is "Come again, sir?". This might be said by a student to a lecturer with the meaning "Could you repeat what you said, sir?". In British English the mixture of formality and informality would sound odd. Oji (1988) and Eyisi (2003) say it is disrespectful.

4.4.5 Religiosity

Nigeria is a highly religious country, at least in the sense that the average Nigerian appears to be far more conscious of the existence and reality of a supernatural 'realm' than is the case in, say, the Western world today. Attendance at church or mosque is at a very high level; every public meeting of any sort begins and ends with prayer; when a religious festival takes place, newspapers devote much space to relating how it has been celebrated.

One major piece of linguistic evidence for this religiosity is that in their English discourse (and in their discourse in any other language) Nigerians constantly refer to divine power. Thus Chiluwa (2010) in his analysis of 133 informal email messages finds that most of them end on a religious note, such as 'Remain blessed', 'We give God all the glory', 'The peace of the Lord be with you', 'Yours in HIM!'. 'In sha Allah(u)' ('God willing') is frequent in Nigerian Islamic discourse. The evidence from the corpus is striking: for the word 'god' (in this context usually 'God'), there are no fewer than 976 hits. Together with 35 hits for 'Allah' the total number of references to the Almighty thus comes to over 1,000. This easily outdistances the total for almost any other 'content' word for which the frequency can be expected to be high in an African culture: thus for 'child' and 'children' there are 209 and 511 hits respectively. Moreover, over half the total number of hits (for both 'God' and 'Allah') occur in just three text categories, in all of which the use of language is on the whole relatively informal: 'conversations' (239), 'unscripted speeches' (146), and 'social letters' (141). There are few text types in which no instances appear, and they occur even in 'business letters', for example: 'I have not been able to give the work the needed attention owing to a number of factors. But by the special grace of God I am set for the work' (bl_47).

Using GlobWe to compare varieties, we find that the percentage of hits for 'God' is 0.1415 in Nigerian English, approximately three times greater than in US English (0.0537) and seven times greater than in British English (0.0247).

It is difficult to think of more eloquent testimonies to the pervasiveness of religiosity in Nigerian English discourse.

4.5 The Nigerian linguistic landscape

The end of this chapter seems a suitable place to make some observations about the Nigerian linguistic landscape.

'Linguistic landscape' refers to the 'visibility and salience of languages on public and commercial signs in a given territory or region' (Landry and Bourkis 1997), and in recent decades such landscapes, especially those found in multilingual countries, have been the subject of intensive study. Attention has been drawn to the Nigerian landscape by Adetunji (2015). It is manifested in roadside boards advertising small businesses, churches, schools, etc., in hoardings that advertise the products of larger commercial companies, and in the colourful inscriptions that, as in other parts of West Africa, are frequently displayed on the back or sides of buses and lorries. They are normally painted in large capital letters, and cannot escape the notice of any passer-by or traveller.

In his study of such inscriptions, Nwagbara (2008) says that such inscriptions give insight into 'the beliefs, world-view, thought patterns and ideologies of mostly the common people in Nigeria'. They are normally composed and inscribed by persons of lesser education. English, often non-Standard, often elliptical, is the language principally used, along with indigenous languages and

Pidgin, which are sometimes mixed with English. Nwagbara classifies inscriptions into these groups: (i) religious messages; (ii) humour; (iii) folk wisdom; (iv) panegyrics, or praise expressions; (v) regulatory traffic signs.

A selection using this classification and mentioning a few mainly English-language inscriptions not found in Nwagbara's article is as follows (with only the first letter of each word capitalized):

(i) 'God Dey', 'Allah De', 'God's Time Is The Best', 'God Case No Appeal', 'God No Be Man', 'If Not God Mmadu Anaa' (where English is mixed with Igbo and the meaning is "If there is no God, man is lost")

(ii) 'Fine Boy' (suggesting, Nwagbara says, that the owner is attractive to women)

(iii) 'No Condition Is Permanent', 'No Hurry In Life', 'No Food For Lazy Man', 'Nobody Knows Tomorrow', '(Beware) Many Have Gone', 'No Money No Friend'

(iv) 'Yellow Man' (perhaps meaning that a 'yellow-', i.e. light-skinned man is handsome)

(v) 'Horn Before Overtaking', 'No Standing'

Categories (ii) and (iv) could be brought together. The most productive category is probably (iii). There are other signs that are not easily classifiable, such as 'Let Them Say' (i.e. "Let them say what they like about me"); 'You Hate Me! Why?'; 'Patient Man'.

Occasionally the regulatory sign 'Horn Before Overtaking' is rendered as 'Horn Before Overtaken' (in this form of course describing a situation hard to imagine). It is worth noting here that, in general discourse (–), the –ing and –en suffixes of other words are also sometimes confused. Thus *thanksgiven* and *haven* may be used in place of *thanksgiving* and *having* respectively.

5 History and Changes in Progress

The history of the English language in Nigeria might be told in a few words as follows: English was brought to Nigeria in the eighteenth and nineteenth centuries, it became firmly established after 1900 in the era of colonial rule, and it remained so after independence was attained in 1960. Such a summary would resemble that of the history of English in many other ESL countries. But every country being actually unique, a detailed re-telling of the Nigerian story, especially the early part of it, soon becomes less simple and straightforward.

No extensive study of this subject has been carried out, however. Ogu (1992) has two chapters on it, and Igboanusi (2002a) eight pages. Schneider (2007) has rather more, and he relates the history of English in Nigeria, and of Pidgin, to the operation of his Dynamic Model. Omolewa (1979) is a lone specialist study of one formative period.

What can be known about the history of English in Nigeria at present is largely what can be inferred or in some way gleaned from books or articles that are primarily concerned with wider matters, such as the history of education in the country (Fafunwa 1991), or from general histories. The latter include Crowder (1962), Isichei (1983), Falola (1998), Afigbo (2005), Ikime (2005), and Falola and Heaton (2008).

5.1 The pre-colonial era

5.1.1 The slave trade and its abolition

As in many other parts of the world, the English language came to Nigeria as a result of English commercial enterprise. It is impossible to be certain exactly when it was first heard in the country, or generally in West Africa (Spencer 1971). However, in 1553, in the reign of England's Queen Mary I, a certain Captain Windham arrived with two ships and a crew of well over one hundred off the coast of the Gulf of Guinea, seeking to trade with the Oba of Benin, whose ancient kingdom was the most powerful and extensive in the region at the time. The English visitors must have spoken English among themselves, to the hearing of the Oba and his court. One Richard Eden later wrote a report of the visit that appeared in Hakluyt's compendium of various voyages made at this time by Englishmen (Crowder 1962).

Windham's expedition was not a great success, and for some time to come English trading expeditions to the Gulf of Guinea were rare. This English enterprise was moreover was just one small manifestation of the movement of Europeans to

https://doi.org/10.1515/9781501504600-005

continents beyond their own that had begun in the 1400s. On the coast and at the court of the Oba, Windham and his men had been preceded by the Portuguese: they had reached the Gulf in 1472 and Benin, some distance inland, in 1485. Cordial trading relations were established between Portugal and Benin, and Catholic missionary activity was started, which continued at Benin and at Warri until the eighteenth century. The first European language that Nigerians began to hear therefore was Portuguese.

It must have been as a result of this contact that Nigerian Pidgin began to develop. A few lexical items in the Pidgin of today are a reminder that the first superstrate language was Portuguese, notably such words as *dash* (though an African source has been claimed for this), *palaver* and *pikin*, and the Portuguese also left their mark in place-names such as *Lagos* and *Forcados*. Nevertheless, Spencer (1971) expresses doubt that Portuguese retained this role, as the principal lexifier of Pidgin, for any great length of time.

By the seventeenth century, slaves, transported to the New World, had become the principal commodity sought after by the Europeans active along the West African coast. Moreover, as well as Portuguese, there were now French, Dutch, and English traders, the latter mainly under the auspices of the Royal African Company. In the eighteenth century, the beginning of which was marked by the emergence of Britain from the union of England and Scotland, British traders and British merchant ships came to dominate the trade; in what are now Nigerian waters they operated off such increasingly thriving ports as Old Calabar, Bonny and Brass. Undoubtedly for this reason, coastal Pidgin included a steadily increasing number of English words.

By the eighteenth century, numerous Africans, undoubtedly including some from Nigeria, resided in Britain and other European countries, often employed as domestic servants. Moreover, for commercial reasons some Nigerians from the coastal region were sent to England to learn English and book-keeping; some on their return set up elementary schools to impart these skills to others, as observed at Calabar by the late eighteenth-century traveller Captain John Adams (Hodgkin 1975). Thus along the coast the knowledge of English spread, as well as that of Pidgin. One Efik trader, Antera Duke, actually kept a diary of his commercial transactions; the first surviving entries date from 1767. The language is imperfect, is 'broken'; but it is not Pidgin, and the diary counts as the first recorded writing carried out in English by a Nigerian. An extract appears in Chapter Seven.

By the late eighteenth century, Britain with its naval power was foremost among the European states involved in the Atlantic slave trade; but it was in Britain that the movement arose at the same time to bring it and its attendant horrors to an end. An Act of Parliament of 1807 made it illegal for British subjects to engage in the trade. Economic motives blended with humanitarian motives, since the certainty grew that, with Britain's Industrial Revolution under way, 'legitimate' trade in such products as palm-oil would prove more profitable to Britain than the slave trade. Nigerian suppliers of slaves were naturally baffled by Britain's volte-face, and when a former British slaver, Captain Hugh Crow, told King Opobo Pepple of Bonny that there was to be no more such trade, the King replied, in Crow's rendering of his Pidgin, 'We tink trade no stop, for all the Ju-Ju men tell we so, for demn say you country can niber pass God A'mighty' ('We think the trade has not stopped/will not stop, because all the juju men tell us so, because they say that your country can never be greater than God Almighty'; cited in Crowder 1962).

One by-product of the movement was the appearance of the first published book written in Standard English by a Nigerian, *The Interesting Narrative of the Life of Olaudah Equiano*, which appeared in 1789 and is Equiano's autobiography. A modern edition was prepared for Heinemann's African Writers Series by Edwards (1967), and it led to intense fresh interest in the book and its author. There has been controversy over Equiano's origins, but he was probably born somewhere in Igboland. Though taken into slavery and transported to the Americas, where he embraced Christianity and learned to read and write, he later reached England, so becoming a free man, and lived there for the rest of his life until he died in 1797, survived by his English wife. Undoubtedly determined and resourceful, his education combined with his Christian faith to make him a vocal opponent of the slave trade, and he took a prominent part in the abolitionist movement along with William Wilberforce and others. His book is written in the elevated, sometimes sentimental neo-classical style fashionable in the eighteenth century; an extract appears in Chapter Seven.

A number of former slaves from West Africa wrote narratives of the same sort in the late eighteenth and early nineteenth centuries; but although Ogede (1991) is probably right to call Equiano's memoir the 'true beginning of modern African literature', its publication was a rather isolated event in the history of the English language in Nigeria. Another by-product of the anti-slavery movement had a permanent, though indirect impact on this history. In 1787, British humanitarian enterprise, in which Equiano was involved, led to the settlement of some liberated African slaves at Freetown in Sierra Leone, and Sierra Leone began its development as a British, English-speaking colony. The population of ex-slaves grew there because after 1807 the British Navy was used not only to prevent British ships from carrying on the trade but also to stop those of other nations, liberating any slaves who might be on board and putting them ashore in Sierra Leone. Among these ex-slaves or 'recaptives' were many Nigerians, and in Sierra Leone they learned to speak Creole English or Krio, the rapidly growing lingua franca of the new colony.

At the same time, the Church Missionary Society (CMS), an Anglican evangelical missionary body founded in 1799, converted many recaptives to Christianity. They were encouraged in their frequently expressed wish to return to their lands of origin, where they might spread the Christian Gospel and also help to promote economic development. Partly towards this end, the CMS in 1827 at Freetown established Fourah Bay College, with Standard English as its medium of instruction. Growing into an institution of higher education, Fourah Bay was later affiliated to the University of Durham in England and began to award Durham degrees. It long remained West Africa's one and only university, attended by students from the Gold Coast and elsewhere as well as from Nigeria.

The first student produced by Fourah Bay was Samuel Ajayi Crowther, a Yoruba recaptive and an intellectually gifted and fervent Christian. His surname illustrates a tendency, pronounced among nineteenth-century Nigerian Christians, to adopt names from the British culture which had produced first the oppressors, then the liberators of their fellow Africans. From Sierra Leone Crowther went to Britain to study at the CMS missionary college at Islington, then just outside London; undoubtedly he perfected his English language skills, and he was ordained an Anglican priest. He soon began to play a decisive role in fostering the establishment and growth of Protestant Christianity in Nigeria. Later, he became the first African Anglican bishop. A good summary of his life and work is provided by Owadayo (1995).

5.1.2 The coming of Christian missionaries

The date 1842 is commonly regarded by Nigerian scholars today as marking the simultaneous arrival of Christianity and the arrival of the English language on Nigerian soil. In that year Methodist missionaries under Thomas Freeman (who was himself partly African) arrived in Badagry, west of Lagos. Anglicans of the CMS, led by the Englishman Henry Townsend but including Crowther soon followed, moving inland to Abeokuta, and American Baptists soon also arrived and moved further inland still, to Ibadan and beyond. A CMS mission was also established at Ibadan by the German-born Hinderers, and a Yoruba convert, Daniel Olubi, later headed the mission there. This was at a time when Yorubaland was racked by a series of wars among various Yoruba groups, the neighbouring kingdom of Dahomey was trying to take advantage of them, and Islam was also making much headway, penetrating down from the North as a result of the jihad of Usman dan Fodio; Ilorin, in the north of Yorubaland, now had a Fulani emir (Crowder 1962).

The deep interior of West Africa was meanwhile being opened to European penetration, and the exploration of the Nigerian interior was largely a British enterprise.

In 1821, Clapperton, Denham and Oudeney crossed the Sahara from Tripoli and established relations with the Shehu of Borno and the Caliph of Sokoto. The course of the River Niger from its source to the sea was finally 'discovered'; and in the 1830s the invention of steam power enabled ships to begin sailing up the river from the delta, facilitating further journeys of exploration and reconnaissance. Crowther took part in one such expedition in 1841 that was financed by the British Government and included scientific experts as well as missionaries. Humanitarian interest in the development of the area grew in Britain; and Dickens famously satirized the do-gooders in the character of Mrs Jellyby in *Bleak House* (published 1852–3): she seeks to bring the benefits of civilization to the natives of 'Borrioboola-Gha'.

Crowther survived the 1841 expedition, but many of its members perished. Generally from this time onwards the enterprise of European traders and missionaries in the Nigerian interior was hindered less by ignorance than by disease, although this too eventually became less and less of a deterrent. On a further expedition up the Niger in 1854 no one died. The leader of the expedition was a Dr William Baikie, and his surname was 'borrowed' into the language of the Igbos, who lived east of the Niger, as *bekee*; in Igbo today it remains a word denoting 'white man', as Blench (2005) notes.

In 1857, Crowther headed another such expedition, with other African-born CMS missionaries, and they established an Anglican mission at Onitsha, the first Christian mission in Igboland. Other CMS missionaries later established a mission and a school further up the Niger, at the confluence with the Benue (then known as the Tchadda) at Lokoja. Earlier, missionaries of the Church of Scotland led by Hope Waddell had brought the Presbyterian form of Protestant Christianity to Calabar in the south-east. In the 1860s, Roman Catholic activity began (or rather was resumed, after the abortive efforts of earlier centuries in the delta region) with the arrival in Lagos of mainly French priests of the SMA (Society for African Missions) and later sisters of the OLA (Our Lady of the Apostles). A SMA mission was later established in Abeokuta. In 1885 another Catholic missionary body, the Congregation of the Holy Spirit (CSSp), or Holy Ghost Fathers, also began working at Onitsha. A fresh focus of CMS attention was Bonny on the coast, where many converts were made from the 1860s onwards. George Pepple I, who ascended the Bonny throne in 1867, had been educated in Britain and as king assiduously promoted Christianity and 'civilization'. Naturally for this reason popular in Britain, which he continued to visit, he was greatly admired, says Ayandele (1966), 'for his erudition and after-dinner speeches'.

Before the twentieth century, however, in spite of all this missionary activity, there were no mass conversions of Nigerians to Christianity. Echeruo (1977) shows that in Victorian Lagos there were more Muslims than Christians. Moreover, some of the new Nigerian Christians found the faith as presented to them too closely associated with European civilization as a whole, and some new 'African' churches were started. Some African Christians renounced the 'European'-sounding names which had become theirs through the conversion of themselves or their parents, and adopted 'indigenous' ones; an example is the Yoruba man formerly known as Dr David Vincent, who founded the Native Baptist church and adopted the name Mojola Agbebi. In his book *Africa and the Gospel*, published in 1889, he asserted that 'To render Christianity indigenous to Africa, it must be watered by native hands, pruned with native hatchet, and tended with native earth' (Olofinjana 2012).

All the missionary bodies made the establishment of schools one of their priorities. Protestant missionaries had a special interest in this task so as to promote literacy, since individual reading of the Bible was fundamental to the Protestant understanding of growth in faith. This meant that either the Bible had rapidly to be translated into 'vernacular' languages – thus one of Crowther's many achievements was to translate the Bible into Yoruba – or Standard English had to be taught, even if the 'vernacular' were used, to some extent, as the medium of oral instruction. Here the Akus played an important role. *Aku* was a Yoruba word denoting a Yoruba receptive who usually came back to Nigeria from Sierra Leone; Akus were therefore uniquely useful as teachers since they knew both Yoruba and English. *Saro* was another word of similar meaning; it denoted someone of any ethnic group who came to Nigeria from Sierra Leone.

From the beginning the English language was in fact taught as a subject to converts, potential or actual, partly because various subjects other than Bible knowledge and Christian doctrine featured in the curriculum, and because materials written in vernacular languages and so available for studying these subjects were at first non-existent. The importance of English in formal education in Nigeria was thus established early on, and it has largely retained this importance to the present day. At the same time, it was presumably taught according to prevailing nineteenth-century assumptions about English language teaching and learning (Howatt and Widdowson 2004); hence there was a strong emphasis on the learning of grammatical rules and little attempt was made to present English as a language of everyday oral communication. Nigerian English thus acquired the features that have been labelled 'bookish' or 'Victorian' by some observers, as discussed in Chapter Four; 'Victorian English' is one of three 'strands' of Nigerian English identified by Bamgbose (1995), along with 'contact' English (i.e. Pidgin or 'broken') and 'school English'. An extract from the writing of the Rev.Dr Samuel Johnson, in which 'Victorian' features can be observed, is given in Chapter Seven.

Early Nigerian learners of English were actually exposed to several varieties of English because the Christian missionary enterprise was quite international. Many missionaries were native speakers of English but they had a wide range of different accents: thus Henry Townsend, Hope Waddell, and Thomas Bowen were respectively English, Scottish, and American. There were a number of West Indians and 'Saros'; there were some non-British Europeans, notably the German-born Hinderers; while Catholic missionaries were mostly French to begin with, later ones being mostly Irish. As mentioned in Chapter Two, when in the twentieth century English began to be taught to the Hausa-Fulani elite in Government schools, they were also taught to acquire an RP-type accent. Although Jibril (2000) may have exaggerated the importance of Germans among Protestant missionaries in the formation of a distinctively 'Southern' Nigerian English accent, it is clear that RP was only one of the accents presented to Southerners who learned English in the latter half of the nineteenth century. As also said in Chapter Two, more research is needed into differences among Nigerian English accents and their possible origins. Thus there has been no study of the impact that Scottish missionaries may have had on the English accent of Efik and other learners in the Calabar area.

The Western-type education that the missionaries at first provided was elementary; but in 1859 what is now Nigeria's oldest post-primary school was established, the CMS Grammar School in Lagos, although it had only four pupils to begin with. It was modelled on the CMS Grammar School in Freetown, and its first principal was Thomas Babington Macaulay, who had been born in Sierra Leone to Yoruba parents and was named after the British nineteenth-century historian (who, as is well known, made an important contribution to the history of the English language in India). The Nigerian Macaulay is an interesting, Janus-like figure in Nigerian history, since he married the daughter of Samuel Ajayi Crowther, while his son Herbert was one of the early twentieth-century nationalist leaders. He had himself acquired, and wished to impart to his fellow Africans what seemed the best kind of education that the nineteenth century could offer, modelled on that of British public schools, designed to refine the mind, and so oriented to the classics of ancient and English literature; hence the new school's curriculum featured Latin and Greek as well as English. Such became the mystique of the classical languages that in the 1880s, when attempts were made to discontinue the teaching of Greek at the CMS Grammar School, the parents of some pupils expressed outrage. The episode suggests that already the teaching of English itself was taken for granted.

5.2 The colonial era

5.2.1 The Lagos colony

Many of the developments outlined above, including the establishment of an English-medium grammar school, occurred in the period before any part of Nigeria became subject to British colonial rule.

It was in 1861 that Britain's efforts to suppress trading in slaves and to promote legitimate trade in the region culminated in its annexation of Lagos and its environs. The Oba of Lagos, Dosunmu, was prevailed upon to surrender his sovereignty in return for a pension, and a Governor of the Colony of Lagos was appointed. The Colony began to prosper, the machinery of modern government was established, and the necessities of modern life in the Victorian era arrived (paved streets, the printing-press, telegraphy, postage stamps, and at the end of the century electric light; motor cars and the cinema followed early in the next century). A lively picture of life in Lagos at the time is provided by Echeruo (1977).

For a long while, however, the British Government was reluctant to extend its commitments and even wanted to reduce them; thus for two decades, from 1866 to 1886, before it became entirely separate again, Lagos was administered along with Britain's other West African colonies, Gambia, Sierra Leone and Gold Coast. Meanwhile, north and east of the Colony the Yoruba civil wars continued, and because they had repercussions on Lagos the colonial government in Lagos could not remain uninvolved. Like the Government in London it would have been glad to see the area opened up for British trade, but conditions were too disturbed for British traders to operate. However, traders became active further afield, especially in the area north, east, and west of the confluence of the Niger and Benue now often referred to as the Middle Belt (see Chapter One). Here, the business genius of Sir William Taubman Goldie later led to the amalgamation of four competing British companies into one, which in 1887 obtained a charter from the British Government as the Royal Niger Company. With its headquarters at Asaba on the Niger opposite Onitsha and an outlet to the sea at Akassa, it monopolized trade, driving out all African and non-African competitors, and it had its own courts, a police force, and eventually a military force, headed by one Captain Frederick Lugard.

As the number of government departments, commercial houses and mission stations in the Lagos colony and then in other areas increased, they required locally-recruited clerks, telegraph operators, and other personnel who could at least read and write English. These were at first supplied by the mission schools, because as yet government was not in the business of establishing schools itself. (Even in Britain this did not begin to happen until after 1870.) The number of schools in the Lagos colony grew, and included more secondary schools: the Methodist Boys' High School in 1878, its Girls' counterpart the following year, the Baptist Academy in 1885. Right at the end of the century Lagos Muslims, who did not wish their children to attend Christian mission schools, persuaded the government to fund a primary school for the education of them (Fafunwa 1991).

The colonial government's interest in what school leavers could provide for its own better functioning led it to begin making grants to schools and, as a condition, to lay down guidelines for their operation. In 1882 for the first time a government ordinance on education was issued. It applied to all Britain's West African colonies since at the time they were under one administration; but its provisions were essentially retained when Lagos was again separated from the other colonies and a fresh ordinance was issued there in 1887. A government board of education was set up; grants made by it were related to pupils' performance, and to factors such as organization and discipline; scholarships began to be made available to students from poor families, and certificates to be awarded to meritorious teachers; and an inspectorate of schools was instituted. Most importantly, the ordinance insisted on English as the medium of instruction at all levels, and it was made imperative for schools to include English Language in the curriculum. Nevertheless, the actual educational progress made at this time was rather limited, as Echeruo (1977) shows.

A new impressive personality on the Lagos scene was Dr Henry Rawlinson Carr. Like T.B.Macaulay he can be called Janus-like, since he was born in 1863 when the colonial period had just begun, and died in 1945 when it was entering its last phase. A Lagosian and raised as an Anglican, he took the usual road to Fourah Bay for an education, and was the first student there to be awarded an honours degree. From Sierra Leone he went to London, where he studied law and other subjects; back in Lagos, he taught for a while at the CMS Grammar School. Then he joined the new education department of the colonial civil service, and rose to become Inspector of Schools for the Colony of Lagos. Later he became the first Acting Director of Education in the South. A balanced assessment of Carr is provided by Fajana (1984).

Carr's achievements were remarkable but not unique. By 1900 a number of Nigerians, mostly Lagos Yorubas to begin with, were managing to raise the funds to obtain a higher education, at Fourah Bay or sometimes in Britain. Among those who went to Britain were J.K.Randle and Orisadipe Obasa, who studied medicine, and Kitoye Ajasa, who studied law and was called to the bar in England. Back in the colonial society of Lagos they encountered prejudice, which was partly due to the unfortunate rise of a new kind of racism. Associated with social Darwinism, it became influential at this time in the Western world, and it made many whites in Nigeria, as in the other European colonies in Africa, hostile to any kind of African advancement beyond the performance of menial jobs. Lawyers could not get legal appointments and had to be content with advocacy. Randle was appointed Assistant Surgeon at the Lagos Colonial Hospital but later resigned because the salary he received was half that of a European doing the same job .

The careers of these men – women as yet had less hope of emulating men than in the Western world, where women were just beginning to fight for their rights – are symptomatic of the steady growth of a new, educated, Westernized elite in Lagos, Calabar, Bonny and soon other places in the South. Both by choice and of necessity, especially in the context of dialoguing with the British, it was English-speaking.

Along with doctors, surgeons and lawyers it included journalists, engineers, survey-ors, and priests and pastors. Lawyers and journalists were of particular importance for the steady strengthening of the position of English because the practice of their forensic skills through the medium of English was a daily necessity in their work.

The beginnings of a Nigerian English-language press can be traced to the period soon after the annexation of 1861, although the first Nigerian newspaper is said to be the twice-weekly *Iwe Irohin* (Yoruba, literally meaning 'book of news'). Written partly in Yoruba, partly in English, it was launched at Abeokuta in 1859 by Henry Townsend, the CMS missionary. Newspapers written entirely in English naturally had a limited circulation, and publishers and editors needed to attract both Euro-pean and Nigerian readers. This exercised a constraint on what could be written, and for some time they mostly carried factual reports and advertisements. A number of them were nevertheless started, especially after 1880, including the *Lagos Times*, the *Lagos Observer*, the *Anglo-African*, the *Eagle*, the *Mirror* (Echeruo 1977).

A striking figure of this early period of Nigerian journalism was John Payne Jackson, a Liberian who came to settle in Nigeria around 1880 and in 1891 started the *Lagos Weekly Record*. After his death in 1915 it was edited by his son Horatio. For many years, in dignified but sometimes scurrilous language, it asserted African rights and the worth of African culture; and although it also expressed support for some of the colonial government's measures, it was the government's constant critic. Thus it agitated against the imposition of a water rate, which the government said would be used to supply piped water to all parts of Lagos and the critics said would only benefit Europeans. A more conservative rival to it, the *Nigerian Pioneer*, was started by Kitoye Ajasa in 1914, whom the more radical papers attacked for his alleged subservience to the British. All these arguments and debates of public inter-est were of course largely conducted in English, and this is a measure of the progress that English had made, even if only a tiny minority of Nigerians were as yet familiar with it.

The intellectual awakening represented by the rise of journalism was stimulated by visits to Lagos made by pan-Africanists such as Africanus Horton, Edward Blyden and, later, Marcus Garvey. Igbo descent has been claimed for at least two of these. Since they wrote their books in English, English was the lin-guistic medium by which their views spread within the Black diaspora of North America, the British Caribbean, Liberia, and British West Africa.

5.2.2 The creation of Nigeria, 1900

Meanwhile, the political landscape of Nigeria and of Africa as a whole had rapidly and radically changed, fundamentally because of the intensifying rivalry of the

European powers as they pursued their commercial and strategic interests. In 1884 the Conference of Berlin had met to regulate the 'partition' of the continent, which was already under way. 'Spheres of influence' of the different powers were recognized, although because these were vaguely defined the ensuing 'scramble' nearly resulted in war between this or that pair of powers on more than one occasion. Britain regarded the area now represented by Nigeria as one of its spheres of influence, which meant both ending the unfettered independence of African states and the exclusion of other powers. What is roughly now the South-East and the South-South of Nigeria was proclaimed the Oil Rivers Protectorate (later renamed the Niger Coast Protectorate) and recalcitrant African rulers such as Jaja of Opobo, Nana of Warri and Overamwen of Benin were deposed and exiled. The whole of Yorubaland came under British 'protection', in effect being annexed to the Lagos colony, and the new *pax Britannica* brought the civil wars to an end; only Egbaland, with Abeokuta as its capital, remained for a while semi-independent. Finally, to secure greater control of the area to the north where the Royal Niger Company operated or hoped to operate, the British Government revoked the charter of the company and assumed direct control.

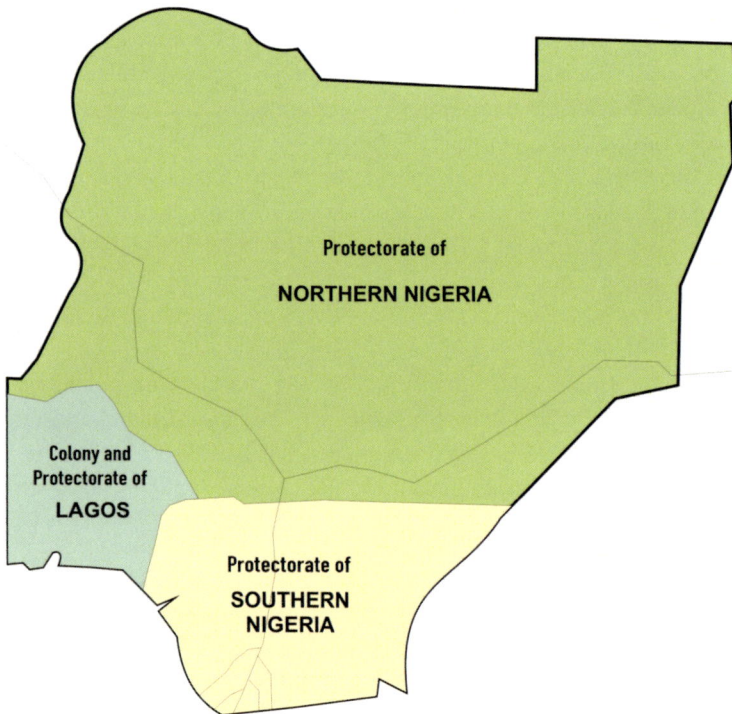

Map 5: Map of Nigeria in 1906

The logic of the hour was reached in 1900 when the British Government proclaimed the two 'protectorates' of Northern Nigeria and Southern Nigeria respectively, the name 'Nigeria' having recently been invented by a British journalist, Flora Shaw. Lagos was soon merged with the South. Several military expeditions in both North and South – in Igboland as late as 1918 – were mounted by the British before armed opposition to their rule was brought to an end. Further logic, of an administrative sort, led to the amalgamation of the North and the South in 1914, with Sir Frederick Lugard, already since 1900 the Governor of the North, as the Governor-General. The North and the South nevertheless continued to have separate administrations, each under a Lieutenant-Governor, and with capitals at Lagos and Kaduna respectively. At a lower level, twenty-two provinces were created, eleven each in the North and the South respectively and each under a British 'Resident'. In the South, the River Niger was a natural dividing line between the 'Eastern provinces' and the 'Western provinces', and eventually, in 1939, each of these groups was given a separate administration. This fostered the 'triangular' politics of the nationalist and immediate post-independence era.

The logic of the unification of North and South was challenged by the educated Lagos elite, especially through the medium of the newspapers. In their view, it made no sense to bring together two areas so unequal in their development: in the North, at the time of the British take-over, almost no Western education existed, and almost no English was spoken. Naturally the newspapers were an important outlet for their criticism. Lugard was infuriated, and expressed great contempt for his critics, for their claims to be educated, and for what he regarded as their mimicry of Western ways. He and his fellow British administrators in the North had embarked upon their long-enduring partnership with the Hausa-Fulani Muslim ruling class, epitomized in the system of 'indirect rule' (first mentioned in Chapter One), which reinforced the authority of the emirs and hindered certain kinds of progress. For their part the Northern emirs, now enjoying fresh security, were not critics of colonial rule.

The colonial régime introduced a series of measures designed to control the freedom of the Lagos newspapers. Details are given by Olukotun (2003). Thus the Seditious Offences Ordinance of 1909 threatened fines or imprisonment for anyone whose spoken or written words brought 'the Government established by law in southern Nigeria' into contempt. Further repressive legislation was introduced in the First World War when it began in 1914. Yet despite the continuing mutual animosity of the government and parts of the Lagos elite, the latter on the whole expressed loyal support for Britain during the War.

The contrast between the North and the South seemed to become starker with the passing of time. Linguistic differences accentuated it: although English was now the language of officialdom, in the North the colonial government also promoted Hausa as a lingua franca and used it to some extent for official purposes. No other indigenous language in the country was favoured in the same way, even though Yoruba for one had been considerably developed for written purposes and became a lingua franca in non-Yoruba areas west of the Niger, as Igbo did in non-Igbo areas east of it.

With the colonial regime now providing settled conditions, the peoples of Nigeria began to interact with one another as never before. An extensive railway network was laid down, along with a network of roads, many of them tarred, both of which facilitated commerce and stimulated production, and postal and telegraphic services were extended to the entire country. People began to move from one part of the country to another to look for work or to trade, especially in the growing cities. This became notably true of the Igbos, who in large numbers left their densely populated eastern homeland and went to the West and the North, but other easterners such as the Ibibios also became migrants, as did Yorubas, many of whom went to the North. The great linguistic importance of this internal migration is that it encouraged the spread of Standard English and of Pidgin as lingua francas for the rather better educated and the not-so-well educated respectively. In the First World War Nigerian soldiers fought for Britain against the Germans in Cameroon and East Africa, and since they served in the ranks and came from different tribes, Pidgin was their common language. Army barracks thus became permanently one of the locales for the use of Pidgin in Nigeria.

Probably the first novel in English with a Nigerian setting is Joyce Cary's *Mister Johnson*, published in 1939. Reflecting Cary's experience as a colonial officer in Northern Nigeria during the period of the War more than twenty years earlier, it has as its central character a clerk from Lagos who has found work in colonial service in a Northern emirate. One criticism to be made of the novel is that the English that Cary puts into the mouth of Johnson does not sound authentic as the kind of English that a semi-educated Southerner at the time would have spoken.

The population of white people in Nigeria grew, but as in the rest of British West Africa they were temporary residents, not settlers, and apart from some missionaries few stayed for any great length of time. Their presence did not result in the 'borrowing' of more than one or two words from indigenous languages into English (*juju* is a rare example, and is of earlier date). Some government personnel had stayed in other parts of the British Empire, such as India and South Africa, and they were presumably responsible for bringing into the use of English in Nigeria words now common such as *compound* and *trek*. The British in Nigeria also anglicized the names of peoples and places, using phonemes and stress patterns they already knew. Thus the MLH tonal pattern of *Yoruba* became HLL, or even LHL; the voiced labio-velar consonant of *Igbo* was replaced by a more manageable voiced labial, and the spelling 'Ibo' resulted. 'Ibadan', Yor. [ibadã, LLL], became [ɪbædn, LHL]; 'Enugu', Igb. [ɛnugu, HHM] became [ɛnu:gu:, LHL], 'Kano' Hau. [kano, with short vowels] became [kɑ:nəʊ]; 'Makurdi' (probably Hau. [makudi], HHH) became [məkɜ:di, LHL]. The names 'Warri' and 'Bonny' show a higher degree of anglicization, corresponding to 'Iwerre'and 'Ibani' in the respective local languages, and resulting from the greater length of the time that white people had known these places.

5.2.3 The growth of schools

Knowledge of English steadily grew in Nigeria in the early twentieth century. Since the government was now 'English-speaking' this is not surprising; but a major contributory if indirect cause is that, with the coming of colonial rule, the number of schools began to increase rapidly. In the South, by 1912 there were at primary level 59 government and 91 'assisted' mission schools – assisted, that is, by government grants (Fafunwa 1974) and subject like government schools to certain policies laid down by the government. There was a much larger number of 'unassisted' schools, often founded by private enterprise and often having untrained teachers and few facilities. Sir Hugh Clifford, who succeeded Lugard as Governor-General in 1919, voiced a patrician contempt for their products, many of whom acted as 'letter-writers' on behalf of those unable to write: '(They) prefer to pick up a precarious and demoralizing living by writing more or less unintelligible letters for persons whose ignorance is even deeper than their own' (quoted by Fafunwa).

The growth of all types of school was especially remarkable in the East, and the figures for 1932 illustrate both the thirst for education and the gross imbalance between 'assisted' (government and assisted mission) and 'unassisted' schools there: in that year there were 18 government, 128 mission, and 1,729 unassisted schools. Now in the forefront of missionary bodies establishing schools in the East, and particularly in Igboland, were the Catholic Holy Ghost Fathers, with Fr (later Bishop) Joseph Shanahan as the leading, indefatigable builder. In the new era Irish priests had a huge advantage over Catholic priests from other parts of the Catholic world: they were native speakers of English (or were generally more at home with English than with Irish Gaelic).

In the East, too, as in some parts of the Western provinces, the foundation of schools was accompanied by mass conversion to Christianity and the abandonment of traditional religion (or at least the profession of it). Each of Chinua Achebe's two novels set in the early twentieth century, *Things Fall Apart* and *Arrow of God*, ends with a description of this phenomenon.

The number of secondary, grammar schools in the South also began to increase steadily, and several missionary bodies also established teachers' training colleges, so as to produce a supply of primary-school teachers. CMS grammar schools were established in Yorubaland at Abeokuta (1908), Ijebu-Ode (1913), and Ado-Ekiti (1933), and in Igboland at Onitsha (1925). Methodist schools were established at Ibadan and at Uzuakoli in Igboland, a Qua Iboe mission school at Etinan in Ibibioland (1915), and, somewhat later, Catholic schools in Lagos and at Onitsha; and some 'private venture' secondary schools also began to be established. The colonial government also felt compelled to take an interest in the intellectual development of Nigerians, partly thanks to the efforts of Dr Henry Carr: he was instrumental in the establishment in 1909 of King's College, Lagos, the first government secondary school in Nigeria. Before long it was known as 'the Eton of Nigeria' (and its boys played cricket). All the schools mentioned were boarding-schools for boys only, but in 1928 the government started Queen's College for girls in Lagos, as a counterpart to King's; the Holy Ghost Fathers established Holy Rosary College for girls at Enugu in the 1930s; other girls' schools followed. To help to maintain standards, enrolment in schools was kept low: Banjo (1996) points out that, twenty-five years after the foundation of Igbobi College, Lagos in 1932, the number of pupils was still only 120. At the same time, British examining bodies set up local branches so that Nigerian boys and girls could sit for the School Certificate examination, and the name 'Cambridge' began to acquire a special lustre among secondary-school teachers and students.

In the North the story was different. As Governor of the North and then as Governor-General of Nigeria, Lugard wanted to promote education – of a certain type and up to a certain level – and in education as in government he believed in 'dual control': he saw educational progress as depending on a partnership of government and the missions. In 1916, his government promulgated an education ordinance which, based on this principle, was now applied to the whole country. It was largely identical to the ordinance of 1887 but made government grants to 'assisted' schools dependent on examination performance.

The problem in the North was that the colonial government had promised the emirs that missionaries would not be allowed into their territories, while for their part the churches could not be content with offering a purely secular education. The Emir of Zaria did allow the CMS to establish a mission at Zaria, under Dr Walter Miller, but the schools he set up were a failure. Likewise a CMS school started early on at Bida, in Muslim Nupeland, was not a great success.

In non-Muslim, 'pagan' parts of the North, however, especially in the Middle Belt, missionaries soon became active after 1900. Protestant bodies included the new Sudan Inland Mission (SIM), the Sudan United Mission (SUM), the Dutch Reformed Church Mission (DRCM) in Tivland along the upper Benue, and in the north-east the Christian Brothers Mission (CBM); while Catholic mission work was carried out mainly by the SMA to begin with and later, in the remote north-east, by the Irish province of the Augustinian order (Crampton 1975). As in other parts of the country, the establishment of schools and the promotion of literacy were among missionaries' major activities, even if evangelization was the overall objective. English was taught, but for a long while mainly at an elementary level. The language policies of different missionary bodies in the North were mentioned in Chapter One: for a long some of them did not give any special attention to English at all, and in some areas they vigorously promoted the indigenous language. The DRCM, who encouraged the production of the Tiv Bible, is one example.

Lugard's administration in the North recognized soon after 1900 that if the predominantly Muslim parts of the North were not to be left behind, it must embark on its own educational policy. In 1909, therefore, before the amalgamation of North and South, it appointed the Swiss-born Dr Hans Vischer, a former missionary, as Director of Education in the North, with a mandate to establish schools. Progress was not spectacular, and it was a long while before any education for girls was started. By 1913 there were in Muslim areas of the North twelve government primary schools, providing some Western education, including teaching of the English language. At the same time there were twenty-nine mission schools in non-Muslim areas. In addition there were in the North no fewer than 19,073 Qur'anic, Arabic-medium schools. In these early years a few government secondary schools were also established in the North, all in the Middle Belt, at Katsina-Ala, Yola, and Ilorin respectively.

By the 1920s, because of the general slowness of progress in the North, even with government encouragement, and the rapidity of progress in the South, largely in the absence of it, the gap between North and South seemed more striking than ever. In 1921, however, the colonial government, anxious that the 'conservative' North should become more 'modern', more vocal, and so a balance to the 'progressive' South, founded Katsina Teachers' College, which after undergoing several changes of location and name over the years finally became Barewa College, Zaria. It was the first of what was eventually a number of government secondary schools in Hausaland that educated the sons of the traditional Northern elite and among other aspects of Western education gave them a thorough grounding in the English language. Barewa was always the most distinguished among them, producing five Northern Heads of State or of government and several governors of regions or states in the post-independence era.

5.2.4 The elite in the inter-war era

The period following the end of the First World War saw the steady growth, in numbers and self-confidence, of the educated, English-speaking elite (Zachernuk

2000). An increasing number of Nigerians went 'overseas' to obtain a higher education, usually after passing through secondary school in Nigeria. Along with Lagos Yorubas, they now included Yorubas and non-Yorubas from the West, and Igbos, Ibibios and others from the East. Government or mission scholarships not being available, the finance was usually put up by families or by town associations. A trailblazing non-Yoruba example is Nnamdi Azikiwe, an Onitsha Igbo, later to be the first President of the Federal Republic. He made his way to the USA and some years later graduated from Lincoln University, Pennsylvania.

Some of the leading members of the elite enjoyed a new measure of respect from or at least developed a closeness to the colonial régime. Thus Dr Carr, who enjoyed Lugard's confidence and who during the War acted as Director of Education for the Southern provinces, was after it appointed Resident for Lagos. Kitoye Ajasa, one of the most distinguished of the Lagos lawyers, was appointed a judge of the Supreme Court and later received a British knighthood, and he was naturally derided for it by the more radical members of the elite. In political and intellectual circles in Britain at this time there was a certain retreat from the imperialistic attitudes of the pre-War era; one sign is that the word 'native', hitherto used by British people to refer to colonial subjects around the world, became stigmatized in educated British English usage, although it continued to be used by Africans to refer to themselves.

The Nigerian educated elite had a freshly heightened political consciousness resulting, partly, from the professed commitment of the Allied victors of the War to democratic principles such as the right of peoples to self-determination. The Treaty of Versailles that marked the end of the War did not regard these principles as applicable to the colonial subjects of Britain, France and other colonial powers. Moreover, under the fiction of a League of Nations (later a United Nations) mandate, Germany's former African colonies were shared among them (predictably without the wishes of the peoples concerned being consulted): thus German Cameroon was shared between Britain and France, and the western part of it, with its capital at Victoria, became, and remained, 'English-speaking'.

The Bolshevik revolution of October 1917 in Russia, with its professed socialist and anti-imperialist ideals, also soon had an impact in Nigeria. In the 1920s the colonial government began to censor socialist literature and prevent its importation, as demonstrated by Iweriebor (2003b). However, for some while the nationalism of the elite did not take the form of demanding the independence of Nigeria. The objective, rather, was to compel the colonial government to allow Nigerians to have some say in the government of their country, and it was shared by nationalists in other colonial territories.

In 1920, representatives from Nigeria, the Gold Coast, Sierra Leone and Gambia came together in Accra to form the National Congress of British West

Africa. Significantly only British West Africa was represented there because a common language was needed, and that could only be English. The most important demand of the Conference was that in each territory a legislative council should be established, with some elected African members. Any racial discrimination in the civil service should be abolished; and a university for West Africa should be set up.

Sir Hugh Clifford, the Governor-General of Nigeria, predictably rejected their demands. Yet in 1922 he introduced a constitution under which a new Legislative Council was established. Its great novelty was that, although it consisted mostly of appointees, official or unofficial, British or Nigerian, it had four elected Nigerian members, three for Lagos and one for Calabar. Thus for the first time at national level in Nigeria the elective principle was established, and soon there came with it the democratic paraphernalia of parties, campaigns, and newspaper partisanship, with English as the principal (if not the exclusive) language used. The new politics was nevertheless still largely an exclusive concern of Lagos and its inhabitants.

The first elections, in 1923, were won by the National Democratic Party led by Herbert Macaulay, whose views naturally found expression in the newspaper he set up, the *Lagos Daily News*. Supporters of the government, expatriate and Nigerian, reacted with the establishment in 1926 of the *Daily Times*. When Macaulay was imprisoned under one of the press laws, the *Times* attacked him as 'a seditious monger, an exploiter of the poor and ignorant in the name of patriotism'. It was later acquired by the London-based Mirror Group, which in Britain published the *Daily Mirror* and also *West Africa* magazine, which was later to be the principal source of news about independent West African countries for a non-West-African audience.

5.2.5 The colonial government and education

The account presented above of various developments of the early decades of colonial rule suggests that the English language became entrenched in Nigeria rather by default than as a result of any deliberate policy on the part of either government or the missions. The idea that English could play or did already play a crucial role in the education of the Nigerian child, and so in fostering the development of the country, was not emphasized by a major report on education in Britain's African colonies that was published in 1922.

The 'Phelps-Stokes' report, as it was called, had been produced by a commission set up by the Phelps-Stokes Fund, an American philanthropic organization. There were actually two reports, one of which concerned Nigeria. The Fund had been approached by American missionaries who, with the explosive growth of education in Africa, found that they lacked the resources to meet the demand, and that the governments of the colonies, for their part, were not doing enough to meet it. The report complained that the government had no overall educational objective. Moreover, the education hitherto provided was too literary, it was suitable only for the production of clerks, and the methods used were outdated. Health and other practical subjects had been neglected; the education of girls had been neglected. The report talked of the need for secondary schools to prepare students for higher studies of a vocational sort, although it was silent on the subject of the need for a university. It asserted that the use of the vernacular language was essential as the medium of instruction, although it did not propose that it could or should be used at all levels.

The Government in London took the two reports seriously. In 1925 it issued a Memorandum the chief importance of which was that it set out the principles on which the education system of each of its African 'dependencies' should be built. It recognized that education must continue to be a joint effort of government and voluntary agencies (which mostly meant Christian missions), and that grants-in-aid should continue to be given to voluntary schools and should not be linked, as in the past, to examination performance. The use of the vernacular, it said, should be promoted. It also foresaw the establishment of institutes of higher education which, in Fafunwa's summary of its provisions, 'might eventually develop into universities'.

In Nigeria, the Memorandum was followed by the issuance of a new Education Code (1926). It strengthened the existing government Departments of Education in the North and South, and the two were soon merged and so came under one Director for the whole country. One major practical task of the Department was to improve the quality of teaching in government or assisted schools, partly through establishing minimum pay for teachers, and correspondingly to limit the growth of unassisted schools.

The new educational thinking in official circles had other important consequences. One was that three new, well-funded, well-staffed government secondary schools were established at Ibadan, Umuahia, and Kaduna in the West, East, and North respectively, where more attention was given to the sciences along with the humanities. Of Nigeria's two most famous writers, as they later became, Wole Soyinka attended the school at Ibadan and Chinua Achebe that at Umuahia. The school at Kaduna was actually the former Katsina Teacher's College, which now became Katsina Higher College (and later, as shown above, Barewa College, Zaria). A second outcome of the new more enlightened thinking was that Nigeria's first higher institution was at last established, Yaba Higher College in Lagos, which was officially opened in 1934. In line with the recommendations of the Phelps-Stokes report it began to provide vocational courses in various technical subjects. Radicals accused the government of not wanting to establish a university.

The onset of the worldwide Great Depression in 1929 had its own important consequences for education in Nigeria. General cuts in government expenditure meant that grants-in-aid for schools had to be reduced and teachers' pay likewise. A number of expatriates working in various government departments, including the Department of Education, lost their jobs and returned to Britain. Yet the thirst for Western education did not diminish. The Director of Education noted in his 1932 report that, while everyone was affected by the Depression, 'one of the last economies of Southern Nigerian parents is school fees'; and with the demand unabated, the number of unassisted schools began to grow again. At secondary level Nigerian teachers were sometimes available to replace expatriate teachers, on lower salaries.

In various government departments, with the increasingly technical nature of their work, the departure and temporary non-recruitment of expatriates made it imperative for training schemes for Nigerians to be rapidly mounted or further developed (Fafunwa 1991). The establishment of Yaba Higher College made possible the coordination of services and standards. Thus a Government Survey School had been established in Lagos as early as 1908; in the 1930s it was affiliated to Yaba Higher College. Technical schools also affiliated to Yaba were established in the South and at Kaduna in the North. The railways department, the marine department, the 'PT&T' (Posts, Telegraphs, and Telephones), all developed their own training courses, as did the agriculture department, with training centres at Ibadan and at Vom on the Jos plateau. Admission to all these programmes was nevertheless strictly controlled, because of the need to maintain professional standards, and the School Certificate was the basic requirement.

Thus came about, in the words of Fafunwa, 'the Nigerianisation of the civil service', though not immediately of its higher ranks. English was inevitably the language of communication within it.

5.2.6 The development of non-Standard English

It can be claimed, as a generalization, that the English taught to Nigerians in the period so far covered in this chapter was Standard English, Standard British English, 'the Queen's' or 'King's' English. Many of the expatriate teachers in secondary schools were British; British personnel staffed the colonial government's Education Department, and the standards they promoted, in English and other subjects, emanated from Britain; the highest examination in English that

Nigerians could sit for, the School Certificate, was set by a British examining body. In many ways just as important is the fact that British personnel in various government departments, from the Governor-General downwards, together with Anglican missionaries, who in the twentieth century mostly came from Britain, served as models which Nigerians emulated. The claim applies more to higher reaches of the education system than to lower ones. It also applies more to written than to spoken English, although Nigerians who were regularly in contact with colonial officers would have been influenced by their predominantly RP accent.

The English that many Nigerians actually learned to speak and write nevertheless became rather different in certain ways from Standard English: in other words, Nigerian English began to develop as a variety, with 'standard' forms and features that have been described in earlier chapters. Many of these 'standard' forms are of course 'non-Standard'.

The causes of this development are presumably similar to those which explain the rise of ESL varieties elsewhere, but in Nigeria one stands out in its plausibility: the rapid growth in the number of primary schools, especially after the extension of colonial rule to the whole country. This is coupled with the fact that so many of the schools were 'unassisted' – soon they were called 'bush' schools – and often employed unqualified teachers whose English competence was very limited and was strongly influenced by the mother tongue, as Odu (1992) points out. Their non-Standard forms would have been passed on to learners, many of whom became teachers later, and thus a cycle of the use of such forms was established, often early in the life of an individual learner.

The history of the development of Nigerian English has been studied even less than the broader subject of the history of English in Nigeria. One brief study is that of Omolewa (1979), who examines the rise in the period 1842–1926 of 'non-standard' or, as he calls it, 'working' English. He contrasts this with two 'standard' types of English used by educated Nigerians, one represented by the 'piquant' style of Dr David Vincent (who, as mentioned above, changed his name to Mojola Agbebi), the other being the 'stiff, inflexible and inelegant' type that was more representative of Nigerian writing at the time. The earliest example he gives of the 'non-standard' type comes from a report written in 1899 by Dr Carr while serving as an inspector of schools in the Lagos colony. Carr observed that some students summarizing the Old Testament story of King Ahab and Naboth's vineyard (I Kings 21) wrote very poor English, such as:

> And it came to pass Naboth have a garden, and Ahab asked him to gave him for his own if he can gave me for present he will gave him money because the garden is near to house and Naboth said I cannot gave you the garden. And Naboth went home he began to angry.

The extract is written in Standard English, but it becomes rather incoherent in the middle, partly because of lack of punctuation; the writer is careless about verbal inflection, misusing 'have' and 'gave'; and he uses 'angry' as a verb. Such errors remain common in more contemporary non-Standard writing.

Unfortunately, the actual number of examples of 'non-standard' English given by Omolewa in this article is very limited, it is not clear how representative they are, and perhaps they are not always relevant. He cites a letter that was sent in 1926 by the then Alaafin of Oyo in the Western provinces to the then local British Resident, requesting that piped water be supplied to Oyo, and presumably because the Alaafin could not do it himself, the writing was done by a letter-writer. The body begins as follows:

> I have just received your letter of even date. It rejoices me that the water is flowing on your hill, and it will please me if a portion of the town could be supplied with water.

Although Omolewa regards this as another example of 'non-standard', 'working' English – and although Governor-General Clifford had recently expressed his disgust at the incompetence of letter-writers – the text is largely 'Standard', containing few infelicities. Another example given by Omolewa is the reproduction by a colonial officer of what his steward said to him one Christmas morning in the 1920s:

> Massa, no fit make morning tea, wood he be too wet, no fit make fire.

But this is clearly Pidgin, not 'non-standard' English. It needs translation, perhaps thus: 'Master, I cannot make your morning tea. The wood is too wet, it cannot be used to light a fire.'

Omolewa also cites some examples of language used in letters exchanged between friends that again seems to be decidedly 'Standard' in grammar, although the lexis may raise questions, such as 'I hope you are swimming majestically in the ocean of good health'. The adverb here has been commented on in Chapter Four. Its popularity in Nigerian English many decades ago as well as today suggests a process at work that might be termed 'the fossilization of overuse'.

Some Nigerians kept diaries, and although those that survive are yet to be exploited for this purpose they are obviously a useful source for studying Nigerian English usage during this period. Examples appear in Adeboye (2003). This is a study of the Ibadan elite, with a special focus on one Akinpelu Obisesan, who for most of his adult life managed his family's business interests in Ibadan but also kept a diary in English over a period of several decades. His biographical details again illustrate the brevity of time from the first implanting of Christianity and

Western education in Nigeria to the attainment of independence: for as a boy in the 1890s Obisesan had Daniel Olubi (see above) as one of his teachers, while he lived until 1963.

Obisesan did not enjoy a higher education, but he was anxious to improve his English, and after the First World War some of his friends helped him write articles for newspapers. His diary gives colourful details of some of the Ibadan personalities of his day, such as Salami Agbaje, the first Ibadan man to build a two-storey house and the first to own a car. Obisesan admired those who had money and wished he had more of it himself; thus in one entry, commenting on a funeral he has just attended he says:

> It is indeed a great burial feast. I have said often times that money is worth having.

The first 'is' appears here where 'was' would probably appear in Standard English; while 'often times' is well established in Nigerian English today in preference to the 'often' of British English.

In another, reflective entry, Obisesan says:

> I regard my past and present life as being indolent and lazy one. Nobody in this town will revere anyone of no means; he would be counted as no-man.

The first sentence after 'as' is awkward and lacks the articles that Standard English would require; while the 'no-man' of the second is a kind of coinage. Standard English might use 'a nobody' here but Obisesan has already used 'Nobody' at the beginning of the sentence. Both sentences are undeniably written in what is fundamentally Standard English, and Obisesan, despite a certain inferiority complex evident in his diary entries, was entitled to count himself among the educated elite who, in Adeboye's words, 'saw the English language, the medium of communication used by the colonial state, as a crucial tool in their hands'; it was seen by them as 'a means of acquiring a meaningful say among the decision makers in the Ibadan community, knowing fully well that the traditional elite lacked this skill'.

5.2.7 The nationalist movement

5.2.7.1 From 1930 to 1945
The development of the nationalist movement from 1880 to 1960 is summarized by Iweriebor (2003a), who points out that there has been no recent major history of the subject. A summary, with some illuminating details, is also provided by Isichei (1983).

An early editor of the *Daily Times* (see above) was Ernest Ikoli, who was born at Nembe in the Niger delta and thus came from outside the old Lagos elite, although he had been educated at King's College, Lagos. In the 1930s he was one of the founders of the Nigerian Youth Movement, which began to advocate self-government and has been described as 'the first multi-ethnic organisation in Nigeria'; significantly, as indicated, the word 'Nigerian' appeared in its name.

In the East too, with the rapid growth of literacy, a number of newspapers were started in the 1920s and 1930s. They were generally not well-produced and did not have a long life. A new wind began to blow in Nigerian journalism when in 1937 Azikiwe returned to Nigeria. By now he was one of the most highly educated Igbos of his day, and he became renowned among them and other Nigerians for his mastery of English, although his enemies and critics, British or Nigerian, complained that his idiom was too American. Based in Lagos, and a passionate nationalist, he started the *West African Pilot* and other newspapers, which introduced a sharper note into criticism of the colonial government, of the domination of Nigeria's economy by expatriate companies, and of the assumptions that lay behind the whole colonial enterprise, although such criticism was not in fact new. He was not surprisingly regarded by the colonial government as a rabble-rouser. His strident tone also offended some among the old-established Lagos elite, and his relations with the Nigerian Youth Movement were stormy.

The latter part of the inter-war period thus saw the emergence into prominence of a number of Nigerians outside the circle of the old elite. Essentially because of their complete or nearly complete mastery of English, they were able to enter into dialogue with 'the colonial masters' and to do so with a sense of common purpose (even if this was later weakened by disagreements among them). A fairly representative figure of the new elite is Anthony Enahoro, whose story is told in his memoirs (Enahoro 1965). He was born in 1923 and like Ikoli he came from a minority tribe, in his case the Esan (anglicized as 'Ishan') of the eastern part of the West, an area for which Enahoro himself later coined the expression 'the Midwest'. The son of a headmaster who was put in charge of a school at Owo in the Yoruba-speaking area of the West, he describes how at Owo he became more fluent in English and in Yoruba than in Esan, so developing the kind of sociolinguistic profile (see Chapter One) that has been common among 'speakers' of minority languages. His father insisted on his giving major attention to English, to the extent that the young Enahoro had to pore over Michael West's pronouncing dictionary in order to acquire the 'right' kind of vowel length and stress placement in words. Also like Ikoli, he later attended King's College, Lagos. On leaving school he went into journalism, first working for one of Azikiwe's papers and later starting one of his own.

The new level of agitation was inspired partly by contemporary developments in the nationalist movement in India, where the Government of India Act of 1935 brought independence closer to realization. During the Second World War, as in India, and as in the First World War, it was muted for a while. Nationalists supported Britain in the struggle with Nazi Germany, because even though British rule in Nigeria did not rest on principles of democracy, nationalists knew that it was utterly different in kind from Nazi tyranny. Distancing itself both from the paternalistic voice of colonial officialdom and from the brutality of the Nazis, Azikiwe's *Pilot* said in 1940:

> The war started with vituperations against Herr Hitler, the beastliness of Nazi methods was explained.... All these were not necessary, the Nazi Government has saved us the trouble.

Notably in this extract 'these' is used as a 'summative' pronoun (other varieties preferring 'this' even when the antecedent is plural), which is normal in Nigerian English today (and is mentioned in Chapter Three).

5.2.7.2 The nationalist movement after 1945: the approach of independence

Falola and Heaton (2008) summarize the complicated story of the rapid succession of constitutional experiments between 1945 and 1960, as does Isichei (1983), and a critical account is also given by Onwuekwe (2003).

Deriving fresh inspiration from the principles stated in Roosevelt's Atlantic Charter, nationalist agitation in Nigeria was resumed as peace approached, and on a more vociferous scale. In 1944 Azikiwe, together with the aged Herbert Macaulay, founded the National Council of Nigeria and the Cameroons (NCNC) to campaign for independence with more vigour than the now defunct Nigerian Youth Movement had displayed. The NCNC was the first nationalist organization that could claim a mass following, in various parts of the country or at least in the cities, and its activities changed the political climate.

At the same time, with the War ended the new Labour Government in power in Britain adopted a new approach to 'the Empire'. The changes it proceeded to effect clearly indicated that Nigeria and the other West African colonies would before very long take the same road as the Indian sub-continent, which attained independence in 1947. The fact that Nigeria and the other West African colonies lacked white settler communities, unlike East and Central Africa, made the process easier. Although in Nigeria some bloody incidents occurred, notably when the Enugu coal-miners went on strike in 1949 and the colonial police opened fire and killed several of them, Nigeria's struggle for independence was largely free of violence.

As soon as the British Government took the decision that it must assist Nigeria to advance towards independence, it also decided to build federalism into the arrangements. The so-called Richards constitution, introduced in 1947, set up regional councils, with nominated members, in the North, East, and West respectively. Nationalists were indignant because the elective principle was thus not extended. The NCNC also attacked the new arrangements because it demanded that the Nigeria of the future should have a unitary form of government; but the British were insistent that the disparity between the North and the South, which had been intensified by colonial policies, required a federal structure.

Largely owing to nationalist agitation, the Richards constitution was soon replaced by the Macpherson constitution, which came into effect in 1952. It was the outcome, partly, of nationwide consultation and discussion, which had never before happened in Nigeria's history; and at least at higher levels, especially in the South, the debates were conducted in English. The constitution provided for elections to regional assemblies, each of which would in turn send some of its members to form a central legislature, and for a central Council of Ministers which would be formed from the legislature. As mentioned in Chapter One, the North secured half the seats in the legislature, and here lay the seeds of future trouble. The regional elections provided for by the new constitution took place in 1951, and were the first democratic elections ever held in Nigeria that involved the entire country. English was rather inevitably accepted as the language of debate in the new assemblies, and in the central legislature; but in the Northern House of Assembly Hausa as well as English was officially recognized as usable.

By now the NCNC was not the only political party in existence. Though it remained strong in the West as well as in the East, it looked increasingly like an Igbo, Easterners' party, and it was damaged by the extremism of the youthful 'Zikist' movement that arose within it and was eventually proscribed by the colonial government. At the same time, the Action Group (AG) under the Yoruba Obafemi Awolowo emerged as a major party in the West and, although it had pan-Nigerian credentials, it had a special appeal to Yoruba interests. *The Nigerian Tribune*, founded in 1949 and still published over sixty years later, represented its views. In the North, where political consciousness was fast developing, in a Nigerian context and with expression in English, the Northern Peoples' Congress (NPC) emerged; unashamedly it promoted 'Northern' interests under the slogan 'One North, one people....' Its leaders, Ahmadu Bello and Abubakar Tafawa Balewa, were both products of Barewa College, but while Bello came from the ruling aristocracy, Balewa, a former headmaster, was of humble birth. Its Southern critics claimed that the NPC's underlying concern was to protect Hausa-Fulani conservative interests and that because of its lack of radicalism it enjoyed the patronage and support of the British. In the North itself, the party was challenged by younger and more radical Hausa-Fulanis who formed the Northern Elements' Progressive Union (NEPU) and also by the United Middle Belt Congress (UMBC), in which the Tiv leader Joseph Tarka was a leading figure; but in the North, as in the East, opposition parties did not make headway.

The momentum towards independence was now unstoppable, although it was far from being without friction. When in 1953 Enahoro on behalf of Southerners in the legislature proposed a motion calling for independence in 1956, the Northerners in the legislature walked out. Riots against Southerners in Northern cities followed, and Nigeria's future as a single entity hovered in the balance. However, a compromise was reached: a further constitution introduced in 1954 provided for direct elections to the central legislature, the National Assembly; but it also strengthened the regions, each of which now had its own government under a Premier, and it was stipulated that each region could advance to self-government when it wished. Azikiwe became the Premier of the East, Awolowo of the West, Ahmadu Bello of the North. In public all the nationalist politicians in fact now looked forward to self-government at an early date. Before long, the post of Federal Prime Minister was created, at the head of a Federal Cabinet; and a Federal Senate was also established.

On October 1 1960, independence was declared. Azikiwe, now more of a national statesman than a nationalist politician, became the new Governor-General and in turn the first President of the Republic when this was proclaimed in 1963. As generally in a 'Westminster' type of government, real power was exercised by the Federal Prime Minister, and this post was held by Sir Abubakar Tafawa Balewa. The fate of the part of Cameroon mandated to Britain under the Treaty of Versailles was determined by a plebiscite in 1961: while the northern half of it voted to stay with Nigeria, the southern half preferred to join the new independent Republic of Cameroon. After forty years of British colonial rule it had become 'English-speaking', with a variety of English close to that of south-eastern Nigeria.

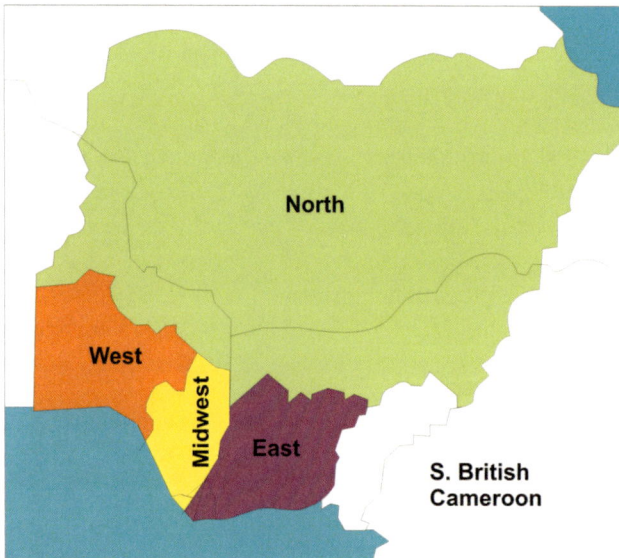

Map 6: The regions of Nigeria, 1965

5.2.7.3 The consolidation of English after 1945

The position of English in Nigeria was inevitably consolidated during these years, since the political developments intensified dialogue between the British Government and its agencies on the one hand and Nigerian nationalists on the other; in addition, the nationalists of different regions and ethnic groups naturally used English to dialogue among themselves. Tafawa Balewa was nicknamed by his admirers 'the Golden Voice of Africa' because of the quality of his spoken English, in which he was deliberately coached by his British friends (Clark 1991). The accent that he acquired, like that of other prominent Northerners, could be described as 'conservative RP' (as of the 1950s) with some Hausa features such as have been described in Chapter Two. An extract can be heard on YouTube (a link is indicated in References). What stands out, predictably, is the highly 'refined' pronunciation of certain vowels: thus /æ/ is raised towards [ɛ], with *African* pronounced as if written 'Efrican', and final /ɪ/ is lowered also towards [ɛ], with *country* pronounced as if written something like 'kun-treh'.

In general, Nigeria's rapidly developing political (and military, administrative, etc.) elite of the post-War era used Standard English with confidence and ease, and 'RP with certain MT-influenced features' (in other words, 'near-RP') could be said generally to characterize its accent. Though there have been exceptions to the rule, some of them spectacular, this has remained true of the elite during the post-independence era up to the present time. Some of its representatives may have been taken aback when (perhaps because of racist stereotyping) their mastery of English caused some surprise outside Nigeria, even if their reaction might be a Nigerian kind of sang-froid. Enahoro amusingly relates how, on a visit to Britain in 1954, he went wearing African robes to Simpson's, a famous department store in the heart of London, and a shop assistant asked him 'Er, speak English?', to which Enahoro laconically replied 'Some'.

English was further strengthened in Nigeria by the accelerated economic and social developments of the period 1945–60. Some developments particularly relevant to this consolidation lay in education and in the media. More and more government and mission or other 'private venture' schools were established, notably in the North, where Sir Ahmadu Bello as Premier encouraged the traditional elite to embrace modern education wholeheartedly. The number of children enrolled in primary schools in the North rose from 66,000 in 1947 to 205,769 in 1957 (Fafunwa), a roughly three-fold increase, although in the West and the East respectively the increase was more like four-fold, and the 1947 base there was higher. In the 1950s Awolowo introduced free primary education in the West, in spite of a lack of trained teachers; in the East the same policy had less apparent success. A major move towards independence from Britain in the educational sphere was the establishment in 1952 of the West African Examinations Council

(WAEC), which began to set and conduct the external examinations marking the end of the secondary-school programme in English-speaking West African countries. The award of a WAEC Certificate was made dependent on a pass in English (and also Mathematics).

By now, too, Nigeria at last had a university. The demand for one – for a university, not a mere 'higher college' – had a long history; to nationalists it was obvious that a university was needed for the creation of the kind of leadership that an independent Nigeria would require (Okafor 1971). During the War the British Government set up the Elliott Commission to investigate and report. Its members debated whether there should be one university serving the whole of English-speaking West Africa, or whether each of the four countries concerned should have its own. The majority favoured the latter view.

In 1948, therefore, University College, Ibadan was established. It was predictably organized along the lines of a British university, initially had a mainly expatriate staff, and initially awarded University of London degrees. It soon acquired an international reputation, and it began to produce the first generation of senior civil servants, academics, and other leaders of thought that governed Nigeria's affairs in the post-independence era. Its curriculum nevertheless encountered much criticism as being too narrow and academic; and as independence approached the demand for more universities was increasingly voiced. This was one of the major recommendations of another Commission, headed by Sir Eric Ashby, and in the nineteen-sixties more universities came into existence, at Nsukka (the University of Nigeria) in the East, at Zaria (Ahmadu Bello University, ABU) in the North, at Lagos, and at Ile-Ife (Obafemi Awolowo University, OAU) in the West. As mentioned below, many more followed.

Where journalism is concerned, in the 1950s sales of the *Pilot* declined, probably because Azikiwe himself became less radical, and the *Daily Times* remained the one newspaper with a nationwide readership. After independence, the Gaskiya Corporation started publication in Kaduna of the *New Nigerian*, which became the principal newspaper in the North and the expression of Northern government interests. Another notable media event was the establishment in 1950 of the Nigerian Broadcasting Service (NBC). Chinua Achebe worked for the NBC for some years after graduating from Ibadan, and it was while working there that he wrote *Things Fall Apart*. Published in 1958, it was the first Nigerian novel written in Standard English that was published outside Nigeria and achieved international renown. As shown in Chapter One, the event marked the beginning of a literary avalanche.

At the same time during these years, decidedly non-Standard varieties were adding colour to the increasingly complex English-language scene. Mention was made in Chapter One of the fiction of Amos Tutuola, a Yoruba, and of 'Onitsha market literature', i.e. short works or chapbooks that were typically written by Igbos of limited education and were published at Onitsha. Some of these were novelettes; others, in the words of Isichei (1983), offered a guide 'through all the complexities of urban life: how to write letters, how to sit examinations, how to become rich (hard work), how to stay rich (sobriety, trust in God, and avoidance of designing women)'. Extracts from Tutuola and Onitsha market literature appear in Chapter Seven (32 and 33 respectively).

5.3 The post-independence era and current developments

5.3.1 General developments since 1960 and the further growth of English

A very brief sketch of the political history of Nigeria in the period since 1960 was given in Chapter One, and summaries are found in Falola and Heaton (2008) and Falola and Oyeniyi (2015). There is no need to repeat or expand this history here, since the political changes that the country has undergone have not had any noticeable bearing upon the role of English in Nigerian national life. The political and other elites who took over from the British did not seriously question the role that English already played; if they reflected on the matter, they took it as axiomatic that the English language was indispensable for the functioning of a country of such diversity. At least at national level, the language chiefly used to express and reflect change and conflict – the conflict between the Federal Government and the secessionist Biafrans in the late 1960s, or the stand-off between the military regimes and their democracy-minded critics in the 1990s, to take just two examples – remained English.

Since independence, as before it, government pronouncements, and public pronouncements in general, have reached the greatest number of Nigerians through the medium of English. As in other English-speaking countries, things said by those in authority have been taken up by the media and much quoted. 'To keep Nigeria one/Is a task that must be done' was an inspirational slogan used by the Federal Government during the civil war of the late 1960s; 'No victors, no vanquished' was how General Gowon expressed his conciliatory policy at the end of the war; 'War against indiscipline' was a slogan of the regime of General Buhari that held power from 1983 to 1985; 'My friend, where is Anini?' was a question jocularly put by General Babangida (who replaced Buhari in 1985) to the Inspector-General of Police when the security agencies were trying to track down George Anini, a notorious robber – Adegbija (1988) devotes a whole article to an analysis of it; 'third term' was an expression constantly heard during the period 2003–07, when President Obasanjo was serving his second term in office and was alleged to be interested in getting the constitution altered so as to enable him to remain in power; 'Good people, great nation' was the slogan of the campaign to 're-brand' Nigeria directed by Mrs Dora Akunyili, Minister of Information in the government of President Yar'Adua (2007–10).

The coming to Nigeria of short text messaging by mobile phone and the internet in the early 2000s has continued to reinforce the position of English. Thus, although English was naturally not the only language to feature in Nigerian discussion of the Boko Haram insurgency that disturbed the country after 2009, it was in English that the most widely influential statements about it were made. A major example is the social media message 'Bring back our girls', which helped to keep in the forefront of public consciousness the fate of the more than 200 schoolgirls who were kidnapped at Chibok in Borno State in May, 2014.

The efflorescence of Nigerian literature in English, which began in the 1950s, was also discussed in Chapter One. As pointed out there, a great number of novels, plays and poetry have been written and continue to be written by Nigerians; and this remains true even if the reading culture in Nigeria is on the decline. Other genres of writing have also flourished: thus a number of public figures have written their autobiographies or have been the subject of a biography written by someone else.

Newspapers and weekly magazines have come and gone in Nigeria; papers that are published today and have been founded since 1980 include *The Guardian*, *ThisDay*, *Daily Trust*, *Vanguard*, and *The Nation*. A number of Nigerian journalists have been famous, at home and abroad, for the quality of their writing, for example Peter Enahoro (brother of the politician), who in the early 1960s wrote the column 'Peter Pan' in the *Daily Times* and later also famous satirical books, *How to be a Nigerian* and *The Complete Nigerian*; while Olatunji Dare, who writes in *The Nation*, is a more recent representative of this satirical tradition. Extracts from their writing appear in Chapter Seven (12 and 17 respectively). Several newspapers feature satirical cartoons, with witty captions; extract 39 in Chapter Seven is the text accompanying a comic strip.

Certain important social developments of the post-1960 era that demonstrate and underline the continued strengthening of English in Nigeria have already been discussed in Chapter One. Surely the most important of these is simply the steady increase in the number of Nigerians with some degree of English competence, and in the proportion of this number to the population. As argued earlier, even if English continues to be associated with the elite more than with any other social group, it has become less and less justifiable to label it 'elitist'.

Another development, closely associated with this one and helping to account for it, is the steady rise in the number of higher institutions and of the number of lecturers and students in the country. Thus in the 1970s a number of 'second generation'

Federal universities were added to the existing ones; subsequently still more Federal universities, along with State universities (i.e. financed by State governments), and private universities (licensed under the Constitution of 1979) were created; and even military and police academies became degree-awarding. By 2015, there were 40 Federal, 40 State, and 61 private universities, a total of 141, and still more followed.

Federal or State colleges of education and polytechnics offering technical courses also proliferated; and the organization of higher education was intensified. Thus a National Universities Commission (NUC), with overall responsibility for policy, was established, along with a National Teachers' Institute (NTI), a National Board for Technical Education, and professional associations (such as the Nigeria English Studies Association, in 2015 renamed the English Scholars Association of Nigeria), with their associated journals and annual conferences; the Joint Admissions Matriculation Board (JAMB) was set up to regulate admission to universities (and the acronym, pronounced [ʤam], became common usage); while unions such as the Academic Staff of Universities Union (ASUU) fought to improve conditions of service, often invoking the strike weapon and usually seeing themselves as standing in a tradition of opposition to government that went back to colonial times.

This expansion at tertiary level was matched by continued expansion at lower levels, and a landmark on the road of the development of primary education was reached in 1976 with the introduction of Universal Primary Education (UPE), i.e. primary education that became available to every Nigerian child because it was free. Comprehensive fresh thinking at official levels about the kind of education that independent Nigeria needed led to the promulgation of the first National Policy on Education (NPE) in 1977, discussed in Chapter One. The NPE also brought about a new American-style '6-3-3-4' (primary – junior secondary – senior secondary – university) education system, and the old British-style pre-university sixth form was abolished. Here can be observed, perhaps, a certain Americanization of Nigerian life in the post-independence era, to some extent a reflection of the increasing number of Nigerians who went to the US for further studies, often because there it was easier than in the UK to combine work with studies. American usage also increasingly influenced Nigerian English usage, as shown in earlier chapters. As pointed out in Chapter One, the American presidential system of government was adopted in the constitutions of 1979 and 1999.

The vast expansion of the education sector in the post-independence era was made possible by revenue from oil wealth. Oil was first discovered in the Niger delta in 1958, and by the end of the civil war Nigeria was a major exporter of crude. Over the decades, the revenue has been used to finance many development projects, but much of it has been siphoned off by corruption. In its various forms this has been pervasive at all levels of Nigerian society, and in various sectors including education. It helps to account for the anxiety, frequently expressed by educationists and others, that 'quantity' has been given precedence over 'quality', and that 'standards' have seriously fallen. Nigerians sometimes jocularly, and echoing the Old Testament Book of Exodus, refer to excessive leniency in the award of marks to students for assignments and exams as the 'Let my people go' philosophy.

The anxiety felt by many Nigerian teachers over declining levels of performance in English in particular was discussed in Chapter One. A settled judgment on this important issue is difficult to arrive at; but many observers feel that the kind of English written by students in the 1960s could not be written by their counterparts of the same formal level of education fifty years later.

A test of the hypothesis used the following example of writing of the earlier period. It comes from a set of fourth-form (Grade 10) essays written in the year 1966 by Igbo grammar-school students, the topic being the *dibia* or 'medicine man' of Igbo culture:

> "Dibia" is a general appellation given to that class of people who are skilled in local native medicine-making. They are believed to be messengers of the gods and goddesses. They possess the wonderful power of refining a person from his pitiable state of poverty to a prosperous happy man, by removing the misfortune, which is, as the belief goes, a punishment from the gods, that eclipses the prosperity to one's life. With their god-like powers they could "cook" a person so that he becomes invulnerable; danger passes him by. Or, they are the gods' images on earth.

The passage is not strikingly well-written, but the sentences are generally well constructed, the choice of words is quite advanced, and the spelling and punctuation are Standard. Without being told in what year the writing had in fact been done, thirty Nigerians who in 2016 were mostly graduates were asked to say what category of pupils or students was likely to have written the passage, the options being (A) primary, (B) junior secondary, (C) senior secondary, (D) undergraduate, (E) postgraduate. Most significantly, every one of the thirty respondents thought that the writer belonged to category (D) or (E). They assumed (naturally enough since they were not given the date), that the writing was also of 2016, and that the writer must be of at least undergraduate status to write so well.

The passage does not contain any common non-Standard features; but by the 1960s such features were by now well-established in Nigerian English. This is confirmed by a study of the scripts of other students who wrote the same essay in 1966, and who generally, like the writer above, showed a high degree of Standard English competence. Non-Standard features occurring in them include 'have' or 'has' for 'had'; 'would' for 'will'; 'dinning' for 'dining'; 'lost' for 'loss'; 'greatful' for 'grateful'; 'am' for 'I'm' or 'I am'; 'incidence' for 'incident', and 'such' as a pronoun for 'this' or 'it'. The well-known Nigerian English idiom 'more grease to your elbow' also occurs.

5.3.2 A summary of current trends

In conclusion, certain trends in the history of English in Nigeria can be summarized and emphasized.

The position of English as the official language in Nigeria seems as secure today as it has ever been, and the number of 'speakers of English' in the country looks set to continue to rise. Fundamentally this is because of the huge numbers of younger Nigerians undergoing higher education programmes. As remarked in Chapter One, some of them come from 'educated' homes where English is spoken in preference to any other language. The number of them is likely to increase.

English is a fairly obvious 'threat' to indigenous languages, and defenders of indigenous languages will continue to seek and advocate ways of reducing the threat. Nevertheless, many indigenous languages are threatened by other indigenous languages; and English itself is threatened by the spread of Pidgin.

As reported in the last section and also in Chapter One, many Nigerian educationists believe that English in Nigeria is today threatened by 'falling standards'; and this anxiety is not likely to diminish soon. It is a 'deficit' view of language, and of an L2 variety of English in particular, that is no doubt unfashionable; but it cannot be ignored. It is expressed primarily, however, in relation to pronunciation, spelling and grammar, less often in relation to lexis. To the extent that the indigenization of English in Nigeria is accepted by educated Nigerians, the use by them or their fellow citizens of distinctively Nigerian vocabulary and the associated 'Nigerian' meanings is less problematic.

The picture of 'falling standards' is also offset by the fact that Nigerians have for long shown a high degree of general competence, and of imagination and inventiveness in their use of English. It is manifested in literary production but also in everyday usage, even if non-Standard forms also flourish. In general terms, this creativity suggests a thorough domestication of the language that seems set to endure.

One thing that seems set to change is the nature of research into Nigerian English. Past research has shown that the incidence of the use of non-Standard features of English of the more conspicuous sort is more frequent at the more basilectal end of the spectrum of usage than at the more acrolectal end. Hitherto this has perhaps tended to make the Nigerian English basilect-mesolect more interesting to descriptivists (and more repellent to prescriptivists). But with new research tools, including the creation of more and bigger corpora, the future offers the prospect of more thorough investigation of usage at all levels.

6 Survey of Previous Work and Annotated Bibliography

English in Nigeria has been given serious attention and been made the subject of scholarly study only in the post-independence era. The study of the more narrowly-defined Nigerian English was initially pursued by Nigerians at Nigeria's 'first generation' universities in the South-West: by Banjo, Bamgbose, Adesanoye, Adeniran, Ubahakwe, Kujore, and others at Ibadan, soon followed by Adetugbo, Akere, and others at Lagos. Others, somewhat later, came from other universities further afield: Jibril (Bayero University, Kano), Odumuh (Ahmadu Bello University, Zaria), Adekunle (Jos), Eka (Uyo). Subsequent work has been carried out by others (Adegbija, Bamiro, Igboanusi, Jowitt, Udofot, Chiluwa, Ugorji, etc.) working in various universities around the country and also (Schmied, Gut, Fuchs, Werner, etc.) outside.

The number of persons in Nigeria carrying out research in the field of English studies has increased greatly because of the increased number of universities. The amount of research being carried out into what is distinctively Nigerian about English language use in Nigeria, or into the comparison of Nigerian English with other varieties, is nevertheless now relatively small. Change would require a change in the research environment in Nigeria, since at present the universities, where such research would be done, lack various kinds of resources. Attitudes would also need to change, however, especially the belief of many Nigerians, well-educated or not, that Nigerian English is 'something inferior, botched, tenth-rate' (Jowitt 1991). Only reasoned advocacy is likely to change this belief.

As pointed out earlier, fields of interest other than Nigerian English have come to hold the attention of researchers. Thus in 2015 a doctoral student at one university was writing a dissertation entitled 'A stylistic study of ambiguity in Nigerian newspaper headlines'; but the study did not address the possible 'Nigerian-ness' of the headlines. Pragmatics is a field popular field with researchers, but the topic chosen may have no Nigerian content at all: thus a Master's dissertation of 2014 bears the title 'A speech act analysis of utterances in classical [*sic*] films: a study of *300 Spartans* and *Game of Thrones*'.

Writing about English in Nigeria can be classified according to broad topic: works of a general nature, the position of English in relation to other languages in Nigeria, phonetics and phonology, morphology and syntax, lexis and discourse, history – a list which largely matches the titles and the sequence of chapters in this book. This method of classification is adopted for the purposes of this chapter, where a number of works are reviewed. It will be clear from the details

https://doi.org/10.1515/9781501504600-006

given for each of these, and also from the list of References, in what form each work can be accessed. The review follows.

6.1 General works

Grieve (1964), 'English Language Examining'
'The Grieve Report' does not come in the category of scholarly works; but, published soon after most of the English-speaking West African countries had achieved independence, it proved influential in shaping attitudes to the emerging varieties of West African English and to the possible teaching of them. Grieve, a British English language teaching expert, was asked by the West African Examinations Council (WAEC) chiefly to evaluate the Council's examining of the English Language. In his 129-page report he maintained that hitherto English language teaching, in Britain as well as in Africa, had been too literary, paying little attention to spoken English forms and being insufficiently linked to everyday, real-life situations. He was sceptical about the possibility of teaching and examining Nigerian and other West African varieties, on the grounds that these had not been properly described. Although he showed guarded acceptance of lexical 'variants' (such as Nigerian 'kia-kia bus' and Ghanaian 'outdooring'), he reaffirmed the existence of a 'universal Standard English', and pointed out that 'in structure the educated African departs but rarely from the patterns and forms of Standard English'.

Walsh (1967), 'Distinguishing types and varieties of English in Nigeria'
The article was published in an early issue of the *Journal* of the Nigeria English Studies Association, which held its first Conference in Jos in 1966. Walsh, an expatriate teacher, brought the expression 'Nigerian English' into academic discussion, and believed that, for example, the pluralized *equipments* could be 'legitimately' regarded as one of its forms: a view of non-Standard syntactic forms that was soon countered by **Salami (1968)** in **'Defining a Standard Nigerian English'** in another issue of the journal. This conflict between 'liberal' (or 'liberationist') and 'conservative' approaches to non-Standard syntax was to recur over the decades, not only in Nigerian English studies but in studies of many other varieties of English around the world.

Spencer (1971), *The English Language in West Africa*
This book brought together for the first time articles on various African Englishes – to be specific, on West African Englishes. Spencer's introductory article gives an overview of issues and problems that have remained staples of debate, such as the fact that there exists a considerable 'range of English' in West Africa; it also

provides much information on the history of English in the region. Of the other eight articles, three concern English in Nigeria. Mafeni's is an introduction to Nigerian Pidgin. Kirk-Greene points out in his that the number of words of West African origin in English is tiny (compared to the number that have entered English from Indian languages); he also presents a number of written-medium Nigerianisms, mostly supplied by Hausa speakers of English. Bamgbose's is the first in a series of articles published over the years that give a general view of the subject. He discusses the role of English, estimates the number of English speakers, and also devotes a section to distinctively Nigerian phonological and lexical forms.

Banjo (1971), 'Towards a definition of Standard Nigerian spoken English'
This proved to be a seminal article in the context of attempts to identify and differentiate sub-varieties of Nigerian English and in particular to identify a 'Standard Nigerian English'. It can be related to an article by Brosnahan (1958) that discussed 'levels' of spoken English in Southern Nigeria, where Pidgin is treated as Level One. Banjo is also concerned with using phonological data, though not exclusively. With this wider scope, and because of its theoretical interest, a summary of the content of the article is presented in Chapter One.

Banjo's student Adesanoye adapted Banjo's model for the purposes of his PhD dissertation entitled 'A study of varieties of written English in Nigeria' (1973), relating Banjo's varieties to written texts. A summary of the work is given towards the end of Chapter One.

Adetugbo (1977), 'Nigerian English: Fact or Fiction?'
The late Abiodun Adetugbo of the University of Lagos strongly supported the descriptive approach to Nigerian English, the existence of which is 'fact', not 'fiction'. In this early article he gives a long list of common grammatical and lexical examples of differences between Nigerian English and 'British Standard English', and clearly does not regard the Nigerian forms as 'deviations'.

Ubahakwe (1979), *Varieties and Functions of English in Nigeria*
This was the first book to be published specifically on English in Nigeria, with the Nigerian variety of English as its main focus. It was the outcome of the Ninth Conference of the Nigeria English Studies Association, held in Ibadan in 1978. Banjo provided the introductory chapter, 'Beyond intelligibility'. The subsequent eighteen chapters are grouped under various headings ('On varieties of Nigerian English', 'On characterizing Nigerian English', etc.), and several of them are of abiding interest. Adekunle's 'Non-random variation in the Nigerian English' gives examples of variation in Nigerian English caused by mother-tongue influence, but distinguishes between 'random' and 'non-random' variation. In 'Regional

variation in Nigerian spoken English', Jibril drew attention to differences between 'Northern' (i.e. Hausa) and 'Southern' English accents, but claimed that the distinction between the two was closing. Taiwo in 'Varieties of English in Nkem Nwankwo's novels' identified five varieties, and examined the third of these, which utilizes mother-tongue structure and idiom without doing violence to Standard English, in the fiction of an early Igbo novelist. Adetugbo's substantial 'Appropriateness and Nigerian English' is chiefly a study of the contrast between formality and informality in English language use, showing that Nigerian usage is generally more formal than its British counterpart.

Jibril (1982a), 'Nigerian English: an introduction' and Akere (1982), 'Sociocultural constraints and the emergence of a Standard Nigerian English'
These two articles represent Nigeria in the landmark symposium on various New Englishes edited by John Pride and published in 1982. Each begins by giving an overview of English in Nigeria, of its history and its relation to indigenous languages; each raises some important theoretical issues, such as the possible meaning of 'Nigerian English'. Jibril goes on to present a number of examples that show the distinctiveness of Nigerian usage in the areas of phonology, syntax and semantics; in his conclusion he predicts that the international intelligibility (i.e. comprehensibility) of Nigerian English will decline, but that its 'internal' intelligibility (among Nigerians) is more important (to Nigerians). Akere, who has written extensively on the adaptation of English to the Nigerian cultural environment, and the distinctiveness of Nigerian usage that results, here demonstrates this distinctiveness in the realm of kinship terminology, greetings, and forms of address.

Bamgbose (1982), 'Standard Nigerian English: issues of identification'
With numerous phonological, grammatical and lexical examples, this also gives a general survey of Nigerian English as a chapter in a book devoted to various New Englishes. It is notable chiefly – though unexceptionably – for its neat equations: Banjo's Variety III, Adesanoye's Variety 3, 'Educated Nigerian English' and 'Standard Nigerian English' all refer to the same entity.

Kujore (1985), *English Usage – Some Notable Nigerian Variations*
This was the first full-length book (though a short one) on Nigerian English by a single author. It was designed, the author says in his Preface, 'first and foremost, as a kind of vade-mecum for school pupils and college students'. It remains a valuable source of data. However, from a scholar's point of view it has several drawbacks. Throughout the book the author adopts a listing approach – chiefly to present, first, variations in word-level stress, then variations in lexis and grammar – and more commentary and analysis would

have been welcome. The organization is also muddled: thus phonological variations other than in word-stress placement appear only in 'appendices', and Appendix II, entitled 'On Nigerian usage' (oddly for an appendix, since this is part of the principal theme of the book), includes material on lexis and grammar that has already appeared in the earlier 'section' on these topics. In the one-page essay that begins Appendix II, the author states that he regards 'Standard Nigerian English' as being 'at best, in process of evolution'. He shows that his approach to the variations he so painstakingly lists is fundamentally prescriptive.

Odumuh (1987), *Nigerian English (NigE)*

This short book is a collection of five papers of varying length written by Odumuh and others. It adopts an unreservedly descriptive approach to Nigerian English and treats all its main aspects. The introduction, and chapters 1, 4 and 5 are by Odumuh alone; 2 is by him and Gomwalk; 3 is by Eka. Chapter 1 is a rare excursion into the history of English in Nigeria; 2 explores typologies of language variation; 3, 4, and 5 are concerned respectively with grammatical structure, phonology and lexis and contain a wealth of interesting data demonstrating the existence of Nigerian English. Odumuh's chapter on grammatical structure proved to be the most controversial because he took the radical approach of arguing, in effect, that usages which others would treat as common errors should be regarded as belonging to 'educated' Nigerian English. Unhappily the book, which has for long been out of print, is marred by extremely shoddy production.

Bamiro (1991), 'Nigerian Englishes in Nigerian English literature'

This is the first of several articles by Bamiro that appeared in *World Englishes* in the early 1990s, in which he began to look to literary texts for examples of Nigerian English, here the novels of Achebe and Soyinka. This meant distinguishing between the language of the 'outer frame' (i.e. used by the narrator) and that of the 'inner frame' (used by characters among themselves); the majority of his Nigerian English examples in fact belong to the 'inner frame'. In these articles Bamiro also shows special interest in Nigerian Pidgin, treating it as the linguistic expression of the frustrations of the poorer, less educated, 'dominated' sections of Nigerian society. He also views Pidgin as the Nigerian English 'basilect' of the familiar lectal triad. Interestingly, too, and convincingly, he gives examples from Achebe's characters of what he regards as the mesolect – something which few other scholars, if any, have attempted to do. His view of the acrolect and the examples he gives of it from the speech of a character in Soyinka's *The Interpreters* are more questionable.

Schmied (1991), *English in Africa*

As suggested by the title, the book provides an overview of various aspects of English in 'English-speaking' African countries. Its approach is strictly descriptivist, and its comprehensiveness is suggested by the chapter headings: 'the sociolinguistic situation', 'linguistic forms', 'English in education', 'attitudes towards English', and so on. Given the scope of the book, with data gathered from different regions of the continent, Nigeria's experience of the English language is shown to be part of the wider African experience. In the chapter on linguistic forms Schmied suggests that there are a number of general features found in the emerging varieties of African English: in grammar, for example, the tendency not to add inflectional endings to verbs, the tendency to avoid complex tenses, the omission of articles in front of nouns. General features or strategies suggested in the section on meaning are redundancy, i.e. the repetition of semantic elements; variation in the form of idiomatic expressions; and the use of English word forms 'in other reference contexts' (the main type of this being extension, as in the extended use of kinship terms).

Jowitt (1991), *Nigerian English Usage*

The book aims at comprehensiveness, and is also fundamentally descriptive while taking prescriptive concerns into account: thus one chapter examines the controversy that the idea of 'Nigerian English' has constantly aroused. The chapter on 'varieties' summarizes the attempts made to identify sub-varieties, which have accompanied the search for a 'Standard Nigerian English'. The principal new idea of the book is that, given that non-Standard forms are common at a certain level (and so 'standard' among the large number of Nigerians who use them) they can collectively be said to constitute 'Popular Nigerian English'. By definition this is different from the elusive 'Standard Nigerian English', and until the latter is defined, Popular Nigerian English is in effect equivalent to Nigerian English. Each of several chapters is devoted to a particular language area, and in 'Phonology II' considerable attention is given to intonation. A large part of the book is taken up by a 'glossary' of some 600 (Popular) Nigerian English expressions. An attempt is also made to identify each expression as characteristic of one of Banjo's three varieties.

Bamgbose, Banjo, and Thomas (eds.) (1995), *New Englishes: A West African Perspective*

With a foreword written by the late Braj Kachru, this book was the outcome of an International Conference on 'Communicative competence and the role of English as a second language' held by the British Council, Nigeria and the University of Ibadan in December, 1993. Ghana and Cameroon are represented, but the majority of the chapters concern Nigeria. Banjo summarizes research into Nigerian English carried out 'so far', i.e. up to the time of the conference, and looks forward to the standardization of the variety. Bamgbose identifies three varieties of English that are discernible in the history of English in the country, to which he gives the labels 'contact English', 'Victorian English', and 'bookish English'. Jibril draws attention to the spread of Pidgin in Nigeria and to the thriving use of it in army barracks. Jowitt examines the role of English in Nigeria in relation to the National Language Question and compares India and Nigeria as multilingual nations. Some chapters concern English language teaching in Nigeria: thus Adejare, with a nod to the Conference theme, discusses the difficulty of teaching communicative competence, and Mohammed deplores declining performance in English in public examinations. Simo Bobda describes the phonologies of Nigerian English and Cameroon English. In a paper of broad relevance, Schmied emphasizes the value of electronic corpora for the study of language, and expresses optimism about the development of national components of the International Corpus of English.

Banjo (1996), *Making a Virtue of Necessity: An Overview of the English Language in Nigeria*

Here, in his most substantial publication, Banjo brings his mature judgment and elegant style to explorations of some key aspects of the subject. The first long chapter, 'Determinants', discusses a variety of issues, such as Pidgin, the contrast between the North and the South, and the question of a national language; it is also particularly useful for its historical perspective. Much space is given to 'falling standards' generally in education since independence: Banjo considers this to be sadly a fact. In the second, also long chapter, he examines 'Nigerian use of English'. While seeming reluctant to speak of 'Nigerian English', he does clearly if cautiously support the idea of an endonormative 'standard Nigerian English', provided it can be properly codified. It can be identified with his 'Variety III' and Adesanoye's 'Variety 3', but he deprecates the idea of a neat correlation of the two, since the former fundamentally refers to speech and the latter to writing, and 'Variety III speakers' are not necessarily 'Variety 3 writers'. A third chapter on bilingualism is largely concerned with code-mixing, with showing how Yoruba discourse is mixed with English; it also asserts, with some qualification, that a speaker of Variety III can be regarded as a coordinate bilingual. The fourth and last main chapter has much of permanent interest on the use of English in Nigerian literature. Finally, in 'Prospects', Banjo claims that English in Nigeria is 'alive and vigorous' and that 'the omens for its future are propitious'.

Bamgbose (1998), 'Torn between the norms: innovations in world Englishes'
Not many Nigerian scholars have used their knowledge of Nigerian Englishes as a
basis for discussing Englishes worldwide and for developing theoretical perspectives. Bamgbose (a one-time President of the International Association of World
Englishes) is a notable exception. Here he lends his support to the 'pluricentric'
idea, developed by Clyne (1992) and others, that English worldwide contains
'several interacting centres', and Bamgbose suggests that the norms of non-native
varieties are provided by 'universal language-learning strategies'. Nevertheless,
he recognizes that several issues remain unsettled in the development of such
norms, and underlining them is 'the constant pull' between native and non-native norms (an idea that has been explored in this book). A particular test case in
the area of syntax is the Nigerian English *can(not) be able* (see remarks on this in
Chapters One and Three).

**Awonusi and Babalola (eds.) (2004), *The Domestication of English in Nigeria:
A Festschrift for Abiodun Adetugbo***
This festschrift in honour of Professor Adetugbo brings together thirty-two
papers on a wide range of topics. Collectively they show the great variety of
purposes served by English in Nigeria, which is surely one way of regarding
it as 'domesticated' in Nigeria. The narrower sense in which the language has
itself undergone domestication – has in Nigeria become Nigerian English – is
represented mainly by three articles. Adegbija's 'The domestication of English
in Nigeria' is the longest article in the collection and, with its title matching the
title of the collection itself, arguably the most important. Arguing in favour of
Nigerian English within a New Englishes perspective, Adegbija gives several
examples of domestication under various headings. A 'semantic' example is
the Nigerian English extension of the senses of 'OK' (the subject of a special
article by Adegbija and Bello 2001). Controversial, surely, is his suggestion
that Nigerian Television Authority (NTA) News English should be taken as the
model for a 'standard' variety.

The principal argument of Okoro's 'Codifying Nigerian English: some practical problems and labelling', also a lucid and thought-provoking article discussed
in Chapter Three, is that the proposed sub-varieties of Nigerian English must not
be taken as discrete, since forms supposedly characteristic of one sub-variety
may be found in another.

Udofot in 'Varieties of spoken Nigerian English' proposes a triad of educa-
tionally differentiated sub-varieties and correlates it with the Banjo-Bamgbose
triad; she gives the name 'Standard' to the second of these. A longer summary of
the content of the article is given in Chapter One.

Owolabi and Dasylva (eds.) (2004), *Forms and Functions of English and Indigenous Languages in Nigeria: A Festschrift in Honour of Ayo Banjo*

This festschrift for Professor Banjo comprises forty articles, and many of them are relevant to the study of the distinctiveness of English in Nigeria, including those by Davy, Awonusi, Alo, Fakoye, Adesanoye, Akinjobi, and Bamgbose. Davy in 'A conservative view of the New Englishes' expresses scepticism about the 'newness' of New Englishes; thus many of the alleged innovations in African English can be traced to older forms attested in British English. Awonusi in 'RP and the sociolinguistic realities of non-native English accents', mentioned in Chapter One, challenges the assumption that RP should remain the model for English pronunciation in Nigeria, and foresees the emergence of codified regional models such as 'Standard West African'. Alo in 'Social meaning in Nigerian English' focuses on the use of kinship terms in Nigerian English discourse. Fakoye's 'A mediolect called "Nigerian English"' and Adesanoye's 'The English language in Nigeria: the case of a vanishing model?' were both mentioned in Chapter One as examples of the persistent concern over the decline in 'standards'. Fakoya scathingly refers to the usage even of professors as a 'mediolect', a term which, blending 'mediocre' and 'lect', describes a variety 'exhibiting overt anomalous usage features'. Akinjobi in 'A phonological study of the influence of word stress shift on educated Yoruba English vowels and syllables' shows that educated Yoruba speakers tend not to operate vowel reduction when in native-speaker English this is prompted by a stress shift due to affixation. Bamgbose's 'Negotiating English through Yoruba: implications for Standard Nigerian English' is a fine study of 'nativisation' in Nigerian English, which may be 'linguistic', 'pragmatic', or 'creative'; Bamgbose gives numerous examples taken from Yoruba speakers and writers.

Dadzie and Awonusi (eds.) (2004), *Nigerian English: Influences and Characteristics*

This work seems to have been conceived as a unity, but its seventeen chapters were written by various scholars, all at the University of Lagos, including Adetugbo, Akere and Okoro as well as Dadzie and Awonusi themselves. The chapters are somewhat uneven in quality, generally the work deserved better editing, and few references date from later than 1990. They nevertheless constitute a useful summary of the thinking of a number of Nigerian scholars who in the 1990s were sympathetic to the evolution of Nigerian English while recognizing problems such as the attitude to take towards 'deviant' morphosyntax. Awonusi in 'Some characteristics of Nigerian English phonology' makes use of the expression 'Nigerian English Accent' (NEA), and the expression has been used in Chapter Two. Okoro in 'The identification of Standard Nigerian English usage' proposes, *pace* Jibril, that within the 'Southern' accent, 'eastern' (mainly Igbo) and 'western' (mainly Yoruba) varieties should be recognized. Like other scholars he also sees SNE as showing a distinctiveness from other varieties in phonology and lexis but not in syntax.

Omoniyi (2006), 'West African Englishes'

The article appears as Chapter 11 in the Kachru et. al. *Handbook of World Englishes*, and the title alone is an indicator of a certain tendency on the international scene to withhold recognition of Nigerian English as such. Omoniyi refers to Nigerian English, Ghanaian English, Sierra Leonean English as 'national varieties' but also as 'potential "dialects" of West African English'. Regrettably, the article provides little linguistic evidence to help to decide the issue.

Ndimele (ed.) (2007), *Convergence: English & Nigerian Languages – A Festschrift for Munzali A.Jibril*

The organizer of this festschrift, Professor Ozo-mekuri Ndimele of the University of Port Harcourt, has been a leading figure for many years in the Linguistic Association of Nigeria, which has played a major role in promoting the study of Nigeria's indigenous languages. Of the seventy-three papers making up the festschrift, a large number are predictably concerned with indigenous language matters, and only three or four are focused on issues to do with Nigerian English. Jowitt in 'The fall-rise in Nigerian English intonation' shows that the tone in question is little used in Nigerian English, but is not entirely absent. The title of Elugbe and Mgbemena's 'Offensive Nigerian English' refers to the English spoken by Chief Zebrudaya, more details of which are given in Chapter Three. Ugorji briefly proposes a phoneme inventory for Nigerian English that is specified in greater detail in his 2010 book. Chiluwa seeks to identify grammatical strategies that he believes make mass media English in Nigeria distinctive, although his arguments seem questionable.

Schneider (2007), *Postcolonial English*

Early on in this important book Schneider points out that certain taxonomies of Englishes that have been fashionable over the years – the familiar tripartite categorization into 'ENL-ESL-EFL' varieties, or into 'inner-outer-expanding' circles – overlook common processes that have been at work shaping all of them. He presents a new Dynamic Model offering an explanatory and comprehensive account of 'postcolonial' varieties of English (PCEs). It is based partly on recent language contact theory as developed by, for example Thomason (2001); and fundamental to it also is a historical analysis that suggests how varieties have been formed and what their future might be. It also builds on the idea of the 'life cycle' of a New English developed by Moag (1982).

Two key features of his model are that, first, a PCE is the product of the contact between two "strands", which really means two sets of people: settlers (the 'STL' strand) and indigenes (the 'IDG' strand); secondly, a PCE passes historically through five stages: 'foundation', 'exonormative stabilization', 'nativization', 'endonormative' stabilization, and 'differentiation'.

From the viewpoint of any particular PCE, part of the interest of the book lies in trying to determine to what extent features of the model are exhibited in this PCE. Schneider recognizes that by its very nature a model varies in its applicability, and corresponds more to the facts of some situations than to those of others. His model is in fact convincing in its account of Australia, less so when applied to India and of Nigeria, the two biggest ESL countries in the world today. This is chiefly because in the history of India or Nigeria an 'STL' "strand" is hard to identify: a group of native-speaker settlers and their descendants who initially identified with the "home" country but later with the new country as it advanced towards independence. In Nigeria the government officials, teachers and missionaries who set the exonormative standard during the colonial era rarely identified with Nigeria rather than with Britain, even if they stayed in Nigeria long enough. They were always 'expatriates'.

For all that, the book makes us continue to consider the possibility of one valid, explanatory model accounting for all PCEs. The 'STL strand' concept could probably be adjusted to add to the model's plausibility.

Schneider's account of the history of English in Nigeria (pp.199-211) is rich in its detail; and it rightly gives much space to Nigerian Pidgin. He also makes it clear that Nigerian, like Indian English, has hardly reached the fourth stage (endormative stabilization), let alone the fifth.

Ajani (2007), 'Is there indeed a "Nigerian English"?'
This is a useful, relatively recent 'general survey' article that fundamentally seeks to show (*pace* some of the author's countrymen) that Nigerian English is worthy of attention and cannot be dismissed as merely a collection of errors. Ajani uses the plays of Soyinka as the main source of his morphosyntactic and lexical data (he does not address phonology).

Okoro (ed.) (2010), *Nigerian English in Sociolinguistic Perspectives: Linguistic and Literary Paradigms – A Festschrift for Funso Akere*
This festschrift, comprising thirty-seven articles, honours Professor Funso Akere of the University of Lagos, an early promoter of (Standard) Nigerian English, with a special interest in its sociolinguistic aspects. Several of the articles are directly relevant to Nigerian English studies. Awonusi in 'Revisiting West African English: evidence from Nigerleone' (a blend of 'Nigeria' and 'Sierra Leone') shows support for the idea of recognizing a West African English lect. Ayoola in 'Much ado about Standard Nigerian English: a study of Zulu Sofola's *Wedlock of the Gods*' attacks the concept of '*Standard* Nigerian English', but also identifies a number of

'Nigerian' expressions in a well-known play. Okoro in 'Perceptions and attitudes to emerging features of Nigerian English' shows interestingly, that the Nigerian undergraduates of his study do not consider forms that are usually deemed erroneous to be erroneous; nor, on the other hand, do they consider them to be examples of 'Nigerian English'. Awhefeada and Ojaruega in 'Nigerian English and the literary enterprise in Nigeria' convincingly demonstrate the Nigerian-ness of the language of Nigerian literature in English.

Udofot and Udoudom (eds.) (2011), *English Usage in Nigeria since 1842 – Patterns and Changes: A Festshcrift for Prof. David Eka*

This festschrift is rather poorly edited and the twenty-six constituent articles vary in quality. Azuike on 'the dwindling standard' of English in language and Mustapha on the need to redefine 'deviations' were referred to in Chapter One. The research interests of both Eka and Udofot are reflected in Section 1, which is devoted to phonological issues, and among the substantial articles here are Mgbemena's on the spoken English used in the city of Aba, Olaniyi's on variations within the Nigerian English accent (showing that 'most Nigerians use the articulatory settings of their mother tongues when they speak English'), and Josiah's on word-initial aspiration (showing that in NigE [k^h] is more frequent than [t^h] and much more so than [p^h]). Among the articles making up Section 3, concerned with sociolinguistic issues, Ofuokwu shows that, surprisingly, the use of non-Standard features increases in formal contexts; while Effiong studies the use among 150 university students of fifteen lexical items that have a distinctive NigE meaning (thus *dowry*, used to mean 'money paid by a man to the parents of a woman that the man wants to marry' is used by 85.3% of the students).

Opeibi et al. (eds.) (2015), *Essays on Language in Societal Transformation: A Festschrift in Honour of Segun Awonusi*

The festschrift comprises twenty-three papers, of which five clearly relate to the forms and the distinctiveness of Nigerian English. Anyagwa's on word-stress and Okunsebor's on spelling pronunciation among speakers of Esan were referred to in Chapter Two. Jowitt's paper, entitled 'Nigerian Received Pronunciation', was also discussed in Chapter Two. Adedeji's 'RP in Nigeria: prestige vs. intelligibility' investigates the intelligibility of speakers of British English to Nigerians; she finds that the mean of intelligibility is only 62.2%, with smoothing as the principal cause of intelligibility failure. Bamiro in 'English in Nigerian settings: recent lexicoining in Nigerian English' produces a fresh array of Nigerian English neologisms, many being slang expressions, and Bamiro adds that a number of them 'deliberately dismiss, negatively define, and deprecate the female'.

Kperogi (2015), *Glocal English: The Changing Face and Forms of Nigerian English in a Global World*

The jokey 'glocal' in the title at once sets the tone for this book: it is addressed to a general educated, rather than an academic readership, and the author, whose background is in journalism, affirms as much in his preface. At times it reads like the author's memoir; disconcertingly, too, it seems to treat Nigerian English as a kind of exotic plant that has just come to the notice of the ordinary citizens (especially the American citizens) of the world. It is rather repetitious, the discussion of various items is sometimes too long, and although very many of its examples of Nigerian English have already been recorded, the writer seldom refers to the work of earlier Nigerian scholars. Thus a long entry on the origins of 'OK' says nothing about the extended Nigerian meanings of this expression (Adegbija and Bello 2004). Nevertheless, very many 'new' expressions feature in the book, including *flash, handset, pass out, 'It's a shame', 'Sequel to…', 'All protocols observed'*. For this reason the book should prove useful to the scholar of Nigerian English.

6.2 Phonetics and phonology

Ekong (1980), 'Investigation into the intelligibility of a possible standard model for Nigerian spoken English'

In the interest of trying to establish the intelligibility of Nigerians to non-Nigerians, Ekong used twenty adult, well-educated Nigerian informants of varying ethnic backgrounds. Extracts from their speech were played to seven mostly native-speaker listeners in the form of two different tests. On the dictation test, the mean of intelligibility was 87.36% (higher than the score of the native-speaker control); on the 'impressionistic' test, 75.5% (lower than the score of the control). On the whole these results were gratifying to those hoping to prove that educated Nigerian English – Banjo's Variety 3 – was internationally intelligible. Ekong's findings can be set beside those of **Tiffen (1974)**, whose PhD dissertation **'The intelligibility of Nigerian English'** had an aim similar to Ekong's. He tested the intelligibility of 24 Hausa and Yoruba undergraduates to 240 British listeners, and found that it ranged from 92.7% to 29.9%, with a mean of 64.4%. In his work, the major cause of intelligibility failure was found to lie in the area of rhythm and stress, including sentence stress; less important were the mispronunciation of segments and errors of lexis and syntax.

Jibril (1986), 'Sociolinguistic variation in NigE'

In this article, Jibril presented in published form some of the findings of his PhD dissertation of 1982, which was the first to study Nigerian English phonology and to do so using experimental methods. Here using data gathered from forty-five informants, with an equal number taken from each of the three main ethnic groups, Jibril specifies the English phoneme systems of Hausa, Yoruba and Igbo speakers respectively, although he maintains that the latter two are so similar that they can be brought together, forming one 'Southern' sub-system. The two sub-systems that finally emerge ('Hausa' and 'Southern') are ingeniously combined in a model the details of which are given in Chapter Two. As a sociolinguistic study the article, like the dissertation, is important for pointing out that Nigeria lacks a class system in the Western sense, and Nigerian English accents cannot be correlated with social class.

Jowitt (2000a), 'Patterns of Nigerian English intonation'

Cruttenden's model of English intonation is used for this article, while data are provided by twenty Nigerian undergraduates reading dialogues. Fundamentally the article seeks to test certain existing claims concerning Nigerian English intonation. On the basis of the data the Nigerian English intonation system, i.e. the structure of a typical intonation-group, is shown to have the following features: unidirectional nuclei; 'end-stress', with a corresponding absence of emphatic stress; a head commencing with an initial high pitch, followed by down-drift (or down-step) before the nucleus is reached. Also, all lexical words carry an inherent, relatively high pitch-accent.

Udofot (2003), 'Stress and rhythm in the Nigerian accent of English'

Udofot was a postgraduate student at the University of Uyo under David Eka, whose PhD dissertation of the 1980s was the first to be written on the suprasegmentals of Nigerian English. The subject of Udofot's own PhD dissertation of 1997 was rhythm, and it was followed by several published articles on suprasegmentals. In this article she addresses some of the complex issues involved in the study of rhythm, but her principal objective is to test whether spoken Nigerian English is 'syllable-timed'. As in other articles (such as Udofot 2002, discussed in Chapter Two), her experimental study makes use of a differentiation of varieties. Her principal finding is that the tendency to syllable-timing is more pronounced in her non-Standard variety, the tendency to stress-timing more pronounced in the Sophisticated variety. Generally there are more stressed syllables in Nigerian English speech than in native-speaker speech, and the duration of unstressed syllables is greater. Udofot does not here bring vowel reduction into her discussion, although she observes in her closing remarks that the lack of variance of syllable durations does not reflect 'the distribution between full and reduced vowels'.

(2005), 'Nigerian English prosody'

Gut's principal contribution to the development of Nigerian English studies, a major one, has been the completion of ICE-Nigeria (see Chapter One). She has also published several articles on the suprasegmentals of Nigerian English and, more recently, on other areas too. In this article she uses experimental data to compare the prosodic patterns of British native speakers, Nigerian speakers of English, and Nigerian speakers of indigenous Nigerian languages, and outlines the features of a Nigerian English prosodic system. Her principal general conclusion is that with this system NigE 'stands "between" an intonation/stress language and a tone language". Some of her particular findings on the whole support claims made by other scholars as mentioned in Chapter Two: thus she observes that pitch movements on a syllable are rare in Nigerian English, and although this means disregarding the 'nuclear tone' of 'end-stress', it supports the claim that NigE does not operate emphatic stress.

Ugorji (2010), *Nigerian English Phonology*

Subtitled 'A Preference Grammar', this must rate as the first published book to deal exclusively with the phonology of Nigerian English, both segmental and suprasegmental. Ugorji presents the book as an attempt to formalize the phonological component of the 'standard variety' of Nigerian English, and so to bring about, for Nigerian English phonology, the 'endornormative stabilisation' which is the fourth stage of the Dynamic Model of Schneider (2007). Part of his concern is pedagogical: to propose a model that can be used to teach the sounds of English in Nigeria, in place of RP.

For his analysis Ugorji uses an extensive corpus of spoken data supplied by 401 Nigerians. His theoretical background is, first, the familiar triad of lects. He regards all three lects as constituting 'educated Nigerian usage' when it has been usual to equate the latter with the acrolect only. Secondly, he uses Optimality Theory (OT) for the purposes of deciding which among several 'candidate' sounds should be regarded as optimal, and so teachable. One advantage of this approach is that it allows for regional variation. He thus systematically examines the segmental sounds (and later the suprasegmental sounds) of each of the three lects.

The book could have been better edited, but it contains much of great importance and interest.

Omachonu (2011), *Optimality Account of Stress in Standard British and Nigerian English*

This work was discussed in Chapter Two. It grew out of the author's PhD dissertation, and it explains the differences between the two varieties of the title in word-stress placement using Optimality Theory, as in Ugorji (see above). The arguments are convincing, but the discussion of more examples would have been welcome.

6.3 Morphosyntax

Jowitt and Nnamonu (1985), *Common Errors in English*
A work of pedagogy, not of scholarship, this merits inclusion here because it provides a long list of what are in fact mainly Nigerian and mainly morphosyntactic non-Standard forms. They are grouped partly according to parts of speech, and in each group there are subdivisions according to type of error: thus 'articles' is subdivided into '"A" or "an" wrongly used', '"A" or "an" wrongly omitted', ' "The" wrongly used', etc. The preface asserts, as others have said, that some of the errors are found in the speech and writing even of highly educated people.

Jibril (1991), 'Prepositional usage in Nigerian English'
Jibril here brings his interest in sociolinguistic variation to the syntax of Nigerian English, and examines prepositional usage. For his experimental study he made use of 105 Hausas, varying in educational attainment, occupation, age, and sex. Their use of English prepositions is shown to co-vary with these social variables: thus females are more likely to following Standard usage than males. One interesting discovery is that the use of the bare infinitive after *enable* – 'a widespread Nigerianism' (and see Chapter Three) – is actually more widespread among members of the elite than among lower-income people.

Bamiro (1995), 'Syntactic variation in West African English'
In this article, Bamiro brings his chosen method of data-collection, i.e. the use of literary sources, to a description of syntactic 'variation' in West African English in general (although actually the Ghanaian novelist Ayi Kwei Armah is the sole non-Nigerian representative among the authors whose works are used). He discusses and gives numerous examples in turn of several types of variation, including the omission of function words, the non-operation of subject-verb inversion in question sentences, tag questions, the use of the progressive with verbs denoting mental processes, and focus constructions, which receives the greatest amount of attention.

Jowitt (2002), 'The English subjunctive: is it dying?'
In part, this is a study of the understanding and acceptance by Nigerians of contemporary uses of the English subjunctive. These uses can be divided into two: 'mandative', and the rarer 'formulaic'. The mandative, used in subordinate *that* clauses after verbs of insisting, suggesting, etc., is more common in American than in British English, which prefers introducing the periphrastic *should*. A test administered to eighteen Nigerian postgraduate students revealed that they largely followed British usage, avoiding the mandative subjunctive in the active

voice and using *should*; in the passive, however, they favoured the use of subjunctive *be*.

Eyisi (2003), *Common Errors in the Use of English*

Like Jowitt and Nnamonu (see above), and as the title suggests, this is a compendium of English errors, again chiefly grammatical, and its purpose is chiefly to draw attention to and correct them. Eyisi expresses alarm over the commonness of errors, as evidence of 'falling standards' in the use of English. Her general approach is thus highly prescriptive. It is also very thorough, with a list of examples running to over 2,200; there are perhaps signs of overkill. The work constitutes a useful data-bank for the study of errors common in Nigeria.

Alo and Mesthrie (2008), 'Nigerian English: morphology and syntax'

At the time of its publication in Mesthrie (ed.), this useful article was unprecedented as offering a detailed and comprehensive survey of Nigerian English morphosyntax (and even so it rather anomalously includes a section on lexis). The authors declare that they seek to 'confine ourselves to identifying recurrent features of syntax in NigE, without prescriptive bias', and go on to present a number of such features, under the headings of 'Tense-aspect-modality systems', 'Auxiliaries', 'Negatives', and so on. A large number of their examples come from Jowitt (1991).

Okunrinmeta (2011), 'Izon syntax and the English of Izon-English bilinguals'

This is a rare study of the acceptability of non-Standard English syntax to speakers of a Nigerian minority language, in this case Izon, which is one of seven languages making up the Ijo or Ijaw cluster. Non-Standard usages involving agreement, stative verbs and prepositions are shown through tests to vary in their acceptability.

Kortmann and Lunkenheimer (eds.) (2013), 'The Electronic World Atlas of Varieties of English'

As observed in Chapters One and Three, *eWAVE* is a useful tool for investigating Nigerian English and comparing it with other varieties. It has some fundamental limitations, which the compilers disarmingly point out in their Introduction. Thus the profile of a variety emerging from the specifications given for it is 'unlikely to perfectly match the linguistic behaviour of any particular subgroup of speakers of that variety'. This is true of Nigerian English: notably, for example, *eWAVE* does not help us to pursue the important but elusive goal of distinguishing acrolectal from non-acrolectal usage. Secondly, and related to the first point, 'the frequency-based ratings in most cases reflect the individual experts' judgments', which, frankly, may not be reliable. This is true of many of the judgments offered about

Nigerian English, and some details were given in Chapter Three. With relevance to this argument it is also worth observing that 15 'A's were given for Nigerian English, but that although Nigerian English is undoubtedly closer to Ghanaian English and to Cameroon English than to any other varieties represented, no 'A' rating at all was given for Ghanaian English, while (in rather sharp contrast again) 26 'A's were given for Cameroon English.

Gut and Fuchs (2013), 'Progressive aspect in Nigerian English'

This article is the outcome of the kind of research that the arrival of ICE-Nigeria has made possible. A principal finding is that a comparison of the Nigerian corpus with the British corpus suggests that the present progressive active is used more often by Nigerians, and the corresponding past progressive less often, than by British native speakers, and that other more complex progressive forms have about the same incidence. The greater use of the progressive in Nigerian English is observable in the more 'opinion-expressing' text types of the corpus, such as commentaries and broadcast interviews. Nigerian English also resembles other New Englishes in extending the use of the progressive with durative habitual verbs and stative verbs.

Werner and Fuchs (2016), 'The present perfect in Nigerian English'

This article also uses ICE-Nigeria as its principal source of data. It chiefly seeks to determine the frequency of the present perfect 'tense' in Nigerian English, a topic which has previously not been studied in detail. The present perfect is found to be less frequent in Nigerian than in British English, and in fact Nigerian English has almost the lowest frequency of use among thirteen varieties surveyed by the authors. Possible reasons for the relatively low frequency are suggested, including a variety of early models, more recent American influence, and learning difficulties (which seems the most plausible).

6.4 Lexis and discourse

Bamiro (1994), 'Lexico-semantic variation in Nigerian English'

This is one of several illuminating articles by Bamiro in which he presents the lexical distinctiveness of Nigerian English, employing the general term 'innovation' to refer to it. Here, as in other articles, examples are taken from contemporary Nigerian literature in English, and he groups them into ten categories (as mentioned in Chapter Four): 'loanshift', 'semantic underdifferentiation', 'lexico-semantic reduplication and redundancy', 'ellipsis', 'conversion', 'clipping', 'acronyms', 'translation equivalents', 'analogical creation', and 'coinages'.

Jowitt (2000b), 'Nigerian English lexis: a sentimental investigation'

This article examines the way in which distinctive use is made in Nigeria of a single English word, in this case *sentiment* and its derivative *sentimental*. Using data obtained from tests in which both Nigerians and non-Nigerians (mostly Britons) took part, and from other sources such as newspapers, Jowitt shows that typically in Nigeria, but not among native, non-Nigerian speakers, *sentiment* is synonymous with *strong emotion*, and *sentimental* with *strongly emotional, impassioned*, etc. Also discussed in Chapter Four.

Igboanusi (2002a), *A Dictionary of Nigerian English Usage*

This was the first dictionary of Nigerian English to be published: the first book, that is to say, wholly dedicated to the lexicographical principle of presenting an alphabetical list of words that have a distinctive meaning. It is well produced and lucidly written. The author says that the words, totalling about 1,500, are ones 'used in everyday speech'. While many of them also feature in Kujore (1985) and Jowitt (1991), Igboanusi adds many 'new' ones, and his inventory is particularly rich in loan-words. He adopts Jowitt's method of adding comment, often by way of contextualizing the use of a word. Perhaps wisely, he does not try to correlate words and their meanings with sub-varieties. The lengthy introduction has sections on topics such as 'the history of English in Nigeria', 'the linguistic situation in Nigeria', and 'Standard Nigerian English' – yet, as pointed out in Chapter One, he does not make clear the distinction between 'Standard Nigerian English' and 'Nigerian English'; in fact, except in that section of the introduction, he does not discuss 'Standard Nigerian English' at all. In a final section he discusses his 'research design': he relies on his intuition, he says, but this is supplemented by information gathered from a variety of written and spoken sources. He also shows his awareness of the problems surrounding the use of words such as 'frequently' and 'often'.

Blench (2005), *A dictionary of Nigerian English*

Blench makes it clear in his preface that his online dictionary is meant as an initial draft of what might eventually be a collective product, and individuals are invited to send suggested amendments or additions. He also says that 'many of the most picturesque expressions [*of Nigerian English*] are strictly oral'. This is quite true, and a great many of the expressions listed by others have also been taken partly or largely from speech. In the long run, both speech and writing are surely needed as sources to identify the distinctiveness of any New English variety.

This dictionary lists nearly 1,000 headwords, considerably fewer than in Igboanusi; it is sparse on comment; it is particularly rich in local names for food items and for flora and fauna; and it ignores the question of a 'Standard Nigerian English', perhaps fortunately, and partly because of its descriptive approach. Its principal concern, as suggested above, is to list forms that are found in popular spoken usage; even so, a number of very common colloquial usages are omitted, such as *somehow* meaning "rather" (Jowitt 1991), "strange" (Igboanusi 2002a).

Okoro (2011), *Exploring Nigerian English: A Guide to Usage 1 (A-L)*

In this first part of a projected two-volume work, Okoro in effect produces the first part of another Nigerian English dictionary with headwords listed alphabetically. Each is accompanied by a detailed and extensive commentary. From time to time Okoro departs from lexicographical listing to give attention to a particular area of grammar – 'determiners', for example. His attitude to his entries is a blend of the descriptive and the prescriptive. In many cases he indicates that a Nigerian usage should be considered 'wrong'; in others, such as in his remarks on *escort*, he indicates that the usage under focus is 'Nigerian' and sets the native-speaker usage beside it without evaluative comment. If completed, the work promises to be a most valuable addition to Nigerian English lexicography.

Fuchs, Gut and Soneye (2013), "We just don't even know"

The article is another fine example of the use that can be made of a corpus such as ICE-Nigeria. The writers use data taken from the corpus to examine the frequency and the meaning in Nigerian English of the focus particles *even* and *still*. Their findings in relation to *even* are particularly interesting. In British English, *even* may have a noun phrase as its focus, less often a verb phrase; in Nigerian English these frequencies are reversed. Moreover, whereas in British English *even* expresses unexpectedness, surprise, etc., in Nigerian English the meaning is more simply emphatic, something like "actually", "really", as in 'I was even trying to photocopy some things'. Mother-tongue influence, or 'transfer effects', may account for the shift in the Nigerian meaning: thus *even* may have become established in Yoruba learners' minds at an early date as a translation of Yoruba *ti(l)ẹ*.

Adegbite et al. (2014), *A Dictionary of Nigerian English Usage*

This slim, 128-page book can be described as the best approximation made up to the time of its publication to the ideal of a Nigerian English dictionary. Over 1,100 headwords are listed, each with a brief comment. In their Introduction the editors affirm that in directing the compilation of the dictionary they were taking at his word Jowitt's observation (2008) that such a task needs to be carried out by a team of experts. They clearly regard the inclusion of a headword as indicative of its belonging to 'Standard' Nigerian usage: 'the dictionary presents only the peculiar forms of English acceptable in educated usage in Nigeria, with the exclusion of non-standard forms'. But this expression of policy is likely in the long run to prove controversial because, for example, under 'B' we find *binded:* a form indeed commonly used, at least by undergraduates, as the past tense and 'past' participle of *bind.* By including it the editors presumably regard it as being 'acceptable', but it must be asked how many educated Nigerians would find it so. We thus find ourselves back to the need to define 'Standard' and 'standard'. We might also think that more comment on individual items would have been welcome in the dictionary. This would of course have greatly increased its volume.

6.5 History

Fafunwa (1991), History of Education in Nigeria
As the title indicates, this is not a history of the English language in Nigeria or of any aspect of it. On the other hand, given that English has been learned in Nigeria chiefly through the education system, knowledge of the history of that system is indispensable to understanding the narrower history of the language; and this is a classic book on the subject. It makes for rather dull reading in places, but it has much interesting detail, some of it directly concerned with language matters.

Ogu (1992), A Historical Survey of English and the Nigerian Situation
This short book, for long out of print, has been used by a number of Nigerian scholars seeking to refer to the history of the English language in Nigeria. In fact, it is only in chapters 4 and 5 that this history is discussed, dealing with the pre-independence and post-independence eras respectively.

Doctoral dissertations

As indicated in some of the entries and elsewhere in this book, a number of doctoral dissertations have been written since the 1960s on issues pertaining to Nigerian English, and some of them have had much influence on the work of subsequent scholars. Since in the nature of things they are unpublished and gaining access to them presents special difficulties, they have not been given entries in the survey above; but it seems to be a limitation of such a survey if they are ignored. A list (not comprehensive) therefore follows, arranged to the date of the award of the degree:

1967 Tomori, S. A study in the syntactic structures of the written English of British and Nigerian grammar school pupils. University of London.

1969 Banjo, A. A contrastive study of aspects of the syntactic and lexical rules of English and Yoruba. University of Ibadan.

1971 Agheyisi, R. West African Pidgin English: simplification and simplicity. University of Stanford.

1973 Adesanoye, F. A study of varieties of written English in Nigeria. University of Ibadan.

1974 Tiffen, B. The intelligibility of Nigerian English. University of London.

1978 Ekong, P. On describing the vowel system of a standard variety of Nigerian spoken English. University of Ibadan.

1981 Odumu, A. Aspects of the semantics and syntax of Educated Nigerian English. Ahmadu Bello University, Zaria.

1982 Jibril, M. Phonological variation in Nigerian English. University of Lancaster.

1984 Alo, M. A lexical study of educated Yoruba English. University of Reading.

1985 Awonusi, V.O. Sociolinguistic variation in Nigerian English. University of London.

1985 Eka, D. A phonological study of Standard Nigerian English. Ahmadu Bello University, Zaria.

1997 Omodiaogbe, S.A. An error analysis of the English language of Education students in Edo and Delta States. University of Nigeria, Nsukka.

1997 Udofot, I. The rhythm of spoken Nigerian English. University of Uyo.

2004 Akinjobi, A. A phonological investigation of vowel weakening and unstressed syllable obscuration in Educated Yoruba English. University of Ibadan.

2007 Omachonu, G. From rule-based to constraint-based analysis: issues in English suprasegmental phonology. University of Nigeria, Nsukka.

2007 Soneye, T. Phonological sensitivity of selected NTA newscasters to polyphonic and polygraphic phenomena in English.

2007 Udom, M. Lexical innovations in Nigerian English usage. University of Uyo.

2009 Josiah, U. A synchronic analysis of assimilatory processes in educated Nigerian spoken English. University of Ilorin.

2013 Anyagwa, C. Word stress in Nigerian (Igbo) English. University of Lagos.

7 Samples of Texts

7.1 Diaries, memoirs

(1) Antera Duke

at 5 am in aqua Bakassey Crik and with fine morning and I git for aqua Bakassey Crik in 1 clock time so I find Arshbong Duke and I go Longsider his Canow so I take Bottle Beer to Drink with him and wee have call first for new Town and stay for Landing come way so wee go town in 3 clock time so we walk up to plaver house sam time to putt grandy Egbo in plaver house and play all night Combesboch go way with 639 slave & Toother.

Modernized version by D.Simmons: At 5 am in Aqua Bakassey Creek; it was a fine morning and I arrived at Aqua Bakassey corral at 1 o'clock. I found Archibong Duke and went alongside his canoe. I took a bottle of beer to drink with him and we called first at New Town and stayed at the landing and then went to town at 3 o'clock. We walked up to the palaver house to put the Grand Ekpe in the house and played all night. Combesboch went away with 639 slaves and Toother (proper name).

[From: Antera Duke's diary entry for 8 February, 1786. Antera Duke was a trader in the Calabar area in the south-eastern coastal area of Nigeria in the late eighteenth century. Extracts from his diary were reproduced by Daryll Forde in *Efik Traders of Old Calabar*, published by the International African Institute, London, in 1956.]

(2) Equiano

Yes, thou dear partner of all my childish sports! Thou sharer of joys and sorrows! Happy should I have ever esteemed myself to encounter every misery for you and to procure your freedom by the sacrifice of my own. Though you were early forced from my arms, your image has always been riveted in my heart, from which neither *time* nor *fortune* have been able to remove it; so that while the thoughts of your suffering have damped my prosperity, they have mingled with adversity and increased its bitterness. To that Heaven which protects the weak from the strong I commit the care of your innocence and virtues, if they have not already received their full reward and if your youth and delicacy have not since fallen victims to the violence of the African trader, the pestilential stench of a Guinea ship, the seasoning in the European Colonies or lash and lust of a brutal and unrelenting overseer.

[Olaudah Equiano's autobiography, mentioned on p 150, was first published in London in 1789. A modern edition was prepared by Paul Edwards and published in 1969. In this extract Equiano addresses his sister.]

https://doi.org/10.1515/9781501504600-007

(3) Soyinka

You say here that you formed a committee to campaign against the importation of arms to Nigeria – you realize by the way that that is a very disloyal thing to do?

I don't accept that.

You don't think it helps the rebels? How is a war to be fought without weapons?

The rebels would use the same argument with justice to prove my antagonism to their cause.

We are not particularly concerned with the views of the rebels.

I am. I have declared already that this war is morally unjustified.

What kind of wars would you support for instance?

Any war in defence of liberty.

And what of the Rivers people who have been forcibly brought into the so-called Biafra? You think we have no obligation to give them their liberty.

I do not support Biafran secessions, so I am clearly for the statehood of the minority groups.

How then do you want the secession to be brought to an end?

Not by this particular war.

[From: Wole Soyinka, *The Man Died: Prison Notes of Wole Soyinka*. Rex Collings, 1973, pp 48–9. Soyinka, who had already emerged as a leading figure of the first generation of creative writers, was arrested during the Civil War on charges of having made treasonable contact with the Biafran secessionists. He was never tried but spent several years in prison.]

7.2 Letters

(4) Crowther

The head chief of Itoku said he had no quarrel with us, neither with the Sierra Leone emigrants in his town, they might come to church and do as they pleased but he checked his people from doing so, because they must do as their forefathers used to do, and then have no business with us, they not being emigrants, he said moreover, that we never gave them any person to make Ogboni, not to worship Ifa, nor Sango etc. Moreover that one of us called the worship of their deceased fore-fathers a lie.

[Samuel Adjai Crowther to Henry Venn, 19 Jan. 1852. CMS CA2/031. In Obaro Ikime, ed. *Groundwork in Nigerian History*. Heinemann Educational Books (Nigeria), 1980, p.376. The proper names towards the end refer to gods of Yoruba traditional religion.]

(5) Nanna

Then the Consul Annesley asked me (Nanna) again who... make you a Governor, and Nanna answered him, and said the Consul E.A.Hewett Esq. gave me (Nanna) the staff to be Governor.

And the Consul Annesley take the staff from me (Nanna) and break it to pieces and throw it away in water and go right up in his boat to Bleasby Beach. I am very shamed in the present of all the chiefs; the Consul Annesley do not ask me any word about the river and commerce to make palaver with me, I having done anything wrong by the Europeans or the Natives – Benin (River)...

But Bleasby the Agent at Fort Douglas have given to Consul Annesley all the wrong information.... Annesley told me... You are chief of your own house, you have no business again.

[Written by Chief Nanna, or his clerk Jackson, 1890; reproduced in J.O.S.Ayomike, *A History of Warri*, Ilupeju Press, Benin City, 1988. Nanna, an Itsekiri chief, held the post of Governor of the Benin River, a British Government appointment.]

(6) Omo Ijesha

A thousand times no! Had I not wasted my time and energies on the mastering of Latin and Greek, and learning the histories of those same people, but had been initiated thoroughly in shorthand, typewriting, book-keeping or any foreign language, I would now be able to earn a living. Had I in my spare time, been taught a trade of any sort whatever, I would be better off in this hour of need. How many men are there nowadays who have reached most enviable social and financial positions without this absurd cramming of Latin and Greek or mathematics in their teens?

[Article by 'Omo Ijesha' – i.e. 'an Ijesha man' – in the *Lagos Weekly Record* of Jan.6, 1894 under the title 'Does Education Pay?'; quoted in Echeruo p 59.]

(7) Osho Davies

....if that system stands condemned in Africa, why is it so much admired in every part of the habitable globe! Is the African not human, and is he so dense as not to be able to discern between what is evil and what is good? How many a time since, fifty years ago, Lagos was given the advantage of English justice, has a discordant tune been raised against the system; not once. Our cry is not against English justice, as we are bred to it, and love and admire it, but against the endeavour now being made to deprive us of that justice and relegate us back to the first ages of barbarism... for if English justice stands condemned in Africa it must necessarily be so in England herself, since, what is good for the goose is also good for the gander.

[Osho Davies, a lawyer, writing to Travers Buxton on 20 October 1914 and attacking Lord Lugard, the Governor-General of Nigeria, for saying that the English legal system was unsuitable for Nigeria; cited in A.Osuntokun, *Nigeria in the First World War*; Longman 1979.]

(8) Ekiti

Sir, – News has been received of your success in the final Arts examination of the University of Durham and I am directed to convey to you my Union's expression of felicitation with you on this uniquely happy occasion for Ekiti. No longer can it be said that no person throughout the length and breadth of Ekiti possesses a degree. Well knowing your health troubles while you were at Fourah Bay College and the tough struggles with which you have to put up in this great educational crusade, we must thank God for bringing His work to perfection by giving you the pluck and zeal to cast out the stigma from us as people at a time when all hopes seem forlorn.

While we concede that the letters B.A. connote Bachelor of Arts we shall extend their denotation to include Begin Again. Once Ekiti is blessed with a first degree man in your person we look forward with great relish to the time when she will be blessed with a man with a Master Degree, as only the best is good enough for her. We would esteem it a great delight, therefore, if you would regard this letter as a clarion call to greater duty and redouble your efforts to attain the Master Degree.

[From: S.D.Ogunbiyi, Hon.General Secretary of the Ekiti Progressive Union, Lagos, to E.A. Babalola, Nov.9, 1946; in Chief E.A.Babalola, *My Life Adventures*. Caxton Press, Ibadan, 1978.]

(9) Ifeanyi

I read your letter this morning when I called at our Dept. I am exceedingly joyed to link up with you once more after a long period of four years. What a happy reunion!

There is no doubt that writers and authors, more than any other professionals, are most exposed to frustrations and disappointments. I have, ironically, submitted myself to be trained for this too-demanding a career. In February this year, I had the opportunity of working as a proof-reader with a foreign novelist. The profession is quite patience-tasking and energy absorbing. Yet, many writers and authors do not reap the fruits of their honest labour.

It is shockingly painful that you never heard a word from Dr.O. I enclose a receipt to show that I did register and despatch the copy to him. The date of despatch is no longer quite visible on the receipt but I hope I sent the book out on

30 April, 1975. Had it been you hinted me earlier, I could have gone out to trace it out with the Post-master General.

Please, send me a copy of Gibbon's The Decline of The Roman Empire. I have not succeeded in securing any locally.

[Personal letter dated 10.10.1979, written by an undergraduate student.]

(10) Boniface

Concerning my life immediately I left the College in 1987, it was a chequered one. For five consecutive years, I remained jobless. Do you know that I was teaching in a primary school before I was offered admission at the College? I was also granted a study leave without pay by the Imo State Ministry of Education, that is, at the completion of my course of study, I would automatically be reinstated. But sadly, at the completion of the course, I could not be reinstated by the Ministry; and I was forced to pass through the intolerable and harsh conditions of joblessness for five years. Being born into a family that is immersed in abject poverty definitely made my problem to become a hydra-headed one.

Proverbially speaking, I am just like a man who was shipwrecked alongside others, who, while he was doing his utmost to save his own life, was equally doing his best to save the lives of others. I am the premier person to be educated in our family; and going by the Igbo custom of being one's brother's keeper, I am expected to be in the vanguard of sponsorship of the education of my junior ones. My concerted effort in this regard has paid off. Do you know that my most junior brother studied at the Imo State University and made a second-class upper division in Banking and Finance?

[Personal letter dated 24 February 2005. The writer's highest qualification, which he obtained in 1987, was the Nigerian Certificate of Education (NCE).]

7.3 Journalism

(11) Weekly Record

The effects morally of European civilization upon the native have too often been pointed out by white travellers in Africa to require to be dilated upon. We must admit that upon the whole the effect has been absolutely enervating. The reason of this is not far to seek, in fact it follows as a matter of course that where a man is deprived of all self-dependence which is the basis and germ of all virtuous principle, he must be totally lacking of the latter. Placed by a foreign civilization in a position of suffrance between the white man and the primitive producer, and without any sustaining force, the civilized native's morals become adjusted to the exigencies of his circumstances and are as flexible and shifting as the circumstances which govern them. It is no wonder then that the uncivilized native stands higher in moral worth in the estimation of the observing foreigner than his more civilized and unfortunate brother.

[From the *Lagos Weekly Record*, May 21, 1904.]

(12) Enahoro

Of all the beguiling roles the Complete Nigerian is called upon to perform in his community, none so easily inflates his ego as the invitation to be chairman at a social event. It is his chance to play God.

No social gathering is complete without a chairman. Such is the passion for a presider that a pack of young Nigerian tearaways would elect a chairman to guide them through their first dirty weekend.

A chairman is appointed to direct a public lecture, a wedding reception, a christening party, a wake-keeping, a political rally, or a football match. Even though the doddering fellow may be too infirm to take the ceremonial 'first kick', his presence will excitement and attract hundreds of spectators who might otherwise have stayed home.

Ours is a patriarchal society with a craving for father figures. Hence, a popular chairman is a dictator, a bully and a know-all who is not averse to self-promotion.

A chairman is chosen firstly, for his upright social standing; and then, for his money. The two qualities are considered synonymous in Nigeria, so that a person without money is not considered socially vertical. The chairman is expected to make a large donation, in return for the privilege of the spotlight that will shine on him throughout the proceedings.

[From: Peter Enahoro, *The Complete Nigerian*. Lagos: Malthouse Press Limited 1992, pp 82–3. Enahoro was a leading journalist of the post-independence era; see Chapter Five.]

(13) Health care

For decades, lack of adequate health care facilities in Gusau, the Zamfara State, and surrounding areas have been a source of worry to the government and residents alike. Apart from the fact that Gusau is the capital city of the state, it serves as the commercial nerve centre of the old Sokoto State where people of diverse background reside and carry their day-to-day activities.

The health care problem of the area was compounded by the ceding of the only General Hospital in the state to the Federal Government to establish a

Federal Medical Centre over ten years ago. That decision, though laudable, made the state government reluctant to establish another befitting facility to cater for the populace, while the FMC could not expand due to limited space available at the old General Hospital.

However, in 1991, then Sokoto state government, under the leadership of Malam Yahaya Abdulkarim, laid the foundation for a new FMC located along Sokoto By-Pass in Gusau. Hopes were raised that a medical facility befitting a growing town was on the way. However, 17 years down the line, no single structure was added to the one put on ground on the day of the foundation laying ceremony.

[Imam Imam, 'Zamfara: Burden of Delivering Healthcare to the People', *ThisDay*, Vol.14, No.5303, Thursday October 29, 2009, p 24. *ThisDay* is one of the leading newspapers of the twenty-first century.]

(14) Army convicts

Ostensibly bowing to wide-ranging appeals for clemency from different quarters, the Nigerian Army authorities have commuted the life imprisonment handed over to 27 Nigerian soldiers who served in the United Nations' Mission in Liberia to seven years jail term.

Expectedly, the life sentences handed over to the army officers were condemned by many people across the world as simply excessive, high-handed, punitive and harsh. A massive plea for clemency for the convicts ensured and this resulted in the reduction of the sentence to seven years imprisonment.

While we commend the Nigerian Army authorities for exercising matured discernment, we feel they should have been more magnanimous and kind-hearted enough to grant the convicts unconditional pardon.

[From 'The Pardon for Army Convicts': editorial in *ThisDay*, September 25, 2009, p 19.]

(15) Banks

There is no gain saying the fact that banking business is a sensitive business, highly induced with maximum risk from operations to image making and others.

However, the issue of risk management in the banking sector is gradually gaining light and the consciousness is on the increase, thanks to the global economic meltdown, which has to a greater extent, exposed the inefficiency of bigger financial institutions to manage risks at their disposal, especially that of credit risk.

This adduced to the fact why big banks such as the Lehman Brothers went bankrupt, later taken over by JP Morgan of Washington Mutual (America's largest bank); takeover of Merrill Lynch by Bank of America, U.S. Government takeover of AIG (world's largest insurer), the government bailout of Freddie Mac and Fanny Mae (key U.S. mortgage institutions); and the collapse of Bear Stearns amongst other developments, led to a failure of confidence that led to a credit squeeze and the current meltdown.

[From Adeyemi Adepetun, 'Risk management in banks: Time to move from rhetorics', in *The Guardian*, July 15, 2009, p 24.]

(16) Osundare

What, if not corruption, is responsible for the presence of so many patently non-roadworthy vehicles on Nigerian roads? Time there was when Vehicle Inspection Officers (VIO's) made sure only fit and proper vehicles plied the roads, and the traffic police took care of the sanity and competence of Nigerian drivers. Now, the VIO has literally disappeared, and, with the right bribe to give, you could speed along with your brakeless vehicle and kill as many people as your tyres can crush.

What about those long articulated vehicles and loaded petrol tankers which pummel the roads with their heavy weights and park anywhere that suits their tyrannical fancy? Is it true that we have the bribing generosity of trailer magnates to thank for the untimely demise of the Nigerian railway? Pray, to which cabal do we owe the death of the once active Nigerian railway?

And, regarding the planes, why is the Nigerian air space full of Tokunbo aircraft? (As if the carnage being wrought by Tokunbo automobiles on our roads is not enough!). Why is the Nigerian sky littered with cheap, creaking carriers from foreign scrap-yards, refurbished jalopies imported to serve as shortcut to wealth for their ruthless owners and one-way ticket to death for Nigerian passengers?

[From: Prof.Niyi Osundare, 'Why we no longer blush: Corruption as Grand Commander of the Federal Republic of Nigeria'. Lecture delivered at Sheraton Hotel, Abuja under the auspices of the Save Nigeria Group, July 9; published in The Nation, July 25–26, 2012.]

(17) Dare

You will not find "panelocracy" in a standard dictionary of the English Language.

That term was coined, I believe, by – who else? – Odia Ofeimun, in our Rutam House years to denote the system of government by committee that was the trademark of the regime of military president Ibrahim Babangida in its first year.

On practically every subject under the sun and even beyond it, Babangida put one committee or another to work with a bold, even radical mandate. To leave nobody in any doubt that he meant business, he made sure that the committees comprised some of the most knowledgeable persons in that field.

When that committee was done, Babangida would constitute a fresh panel, again comprising persons with impeccable credentials, to review its submissions.

Following that, another committee, made up exclusively of insiders who may or may not be civil servants, would prepare a White Paper setting out the government's position on the matter. And it was not uncommon that yet another committee would review the White Paper.

That was before Babangida dispensed altogether with the pretence of shared governance and ruled by the ethos of the military that had bred him.

[From: Olatunji Dare, 'Back to "panelocracy"' in *The Nation*, July 31, 2012, p 64. Dare was once on the editorial board of *The Guardian* newspaper; Rutam House is the newspaper's headquarters in Lagos. Odia Ofeimun is a distinguished Nigerian poet.]

(18) Taxi-driver

A taxi driver, Imeh Usuah, yesterday received an award from the National Orientation Agency (NOA) for returning N18 million left in his car by a passenger.

The NOA Director-General Mike Omeri, who eulogized the exemplary life of the taxi driver, said every Nigerian "who toed the path of honesty and displayed rare integrity must be celebrated".

Omeri said the award should be given to any Nigerian, irrespective of status or class.

Usuah, who plies the Abuja airport road, said he was at a car wash, when he discovered there was a bag in the car.

"My mind went back to the man whom I dropped at a hotel and I immediately alerted my chairman and he instructed me to go back to the place where I dropped him. I saw him and delivered his bag to him."

Oche Elias, who represented the Minister of Aviation, said it was a rare display of honesty, adding that it was "a huge integrity and trust exhibited by Usuah".

[Unattributed report entitled 'Taxi driver honoured for returning N18m', in *The Nation*, August 3, 2012, p 7.]

7.4 Academic writing

(19) Johnson

In ancient times the Yorubas were mostly monogamic; not from any enlightened views on the subject however, but rather from necessity; for, although polygamy was not actually forbidden, yet only rich folk could avail themselves of indulgence in that condition of life.

Besides, in a community mainly pastoral and agricultural, where all were peaceful, and no one engaged in any occupation perilous to the lives of its male population e.g. warfare, sea-faring, deep mining, etc., where wants were few, and those easily satisfied, the young men married as soon as they were of an age to support a family, and therefore a superfluous female population was hardly ever known.

The marriage laws and customs have undergone changes brought about by intercourse with other peoples, but the chief features in them are still preserved.

[From Samuel Johnson, *The History of the Yorubas*. Author's preface written 1897; edited by O.Johnson and first published 1921 by C.S.S. Bookshops, Lagos. Johnson belonged to the first generation of Yoruba Anglican clergymen.]

(20) Okonkwo

Murder which is the most grievous kind of homicide is defined in section 316 of the Code which provides as follows:

Except as hereinafter set forth, a person who unlawfully kills another under any of the following circumstances, that is to say:

1. if the offender intends to cause the death of the person killed, or that of some other person;
2. if the offender intends to do to the person killed or to some other person some grievous harm;
3. if death is caused by means of an act done in the prosecution of an unlawful purpose, which act is of such a nature as to be likely to endanger human life;
4. if the offender intends to do grievous harm to some person for the purpose of facilitating the commission of an offence which is such that the offender may be arrested without warrant, or for the purpose of facilitating the flight of an offender who has committed or attempted to commit any such offence;
5. if death is caused by administering any stupefying or overpowering things for either of the purposes last aforesaid;
6. if death is caused by willfully stopping the breath of any person for either of such purposes; is guilty of murder.

[From C.O.Okonkwo (1980), *Criminal Law in Nigeria*, 2nd edition. Ibadan: Spectrum, p 231.]

(21) Hagher

The cultural attitude of the Tiv versus (that of) Hausa/Fulani to dance became the crucial factor in winning party followership. All kinds of dances and songs were employed, but since the UMBC employed ethnic nationalism to attack the NPC any form of the traditional Tiv dances were appropriated by them. The Tiv NPC supporters were referred to as Baja, a pre-colonial slave who, when his slave master freed all the slaves, had crawled back to the master to demand (for) further enslavement. This loss of identity caused the NPC to turn to popular theatre to form a new identity. As if to reflect the contempt that the Moslem Hausa/Fulani elite had for dancing, the Tiv NPC members chose a dramatic anti-Tiv style. Instead of dancing from left to right – the Tiv dance formation – they danced clockwise.

[From Iyorwuese H.Hagher, 'Popular theatre and politics in Tivland since 1900': paper presented at the Faculty of Arts Seminar, University of Jos, 16th February, 1988, p.15; quoted in Mvendaga Jibo, *Tiv Politics since 1959*. Katsina Ala, Benue State: Mandate International Limited, p.50. The background to this piece is the politics of the Northern Region in the period before and after independence, as very briefly outlined in Chapter Five. The Tivs are one of the largest ethnic groups in the Middle Belt – see Chapter One – and their interests were represented in the 1950s and 1960s by the UMBC, the United Middle Belt Congress.]

(22) Ajayi

We have failed in our externally driven, top to bottom approach to development, development that ignores the people. More than that, we have created a cultural void and a moral crisis. It is in filling this cultural void that I see the principal challenge for the Nigerian Academy of Letters. While short term political, administrative, judicial, and economic measures are being taken to prevent a total collapse and a Congo situation, the Academy of Letters must address the medium- and longer-term process towards a cultural and moral reorientation. Perhaps in our approach to development, we have been too hasty and tried to cut too many corners. The cultural and moral void we have created is perhaps the most dangerous consequence. We cannot have science and technology, growth-oriented economy, good governance, principled public officials and honest businessmen without a culture that stresses virtue, integrity, reaching out beyond oneself, working hard, and caring. Several generations of ancestors have built up the concept of Virtue within each separate culture in Nigeria. The Yoruba have the concept of *Omoluabi* who in private and public life has regard for others. If we are serious about building up a Nigerian culture that will sustain an internally generated momentum for growth and adaptation, and provide improved quality of life for our people, we need to build such a culture on the concepts of Virtue in our traditional cultures.

[From J.F.Ade Ajayi, 1999, 'Development is About People' in Banjo (ed.) *Humanity in Context*. Occasional Publications of the Nigerian Academy of Letters, 2000, pp 32–3. The Nigerian Academy of Letters brings together leading academics of different disciplines. Professor Ajayi, of the University College, Ibadan, later the University of Ibadan, was one of Nigeria's earliest academic historians.]

(23) Maitama

General Murtala in February 1976 invited Maitama with a view to giving him an assignment that was tough. He told Maitama that he wanted him to conduct an investigation into cults and secret societies and their influence on the lives of Nigerians and which Nigerians. He was giving the assignment to Maitama, he said, because other people that might be asked to undertake the task were scared of cults and secret societies and were therefore, afraid to go into finding out about cults. Maitama confirmed to the Head of State that he was afraid of nobody except Allah and would therefore conduct the investigation. Maitama investigated the phenomenon of cultism and submitted a report to the Head of State. Among his discoveries were (1) that the bodies derived their power from the initiation ceremonies whose tenets were based on ancient religious practices. (2) that the cults and secret societies were founded by highly placed and highly influential dignitaries in society (3) the rationale that each society or cult operated on the basis of "self-help". For example if a powerful contractor wanted to be awarded a contract he would be made to belong to the cult as a condition for the award if the offender who could make the decision for the award belonged to a cult or society.

[From Ayuba T.Abubakar, *Maitama Sule – Danmasanin Kano*. Zaria: Ahmadu Bello University Press, 2003, pp. 265–6. The late Maitama Sule was a veteran politician, a prominent figure in the traditional Northern elite and one of the founders of the NPC; see Chapter Five. 'Danmasanin' is a traditional Kano title. The passage is written by one of his admirers.]

(24) Lenses

When a beam of light is parallel to principal axis passes through a convex lense it is inverted and then converged to a point F called principal focus. It is a real focus, thus, the focal length of a converging lense is +ve sign. But a concave tense have a virtual principal focus. Since the focuse is virtual, the focus length of such lens is –vc.

The fact that light can fall on both sides of a lens has two principal foci of equidistance from centre C.

[From the Physics (Optics) notes of a pre-degree, "remedial" student of Benue State origin, 2007.]

(25) Aro

The administration also proscribed the publication as well as prohibit from circulation the following Newspapers around 1993: Africa Concord Magazine, Weekend Concord, Sunday Concord, National Concord, The Punch, Saturday Punch, Sunday Punch, Daily Sketch, Sunday Sketch and Nigerian Observer. It is interesting to note that despite all these, the worst and turbulent experience was under General Sanni Abacha's regime of 1994 to 1998 which did not bother to woo or befriend Nigerian Press instead franked at the existence of press and even by act held contrary opinion to Thomas Jefferson's position that where it is left to him to decide whether there should be a government without newspaper or newspaper without government, he will prefer the latter (A. A. Yahaya, 1990). The regime did not rely much on promulgation of any draconian Decrees to attack the press, instead Journalist were being alleged of conspiring in the execution of coup and subsequently jailed, newsprint were been seized in port, newspaper houses were proscribed, vendors of enemy publications were harassed, newspaper proprietors were attacked, publications were proscribed, fake publications became popular which were extended to electronic media.

[From: Olaide Aro, *The Nigerian Press: the Journey So Far*. In Continental Journal of Sustainable Development 2:8–19, 2011.] [Accessed through: WILOLUD Journals 2011.]

7.5 Public addresses

(26) Odutola

The Africans of today are faced with greater and more intricate problems than those of two decades ago. Changing is the Old Order. Africa therefore needs people who will handle her problems practically. Whether such persons are of humble birth or of high birth does not matter. What matters is that they should be men of action, men with broad mind, men able to call a spade a spade. Such people and such only are worthy to be leaders of the New Africa.

[From an address by Timothy Adeola Odutola on behalf of the Nigerian Youth Movement to the Rev.S.O.Odutola, 27 July, 1938; in E.A.Ayandele, *The Ijebu of Yorubaland, 1850–1950: Politics, Economy, and Society*, p.167; Heinemann Educational Books (Nigeria), 1992. The NYM, an early nationalist movement, is described in Chapter Five.]

(27) Tafawa Balewa

Mr President, Sir, – First I must crave the indulgence of the House and make my apologies to you Sir for constantly referring to my notes. My line is direct and the words I have written are frank; and I consider the motion of such fundermental importance that I can take no risk of missing one point or of weakening one statement by impromptu diversions into which I might be led by the strength of my feeling. You will see that the motion concerns the North alone; and as the other Regions are dealing with the same problem in their own way, I hope I shall not be called upon to move this resolution in the Legislative Council: for it is here and now that a remedy for our disease must be found and applied with the least possible delay.

Let there be no misunderstanding. I have no axe to grind and wish for no heads to roll in the gutters. I do not wish to destroy; I call for reform. We must ask ourselves whether the constitutional battles we have fought, and are still fighting, will have been worthwhile if the Victor's laurels are to crown a statue with feet of clay. It would surely be the height of unwisdom were we to disregard the example of other Nations who had suffered similar teething troubles, and fail to appreciate the importance of our relationship with the other Regions of Nigeria and with the World at large. We cannot afford to stagnate, we must go forward.

[Speech by Sir Abubakar Tafawa Balewa in the Northern House of Assembly, July 1950 on a resolution calling for an independent commission to be set up to investigate the system of native administration in the Northern provinces. The handwritten speech is reproduced in full on pages 135–45 of Clark (1991). This extract is taken from pages 135–6. Clark says: "The speech was been mistakenly attributed to Robert Wright [a colonial officer and friend of Sir ATB], but this is a gross misconception. Although he did give some help with the presentation of the speech, the substance of it is entirely Malam Abubakar's."]

(28) Gowon

In spite of the present situation, the Federal Military Government is determined to provide conditions that make continued unity of this country a reality. I also want to take this opportunity to assure everyone, as I have emphasized in my previous statements, that no form of government would be imposed on any section of the community without their wishes being fully ascertained. And I would wish to appeal to all our friends and governments to sympathise with our growing pains and not in any way add to the problems which our young country has to face. I am encouraged by the numerous goodwill messages already received from Heads of Governments and States of African countries, all expressing confidence in the ability of Nigerians to solve their problems and the hope that the country will remain united.

[From a speech by Lt.-Col.Yakubu Gowon, head of the Federal Military Government delivered at a press conference on October 8, 1966 and reported in the *Sunday Times* of October 9, 1966. Gowon had assumed power the previous July after the second military coup of that year.]

(29) Soludo

As we all know, Nigeria has been a country of paradoxes. It is a country abundantly blessed with natural and human resources but in the first four decades of its independence, the potentials remain largely untapped and even mismanaged.

A classic example to underscore the scope of our misfortunes is to compare Nigeria with Indonesia and even Malaysia. By 1972, before Nigeria and Indonesia had the first oil boom, both countries were comparable in almost all counts: agrarian societies, multi-ethnic and religious societies, with comparable size of GDP, etc. Both experienced oil boom in 1973 and thereafter, but took different policy choices. The outcomes of the differences in policy regimes are such that today, while manufactures as percentage of total exports is about 40 per cent in Indonesia, it is less than one per cent in Nigeria – where we were in the 1970s. We hear of how Malaysia got their first palm seedlings from Nigeria in the early 1960s when oil palm produce was already a major export of Nigeria. In the 1990s, it was said that Malaysia's export of palm oil produce earned it more than Nigeria earned from oil exports.

[From a lecture delivered on Founders' Day at the University of Benin, November 23, 2006, by Prof.Chukwuma Soludo, Governor, Central Bank of Nigeria.]

(30) Ebonyi

This brings me to the subsisting national security challenge posed by the Boko Haram insurgency. In this regard, it has become both a fad and a national pastime to charge that the government is not doing anything about the problem.

While nobody can play down the seriousness of the situation, the press must be careful not to lend itself as a vehicle of the opposition which is desperate in its attempt to forge a national consciousness against the government for political goals. While the government at all levels continues to tackle the challenge of Boko Haram, let us not forget that the entire nation was taken by surprise by this particular specie of terrorism which demands courage, time and patience to overcome. In fighting the enemy, we all need to bear in mind that like the proverbial fly on the scrotum, great care is needed to prevent or minimize collateral damage against innocent people so that the victory we are certain to have will not be a pyrrhic one.

[From a Keynote Address, 'Impeachment Threat, Boko Haram and Other Issues', given by the Governor of Ebonyi State on the occasion of the Grand Finale of the 2012 Press Week of the Nigeria Union of Journalists Ebonyi State Council, 26 July 2012; published in The Nation, 30 July 2012, p 51.]

7.6 Religious writing

(31) Ehusani

Human beings in their inordinate crave for autonomy often think that they can achieve happiness, peace, fulfilment and salvation by their own efforts. These efforts, however, often end up in futility. The event of Pentecost demonstrates that peace, fulfilment and salvation are possible only through the bestowal of the Spirit of Christ.

The Spirit of God is the only power that can transcend all the divisions that human history has created between peoples and nations. It is the spirit that can remove the blindness, pull down the walls, and overcome the biases and prejudices that keep people apart. It is the Spirit of God that can inspire forgiveness of past wounds and hurts, and bring people together once again to live as brothers and sisters – children of one God and Father of all.

[From George Omaku Ehusani, *Gospel Reflections for Our Time*. Mumbai: St Pauls. 2006, p 190.]

(32) Tafsir

For centuries after the revelation of the Qur'an,... it was the Arabs who mostly assumed authority on its interpretation. Others like the Persians (present day Iranians), Indians and Africans who tried to compete with the Arabs in that field, could only do so in Arabic language which they first had to learn.

Thus, from the beginning, Arabic had been the authoritative language of Tafsir (exposition of the Qur'an). Whoever wanted to attain scholarship in the field of Tafsir ought to master Arabic. But the anomaly here becomes very conspicuous when it is remembered that over four fifth of the world's Muslim population today are non-Arabic speakers.

There is nothing like being literate in one's own mother tongue. The Arabs have demonstrated this abundantly through Tafsir. But since Tafsir of the Qur'an is not meant for the Arabs alone, shouldn't there be a means of making it available to majority of Muslims in the languages understandable to them?

[From Femi Abbas, 'Abuse of Ramadan', later corrected to 'Features of Ramadan'. *The Nation*, July 27, 2012, p 36.]

7.7 Formal resolutions

(33) Afikpo

In 1950, the Afikpo Clan Union, Lagos branch, formulated a plan for securing financial support from its members.

1. Individuals who donate one hundred or more pounds will have their names used to name our public buildings or any other things of common interest. Their names will be sung as heroes or heroines and a special title, honour and respect planned out for them.
2. Those who donate fifty or more pounds but not up to 100 will have their names in tablets on the walls of our public buildings.
3. Those who donate twenty-five or more pounds but not up to fifty will have their full plate pictures (with creditable footnotes) framed and hung on the walls of our public buildings.
4. Those who donate ten or more pounds but not up to twenty-five will have their postcard pictures (with creditable footnotes) in a special album to be kept in our future public library.
5. Those who donate two or more pounds but not up to ten will have their names written in gold ink in a special register.
6. All donations below two pounds will be entered into an ordinary register.

[From Boniface I.Obichere, *Studies in Southern Nigerian History*. Frank Cass, 1982, pp 160–1. The Afikpo Union is an example of the type of association that brought together for purposes of mutual assistance people living in one town or city far from the place they originated from. Associations of this sort became particularly common in colonial times among the Igbos, with their propensity for internal migration.]

7.8 Literature

(34) Tutuola

I could not blame the lady for following the Skull as a complete gentleman to his house at all. Because if I were a lady, no doubt I would follow him to wherever he would go, and still as I was a man I would jealous him more than that, because if this gentleman went to the battle field, surely, enemy would not kill him or capture him and if bombers saw him in a town which was to be bombed, they would not throw bombs on his presence, and if they did throw it, the bomb itself would not explode until this gentleman would leave that town, because of his beauty.

[From Amos Tutuola, *The Palm-Wine Drinkard*. Faber and Faber, 1952, p 25]

(35) Onitsha

King: How many times have I warned you that your service with me will be terminated if you continue to put eye on my wives and daughters. I have received several complaints against you from outsiders. You are finally warned just now to take time, otherwise you lose your job and become an applicant.

Servant: My Lord, please tell what type of putting eye on your daughters and wives.

King: I mean that you are chasing them about. Were it to be that you have got the opportunity, you would have mixed up with them. You are too fond of female, why? It has came to my observation that, some servants find means to mingle with their masters wives and daughters. When I hold you one day, I will cut off your thing with a knife.(*Laughter*)

Servant: My Lord, your daughters and some of your wives are the people who worry me every now and then.

King: By how?

Servant: They are interested in me and have been asking me for friendship. When I said No! some of your wives started to hate and trouble me. Any thing I do, they find faults in it merely because I refused to be their secret lovers.

[From 'My Seven Daughters Are After Young Boys' a 'Classic Drama' by Nathan Njoku. Onitsha: Njoku & Sons, 196–? Accessed 1/8/2012 in the Kansas University Onitsha Collection.]

(36) Achebe

'Let's go and call a doctor,' I said.

'That's right,' said Chief Nanga with relief and, leaving his friend, rushed towards the telephone. I hadn't thought about the telephone.

'What is the use of a doctor?' moaned our poisoned host. 'Do they know about African poison? They have killed me. What have I done to them? Did I owe them anything? Oh! Oh! Oh! What have I done?'

Meanwhile Chief Nanga had been trying to phone a doctor and was not apparently getting anywhere. He was now shouting threats of immediate sacking at some invisible enemy.

'This is Chief the Honourable Nanga speaking,' he was saying. 'I will see that you are dealt with. Idiot. That is the trouble with this country. Don't worry, you will see. Bloody fool...'

At this point the cowboy bodyguard came in dragging the cook by his shirt collar. The Minister sprang at him with an agility which completely belied his size and condition.

'Wait, Master,' pleaded the cook.

'Wait your head!' screamed his employer, going for him. 'Why you put poison for my coffee?' His huge body was quivering like a jelly.

'Me? Put poison for master? Nevertheless!' said the cook, side-stepping to avoid a heavy blow from the Minister.

[From Chinua Achebe (1966), *A Man of the People*. London: Heinemann.]

(37) Alkali

That evening Li went to her grandfather's hut. Lifting the mat that covered the door, she greeted him. 'Kaka, did you spend the day well?'

'Come in, my wife, come in, my mother,' he said weakly. Inside, she stood for a while trying to focus her eyes in the semi-darkness.

'I want to talk with you about something serious,' Li said.

'I am waiting,' he said simply.

'It is four years now. Four years since the man left us.' Ever since they were formally married, she never referred to Habu by name.

'What am I to do, Kaka?'

'Wait for him child,' he said flatly and Li's heart sank. She had feared this answer.

'Wait for him Kaka?' she said, rather too sharply. 'How long can a woman wait for a man? I am tired and the whole village is laughing behind my back!' A sob rose to her throat.

'Tired of what?' Li looked surprised. Not so much by the sharpness of her grandfather's voice but by the realisation that her boredom to escape sprang from many sources. She experienced an intense desire to escape from them all.

[From Zaynab Alkali, *The Stillborn*. London: Longman, 1984, pp 62–3.]

(38) Saro-Wiwa

One evening, as we were playing football for the church field, we heard the sound of lorry. At first I think that it is my master's lorry that have returned from Pitakwa. Everybody was telling me: 'Ah-ha, you will now go to work again you foolish boy instead to stay here looking for woman to sleep with and playing football without work, chopping your mama chop for nothing.' Myself too I began to glad small small. Because if I can be going to Pitakwa everyday, it means to say that when I return every night, they will begin to ask me of how the world is, what is happening whether there is fight or no fight. Then I can tell that stupid Chief Birabee what other people are doing in the world. And sometimes I can bring Agnes my dear some better thing from the shop which she will like and thank me for it. So I begin to run towards the motor. But when I get there now, soso soza soza. I am telling you when I see these sozamen inside their khaki and all of them holding gun, I was afraid small. My heart begin to cut, *gbum, gbum, gbum.* I stopped and I begin to go back small small.

[From Ken Saro-Wiwa, *Sozaboy*. Port Harcourt: Saros International Publishers, 1985, p 38.]

(39) Aliyu

"Look," said Dija with a giggle, catching hold of the handbrake. "You forgot to release it."

"But it can't make the car jerk or stop the engine. Release the handbrake and let's start the car again."

The car whined and failed to start.

"Don't weaken the battery," said Dija. "What happens in a situation like this is for people to push-start the car for you."

"It has never behaved like this before."

"Even when you drove it with the handbrake up? Let's go out and ask for help."

A veiled woman stood a few yards away waiting for a taxi. She kept flagging them down and they kept going without stopping. The two girls stood in the afternoon heat not knowing what to do, but wait.

"I've never asked strange men for help before," said Husna, suddenly becoming conscious of her sex.

"Neither do I," said Dija. "Or should we stand by the car until a passing motorist who recognises us stops?"

"That may mean staying here forever."

[From Aliyu Kamal, *Silence and a Smile*. Kano: Myrrh, 2005, pp 78–9. Two young Hausa women have a problem with their car.]

(40) Atta

It was a city hard to love; a bedlam of trade. Trade thrived in the smallest of street corners; in stores; on the heads of hawkers; even in the suburbs where family homes were converted into finance houses and hair salons, according to the need. The outcome of this was dirt, piles of it, on the streets, in open gutters, and in the marketplaces, which were tributes to both dirt and trade.

By the Cathedral Church of Christ, I met a bottleneck and was cornered by a group of lepers. One rapped on my window and I rolled it down to put money into his tin cup. A group of refugee children from North Africa, noticing my gesture, scurried to my car. They rubbed my windows and pleaded with feigned expressions. I felt ashamed for wishing them off the streets. Passers-by trespassed the stairs of the Cathedral without regard. Once a monument along the marina, people could now buy fried yams, brassieres, and mosquito coils inches away from her ebony doors.

[From Sefi Atta, *Everything Good Will Come*. Lagos: Farafina, 2005, pp 102–3.]

7.9 Miscellaneous

(41) Pepeiye

Pepeiye: Imagine; if dem say na animal with horns go kill person, na animal like snail? This Beetle owner no know him level. It's getting dark... At this stage, I think I would manage a Passat if I see one again..

It's getting dark...Not only that... the weather is getting cloudy...The cars have all stopped coming. A motor-cyclist stops for Miss Pepeiye.

Pepeiye: Motor cycle? Infra dignitatem! If the worse comes to the worst I'll manage a Beetle.. But I'll hide my face inside it.

The clouds are rumbling in the sky... Rain is about to fall.. A bicycle-rider offers to help our dear city girl.

Pepeiye: Don't worry. I'll rather ride on motor cycle than dirty my expensive clothes on a bicycle.

Bicycle-rider: But you fit manage am now –

Pepeiye: I say no! Abi na by force?

Bicycle-rider: Okay o...

The weather has suddenly turned hostile. The rains come tumbling down with rough winds... And there's no mode of transport in sight. Miss Pepeiye didn't even know when she removed her shoes to do a bit of Ben Johnson on the macadamized thoroughfare!
Pepeiye: Chei! Na me kill myself! God – abeg – wey that bicycle man again? How am I going to cover six kilometres under this heavy downpour?!

['Miss Pepeiye in "A Bird in Hand", in *Ikebe Super* No.119, ? 1991. *Ikebe Super* was a monthly cartoon magazine featuring a number of comic characters, founded in the 1980s by Wale Adenuga.]

(42) Christmas Prayer
My prayers are that all your expectations during this Christmas shall be fulfilled. You shall receive the blessings of the Lord in abundance. And in returns may you give thanks and praises to God. May God protect you and your beloved ones throughout this season and always.

[Anonymous printed message on a Christmas greetings card, 2005.]

(43) Banwell
Here is a life time opportunity to meet Live with Alh. Aliko Dangote, Africa's wealthiest and most successful entrepreneur by participating in the "Ask Alh. Aliko Dangote" quiz.
Youngstars Foundation is partnering with the World Economic Forum – Young Global Leaders (YGLs) in Nigeria to produce a short film documentary featuring Alh. Aliko Dangote titled "**I Believe**". The objective of the film documentary is to spark among youths in Nigeria and Africa the consciousness that we can transform Africa for good in one generation through entrepreneurship and self belief, using Alh. Aliko Dangote's story as a model of mass inspiration and reorientation among emerging young entrepreneurs.

Special Highlight:
Two Nigerian youths, one male and one female shall get the chance to be part of the documentary recording with Alh. Aliko Dangote. To be one of those 2 lucky youths, you have to answer the question below.
If you have a 2 minutes opportunity to meet with Alh.Aliko Dangote, what one question will you like to ask him?

[An online advertisement by Kingsley Banwell 24.7.2012. Alhaji Aliko Dangote, a commercial magnate, has been named by Forbes as Africa's richest man.]

(44) Congratulations

ALHAMDULLILAH!
THE PEOPLE'S GOVERNOR & KHADIMUL ISLAM
is
67

On behalf of myself, family and the entire people of Kano North Senatorial District, I Senator Barau Jibrin rejoice with the Executive Governor of Kano state, His Excellency, Dr Abdullahi Umar Ganduje, OFR (KHADIMUL ISLAM) on his 67th birthday anniversary.

While some states are unable to pay the salaries of their workers due to the current economic recession in the country, Kano state under your leadership is not only paying the salaries of it's workers promptly but also embarking on a massive infrastructural development in all nooks and crannies of our dear state.

We are proud of your performance of the Governor of Kano state. MORE GREASE TO YOUR ELBOW.

May Almighty Allah (SWT) continue to give you good health and wisdom to continue to serve kano state and humanity in general. Amin Ya ALLAH.

[This reproduces a full-page advertisement published in *Daily Trust*, December 26, 2016. Full-page advertisements, congratulations on various occasions, etc. are common in Nigerian newspapers. This one congratulates the Governor of predominantly Muslim Kano State on his birthday. 'Alhamdulillah', meaning "Praise God", is an Islamic (Arabic) prayer. 'Khadimul Islam' is an Islamic title.]

References

Details of doctoral dissertations referred to in the text appear in a special list at the end of Chapter 6

Achebe, Chinua. 1975. *Morning yet on creation day: essays*. London: Heinemann.

Achebe, Chinua. 1984. *The trouble with Nigeria*. Enugu: Fourth Dimension.

Adeboye, Olufunke. 2003. Elite lifestyle and consumption in colonial Ibadan. In Oyebade (ed.), 281–304.

Adegbija, Efurosibina. 1988. 'My friend, where is Anini?': decoding the meaning of utterances. *Journal of Pragmatics* 1(2), 151–160.

Adegbija, Efurosibina. 1989a. Lexico-semantic variation in Nigerian English. *World Englishes* 8:2, 165–177.

Adegbija, Efurosibina. 1989b. A comparative study of politeness phenomena in Nigerian English, Yoruba and Ogori. *Multilingua: Journal of Cross-Cultural and Interlanguage Communication* 8(1), 57–80.

Adegbija, Efurosibina, 2003. Idiomatic variation in Nigerian English. In Peter Lucko, Peter Lothar, and Hans-Georg Wolf (eds.), *Studies in African Varieties of English*, 41–56. Frankfurt am Main: Peter Lang.

Adegbija, Efurosibina, 2004. The domestication of English in Nigeria. In Awonusi and Babalola (eds.), 20–44.

Adegbija, Efursosibina and Janet Bello. 2001. The semantics of *OK* in Nigerian English. *World Englishes* 20(1), 89–98.

Adegbite, Wale. 2010. English language usage, uses and misuse(s) in a non-host second language context, Nigeria. Obafemi Awolowo University Ile-Ife inaugural lecture No. 231, September 14, 2010.

Adegbite, Wale. 2011. Languages and the challenges of education in Nigeria. *Journal of the Nigeria English Studies Association*, 14:1, 11–29.

Adegbite, Wale, Inyang Udofot and Kehinde Ayoola. 2014. *A dictionary of Nigerian English usage*. Ile-Ife: Obafemi Awolowo University Press in collaboration with the Nigeria English Studies Association.

Adegoju, Adeyemi. 2012. Preface to Wale Adegbite, Segun Adekoya, and Adeyemi Adegoju (eds.), *Use of English: A Manual on Communicative Skills for Tertiary Institutions*. Olas Ventures, Mushin, Lagos and Department of English, Obafemi Awolowo University, Ile-Ife.

Adejare, O. 1984. Towards a language-centred English degree programme. In Richard Freeman and Munzali Jibril (eds.), *English language studies in Nigerian higher education*. Papers of the Nigeria English Studies Association/British Council Conference held at Bayero University, Kano, 23–27 September 1984. London: British Council.

Adekunle, Mobolaji. 1974. The standard Nigerian English in sociolinguistic perspective. *Journal of the Nigeria English Studies Association* 6(1), 24–37.

Adekunle, Mobolaji. 1979. Non-random variation in the Nigerian English. In Ebo Ubahakwe (ed.), *Varieties and functions of the English language in Nigeria*. Lagos: Africa Universities Press, in association with the Nigeria English Studies Association.

Ademola-Adeoye, Feyi. 2004. Language, gender and identity: a social, cultural and psychological survey. In Awonusi and Babalola (eds.), 336–362.

https://doi.org/10.1515/9781501504600-008

Adesanoye, Festus. 1973. A study of varieties of written English in Nigeria. University of Ibadan PhD thesis.

Adesanoye, Festus. 2004. The English language in Nigeria: the case of a vanishing model? In Owolabi and Dasylva (eds.), 239–257.

Adetugbo, Abiodun. 1977. Nigerian English: fact or fiction? *Lagos Notes and Records* 6, 128–141.

Adetugbo, Abiodun. 1979. Appropriateness and Nigerian English. In Ubahakwe (ed.), 167–183.

Adetugbo, Abiodun. 2004. Problems of standardization and Nigerian English phonology. In A.B.K. Dadzie and Segun Awonusi (eds.), *Nigerian English: influences and characteristics* 179–199. Lagos: Concept Publications.

Adetugbo, Abiodun and V.O. Awonusi. 1982. Americanisms in Nigerian English. *Calabar Papers on English Language and Literature in Africa*, Vol. I.

Adetunji, Akin. 2015. English in a Nigerian linguistic landscape. *World Englishes* 34:4, 654–668.

Afigbo, Adiele. 2005. *Nigerian history, politics and affairs: the collected essays of Adiele Afigbo.* Trenton, NJ: New World Press.

Afolayan, Adebisi. 1984. The English language in Nigerian education as an agent of proper multilingual and multicultural development. *Journal of Multilingual and Multicultural Development* 5; 1–22.

Agheyisi, R.N. 1971. West African Pidgin English: simplification and simplicity. University of Stanford Ph.D. thesis.

Ajani, Timothy. 2007. Is there indeed a "Nigerian English"? *Journal of Humanities and Social Sciences* 1(1). Accessible at http://scientificjournals.org/journals2007/articles/1084.htm.

Ajulo, S.B. (ed.). 2000. *Language in education and society: a festschrift in honour of Professor C.M.B.Brann.* Lagos: University of Lagos Press.

Akere, Funso. 1982. Sociocultural constraints and the emergence of a Standard Nigerian English. In Pride (ed.), 85–99.

Akinjobi, Adenike. 2004. Language chauvinism and the prospect of an indigenous national language in Nigeria. In Lekan Oyeleye (ed.), *Language and Discourse in Society*, 33–46. Ibadan: Hope Publications.

Akinjobi, Adenike. 2006. A cyclical search for a rhythm description for Nigerian English: the Yoruba (Nigerian) English example. *African Journal of Educational Research* 10(1&2), 7–13.

Akinjobi, Adenike. 2009a. English syllabic consonants and the quantity factor in educated Yoruba English. *African Research Review* 3(2), 45–55.

Akinjobi, Adenike. 2009b. A study of the use of weak forms of English grammatical words. *African Research Review* 3(3), 81–94.

Akinjobi, Adenike. 2010. Consonant cluster simplification by deletion in Nigerian English. *Ibadan Journal of English Studies* 6; 27–38.

Akinjobi, Adenike (ed.). 2014. *English Language Clinic Lecture Series 1 – 5.* Ibadan: Edunjobi Enterprises.

Akinjobi, Adenike and Rotimi Oladipupo. Patterns of intonation of some Nigerian television reporters. *Ibadan Journal of European Studies* 5; 11–16.

Akinremi, Ihuoma. 2015. Form and structure of urban youth varieties of Nigerian Pidgin. A paper presented at the 2nd African Urban and Youth Language Conference (AUYL), Kenyatta University, Nairobi, Kenya.

Akinremi, Ihuoma. 2016. Phonological adaptation and morphosyntactic integration in Igbo-English intersentential codeswitching. *Journal of Universal Language* 17(1); 53–79.

Akinremi, Ihuoma and Polycarp Dajang. 2015. Strategies of linguistic form manipulation in the Nigerian Pidgin-based youth variety. A paper presented at the 28th Conference of the Linguistic Association of Nigeria, Nnamdi Azikiwe University, Awka.

Akinremi, Ihuoma and Adewumi Erin. 2017. Transformation of the linguistic landscape of Central Nigeria: a case study of the Cara language. In Sati Fwatshak (ed.), *The Transformtion of Central Nigeria: Essays in Honor of Toyin Falola*, 299–308. Austin: Pan-African University Press.

Alo, Moses and Rajend Mesthrie. 2008. Nigerian English: morphology and syntax. In R. Mesthrie (ed.), 323–339.

Amayo, Airen. 1980. Tone in Nigerian English. Papers from the 16th Meeting of the Chicago Linguistic Society, April 17–18, 1980, 1–9.

Amayo, Airen. 1986. Teaching English pronunciation in Nigeria for international intelligibility: the suprasegmentals. In Unoh (ed.)

Anyagwa, Carol. 2015. Word stress in Nigerian English. In Opeibi et al. (eds.), 41–54.

Asomugha, C.N.C. 1981. *Nigerian slangs*. Onitsha: ABIC Publishers.

Atoye, Raphael. 2005. Non-native perception and interpretation of English intonation. *Nordic Journal of African Studies* 14(1), 26–42.

Awonusi, V.O. 1985. Sociolinguistic variation in Nigerian (Lagos) English. University of London PhD thesis.

Awonusi, V.O. 1990. Coming of age: English in Nigeria. English Today 22, 31–35.

Awonusi, V.O. 1994. The Americanization of Nigerian English. *World Englishes* 13(1), 75–82.

Awonusi, Segun. 2004. RP and the sociolinguistic realities of non-native English accents. In Owolabi and Dasylva (eds.), 179–192.

Awonusi, Segun and E.A. Babalola (eds.). 2004. *The domestication of English in Nigeria: a festschrift in honour of Abiodun Adetugbo*. Lagos: University of Lagos Press.

Awonusi, Segun. 2007. Good spoken English and national development: sociophonology in the service of man. University of Lagos inaugural lecture, March 14, 2007.

Ayandele, Emmanuel. 1966. *The missionary impact on modern Nigeria, 1842–1914*. London: Longman.

Azuike, Macpherson. 2011. The dwindling standard of the English language: a challenge to the English language teacher. In Udofot and Udoudom (eds.), 128–141.

Babalola, E. and Rotimi Taiwo. 2009. Code switching in contemporary Nigerian hip-hop music. *Itupale Online Journal of African Studies* 1, 1–26.

Baker, C. 2001. *Foundations of Bilingual Education and Bilingualism*. Clevedon: Multilingual Matters.

Bamgbose, Ayo. 1965. *Yoruba orthography*. Ibadan: Ibadan University Press.

Bamgbose, Ayo. 1971. The English language in Nigeria. In Spencer (ed.), 35–48.

Bamgbose, Ayo. 1982. Standard Nigerian English: issues of identification. In Braj.Kachru (ed.), *The other tongue: English across cultures 99–109*. Urbana: University of Illinois Press.

Bamgbose, Ayo. 1989. Issues for a model of language planning. *Language Problems and Language Planning* 13(1).

Bamgbose, Ayo. 1995. English in the Nigerian environment. In Bamgbose et al. (eds.), 9–26.

Bamgbose, Ayo, Ayo Banjo and Andrew Thomas (eds.). 1995. *New Englishes: a West African perspective*. Ibadan: Mosuro.

Bamgbose, Ayo. 1998. Torn between the norms: innovations in world Englishes. *World Englishes* 17(1), 1–14.

Bamiro, Edmund. 1991. Nigerian Englishes in Nigerian English literature. *World Englishes* 10(1), 7–17.

Bamiro, Edmund. 1994. Lexico-semantic variation in Nigerian English. *World Englishes* 13(1), 47–60.

Bamiro, Edmund. 1995. Syntactic variation in West African English. *World Englishes* 14(2), 189–204.

Bamiro, Edmund. 2015. English in Nigerian settings: recent lexicoining in Nigerian English. In Opeibi et al. (eds.), 87–96.

Banjo, Ayo. 1971. Towards a definition of Standard Nigerian spoken English. *Annales de l'Université d'Abidjan, Série* 5(1), 165–175.

Banjo, Ayo. 1976. The university and the standardization of the English language in Nigeria. *West African Journal of Modern Languages* 1.

Banjo, Ayo. 1979. Beyond intelligibility. In Ubahakwe (ed.), 7–13.

Banjo, Ayo. 1993. An endormative model for the teaching of the English language in Nigeria. *International Journal of Applied Linguistics* 3(2), 261–275.

Banjo, Ayo. 1995. On codifying Nigerian English: research so far. In Bamgbose et al. (eds.), 203–231.

Banjo, Ayo. 1996. *Making a virtue of necessity: An overview of the English language in Nigeria*. Ibadan University Press.

Banjo, Ayo. 2014. The deteriorating use of English in Nigeria. In Akinjobi (ed.), 2–13.

Bickerton, Derek. 1975. *The Dynamics of a Creole System*. Cambridge: Cambridge University Press.

Blench, Roger. 2005. *A dictionary of Nigerian English*. www.rogerblench.info/English.

Blench, Roger (ed.). 2014. *Atlas of Nigerian Languages III*. Oxford: Kay Williamson Educational Foundation.

Blommaert, J. 2010. *A Sociolinguistics of Globalization*. Cambridge: Cambridge University Press.

Brann, Conrad Max Benedict. 1990. Language in/for the mass media: a research model for Nigeria. In *Language in education & society: an anthology of selected writings of C. M. B. Brann (1975–2005)*; compiled with the assistance of Baba Mai Bello. Maiduguri: Library of Language in Education and Society, University of Maiduguri.

Brosnahan, L.F. 1958. English in Southern Nigeria. *English Studies* 39, 97–110.

Chiluwa, I. 2010. Nigerian English in informal e-mail messages. *English World-Wide* 31(1), 40–61.

CIA (US Central Intelligence Agency). 2018. The World Factbook. https://www.cia.gov/library/publications/the-world-factbook/geos/print_ni.html.

Clark, Trevor. 1991. A *Right Honourable Gentleman: the Life and Times of Alhaji Sir Abubakar Tafawa Balewa*. Zaria: Hudahuda Publishing Company.

Clyne, Michael (ed.). 1992. *Pluricentric Languages: Differing Norms in Different Nations*. Berlin: Mouton de Gruyter.

Coates, Jennifer. 1993. *Women, Men and Language*. London: Longman.

Corder, S.P. 1981. *Error Analysis and Interlanguage*. Oxford: Oxford University Press.

Crampton, E. P. 1975. *Christianity in Northern Nigeria*. Zaria: Gaskiya Corporation.

Crowder, Michael. 1962. *The story of Nigeria*. London: Faber & Faber.

Crozier, David and Roger Blench. 1992. *An index of Nigerian Languages*. 2nd edn. Dallas: Summer Institute of Linguistics.

Cruttenden, Alan. 2001. *Gimson's pronunciation of English*. Sixth edn., revised. London: Arnold.

Crystal, David. 1997. *English as a Global Language*. Cambridge: Cambridge University Press.

Dada, S.A. 2006. Language contact and language conflict: the case of Yoruba-English bilinguals. In O. Ndimele, C. Ikekeonwu, and B.M. Mbah (eds.), *Language and Economic Reforms in Nigeria 68–85*. Port Harcourt: M & J Grand Orbit Communications & Emhai Press.

Dadzie, A. B. K. and Segun Awonusi (eds.). 2004. *Nigerian English: influences and characteristics*. Lagos: Concept Publications.

Dauer, R. 1983. Stress-timing and syllable-timing reanalyzed. *Journal of Phonetics* 11, 51–62.

Davies, Mark. 2013. *Corpus of Global Web-Based English: 1.9 billion words from speakers in 20 countries (GloWbE)*. https://corpus.byu.edu/glowbe/

Davies, Mark and Robert Fuchs. 2015. Expanding horizons in the study of World Englishes with the 1.9-billion-word global web-based English corpus (GloWbE). *English World-Wide* 36(1), 1–28.

Deuber, Dagmar. 2005. *Nigerian Pidgin in Lagos. Language contact, variation and change in an African urban setting*. London: Battlebridge.

Dunstan, Elizabeth (ed.). 1966. *The sound systems of the main Nigerian Languages and English: A preliminary handbook for teachers of English as a second language*. Published by the Department of Linguistics and Nigerian Languages, University of Ibadan.

Echeruo, M. 1977. *Victorian Lagos*. London: Macmillan.

Edwards, Paul. 1967. *Equiano's travels*. London: Heinemann.

Eka, David. 1985. A phonological study of Standard Nigerian English. Ahmadu Bello University, Zaria PhD thesis.

Eka, David. 1987. Phonology of NigE. In Adama Odumuh, *Nigerian English (NigE): Selected essays, 37–57*. Zaria: Ahmadu Bello University Press.

Eka, David and Inyang Udofot. 1996. *Aspects of spoken language*. Calabar: Bon Universal.

Ekong, Pamela. 1980. Investigation into the intelligibility of a possible standard model for Nigerian spoken English. In Solomon Unoh (ed.), *Journal of Language Arts and Communication*, 1:1, 1–11.

Elugbe, Ben and Augusta Omamor. 1991. *Nigerian Pidgin*. Ibadan: Heinemann Educational Books.

Elugbe, Ben and Judith Mgbemena. 2007. Offensive Nigerian English. In Ndimele (ed.), 29–46.

Emenanjo, Nolue (ed.). 1990. *Multilingualism, Minority Languages and Language Policy in Nigeria*. Central Books, Agbor in collaboration with The Linguistic Association of Nigeria.

Emenanjo, Nolue. 2015. *A grammar of contemporary Igbo*. The Linguistic Association of Nigeria (LAN) in collaboration with M & J Grand Orbit Communications, Port Harcourt.

Enahoro, Anthony. 1965. *Fugitive offender*. London: Cassell.

Essien, Nkereke M. 2011. Deviation as development: a study of the production of English voiced plosives and affricates by Ibibio speakers of English. In Udofot and Udoudom (eds.), 112–126.

Eyisi, Joy. 2003. *Common errors in the use of English*. Onitsha: Africana First Publishers.

Eyisi, Joy. 2015. Accuracy in the use of English. National Open University of Nigeria 9th Inaugural Lecture.

Fafunwa, A. Babs. 1991. *History of Education in Nigeria*. 2nd edn. Ibadan: NPS Educational.

Fafunwa, A. Babs (ed.). 1989. *Education in the mother tongue: The Ife primary education research project 1970–1978*. Ibadan: University Press.

Fajana, Adewumi. 1984. Henry Carr – portrait of a public servant. *Ilorin Journal of Education*, republished in the Internet Archive in Wayback Machine, 2015

Fakoya, Adeleke. 2004. A mediolect called 'Nigerian English.' In Owolabi and Dasylva (eds.), 223–238.

Faleke, Victoria. 2015. The fate of the English language in Nigeria in the cyber age. In Ndimele (ed.), 129–138.

Falola, Toyin. 1998. *The history of Nigeria*. Westport, CT: Greenwood Press.

Falola, Toyin and Matthew Heaton. 2008. *A history of Nigeria*. Cambridge: Cambridge University Press.

Falola, Toyin and Bukola Oyeniyi. 2015. *Nigeria*. Santa Barbara, CA: ABC-CLIO, LLC.

Faraclas, Nicholas. 2008. Nigerian Pidgin English: morphology and syntax. In Mesthrie (ed.), 340–367.

Fuchs, Robert. 2016. *Speech Rhythm in Varieties of English. Evidence from Educated Indian English and British English*. Singapore: Singer.

Fuchs, Robert and Ulrike Gut. 2015. An apparent time study of the progressive in Nigerian English. In Peter Collins (ed.), *Grammatical change in English World-Wide* 373–388. Amsterdam: John Benjamins.

Fuchs, Robert, Ulrike Gut and Taiwo Soneye. 2013. "We just don't even know": the usage of the pragmatic focus particles *even* and *still* in Nigerian English. *English World-Wide* 34(2), 223–245.

Garba, Dantala. 2016. Newspaper revenue and sustainability. In David Jowitt, Godfrey Danaan, and Taye Obateru (eds.), *Understanding the Newspaper Business in Nigeria*, 101–114. Newcastle-upon-Tyne: Cambridge Scholars Publishing.

Greenberg, Joseph. 1966. *The languages of Africa*. Bloomington: Indiana University Press.

Grieve, D.W. 1964. *English language*. Ibadan: African Universities Press for The West African Examinations Council.

Gussenhoven, Carlos and Inyang Udofot. 2010. Word melodies vs pitch accents: A perceptual evaluation of terracing contours in British and Nigerian English. *Proceedings of Speech Prosody*, Chicago, 1–4.

Gut, Ulrike. 2005. Nigerian English prosody. *English World-Wide* 26(2), 153–177.

Gut, Ulrike. 2008. Nigerian English: phonology. In Mesthrie (ed.), 35–54.

Gut, Ulrike. 2012. Towards a codification of Nigerian English – the ICE Nigeria project. *Journal of the Nigeria English Studies Association* 15(1), 1–13.

Gut, Ulrike and Lilian Coronel. 2012. Relatives worldwide. In Marianne. Hundt and Ulrike. Gut (eds.), *Mapping unity and diversity of New Englishes world-wide,* 215–241. Amsterdam: John Benjamins.

Gut, Ulrike and Robert Fuchs. 2013. Progressive aspect in Nigerian English. *Journal of English Linguistics* 41(3), 243–267.

Hansford, Keir, John Bendor-Samuel and Ron Stanford. 1976. *An index of Nigerian languages*. First edition. Dallas: Summer Institute of Linguistics.

Hickey, Raymond. 2000. Language policy of the Roman Catholic Church in Northern Nigeria: 1960–1995. In Ajulo (ed.), 280–290.

Hodgkin, Thomas. 1975. *Nigerian perspectives*. Oxford: Oxford University Press.

Hogg, Richard and C.B. McCully. 1987. *Metrical Phonology: A coursebook*. Cambridge: Cambridge University Press.

Howatt, A. P. R. with H. G. Widdowson. 2004. *A history of English language teaching (ELT)*. 2nd edn. Oxford: Oxford University Press.

Igbineweka, Alex. 1981. *Teach yourself Guosa language*. Lagos: Express Commercial Press.

Igboanusi, Herbert. 2002a. *A dictionary of Nigerian English usage*. Ibadan: Enicrownfit Publishers.

Igboanusi, Herbert. 2002b. *Igbo English in the Nigerian novel*. Ibadan: Enicrownfit Publishers.

Ike, Chukwuemeka. 2004. Book publishing in Nigeria. Sabre Foundation. www.sabre.org/publications/publishing

Ikime, Obaro. 2005. *Groundwork of Nigerian history*. Ibadan: Heinemann Educational Publishers.

Isichei, Elizabeth. 1983. *A history of Nigeria*. London: Longman.

Iweriebor, Ehiedu. 2003. Nationalism and the struggle for freedom, 1880–1960. In Adebayo Oyebade (ed.), 79–106.

Iweriebor, Ehiedu. 2003. Radicalism and the national liberation struggles, 1930–1950. In Oyebade (ed.), 107–125.

Jibril, Munzali. 1979. Regional variation in Nigerian spoken English. In Ubahakwe (ed.), 43–53 *Varieties and functions of the English language in Nigeria*. Lagos: Africa Universities Press, in association with the Nigeria English Studies Association.

Jibril, Munzali. 1982a. Nigerian English: an introduction. In Pride (ed.), 73–84.

Jibril, Munzali. 1982b. Phonological variation in Nigerian English. University of Lancaster PhD thesis.

Jibril, Munzali.1986. Sociolinguistic variation in Nigerian English. *English World-Wide* 7, 47–74.

Jibril, Munzali. 1991. The sociolinguistics of prepositional usage in Nigerian English. In Jenny Cheshire (ed.), *English around the world: sociolinguistic perspectives.*, 518–543 Cambridge: Cambridge University Press.

Jibril, Munzali. 2000. Diachrony and sociolinguistics in Nigerian English. In Ajulo (ed.), 411–420.

Joos, M. 1962. *The Five Clocks*. Bloomington: Indiana University, and The Hague: Mouton.

Josiah, Ubong E. and Sola T. Babatunde. 2011. Standard Nigerian English phonemes: the crisis of modelling and harmonization. *World Englishes* 30(4), 533–550.

Jowitt, David. 1991. *Nigerian English Usage*. Lagos: Longman Nigeria.

Jowitt, David. 2000a. Patterns of intonation in Nigerian English. *English World-Wide* 21:1 , 63–80.

Jowitt, David. 2000b. Nigerian English lexis: a sentimental investigation. *Kakaki: A journal of English Studies.* 1(4), 29–53.

Jowitt, David. 2001. In defence of triphthongs. *English Today* 17(3), 36–41.

Jowitt, David. 2002. The English subjunctive: is it dying? *Kakaki: A Journal of English Studies*, 2(1), 201–232.

Jowitt, David. 2007a. Standard Nigerian English: a re-examination. *Journal of the Nigeria English Studies Association* 3(1), 1–21.

Jowitt, David. 2007b. The rise-fall in Nigerian English intonation. In Ndimele (ed.), 11–28.

Jowitt, David. 2008. Varieties of English: the world and Nigeria. University of Jos inaugural Lecture no. 36, 28 March 2008. Jos: University of Jos Press.

Jowitt, David. 2013. English in Nigeria: some trends observed. *Journal of the Nigeria English Studies Association*, 16: 1&2, 1–12.

Jowitt, David. 2014. Nigerian English lexis: neologisms and archaisms. In Akinjobi (ed.), 63–82.

Jowitt, David. 2015. Nigerian Received Pronunciation. Opeibi et al. (eds.), 3–13.

Jowitt, David and Silas Nnamonu. 1985. *Common errors in English*. Longman Group.

Kachru, Braj. 1985. Standards, codification and sociolinguistic realism: the English language in the outer circle. In Randolph Quirk and H. Widdowson (eds.), *English in the world: teaching and learning the language and literatures*. Cambridge: Cambridge University Press.

Kachru, Braj. 1991. Liberation linguistics and the Quirk Concern. *English Today* 25.

Kager, René. 1999. *Optimality Theory*. Cambridge: Cambridge University Press.

Ker, David. 2002. The choice of English as a national language for Nigeria: a revaluation. In Lawal, A., I. Isiugo-Abanikhe, and I. Ohia (eds.), *Perspectives on Applied Linguistics in Language and Literature*, 114–128. Ibadan: Stirling Horden Publishers.

Kirkpatrick, Andy (ed.). *The Routledge Handbook of World Englishes*, 197–211. London: Routledge.

Kirk-Greene, Anthony. 1971. The influence of West African languages on English. In Spencer (ed.), 123–144.

Kolawole, C.O.O. 2004. Teaching the English language in Nigerian secondary schools: the teacher's dilemma. In Owolabi and Dasylva (eds.), 258–272.

Kortmann, Bernd and Kerstin Lunkenheimer (eds.). 2013. *The electronic world atlas of varieties of English*. Leipzig: Max Planck Institute for Evolutionary Anthropology. http://ewave-atlas.org.

Kperogi, Farooq. 2015. *Glocal English: The changing face and forms of Nigerian English in a global world*. New York: Peter Lang.

Kujore, Obafemi. 1985. *English usage – some notable Nigerian variations*. Lagos: Evans Nigeria.

Lamidi, Mufutau. 2007. The noun phrase structure in Nigerian English. *Studia Anglica Posnaniensia: International review of English Studies* 43, 237–250.

Landry, Rodrigue and Richard Y. Bourhis. 1997. Linguistic landscape and ethnolinguistic vitality: an empirical study. *Journal of Language and Social Psychology* 16(1). 23–49.

Leech, Geoffrey. 1983. *Principles of Pragmatics*. London: Longman.

Lewis, M., G. Simons and C. Fennig (eds.). 2016. *Ethnologue: languages of the world*. 19th edn. Dallas: Summer Institute of Linguistics.

Longe, V. 1999. Student slang from Benin, Nigeria. *English World-Wide* 20(2), 237–249.

Mafeni, B. 1971. Nigerian Pidgin. In Spencer (ed.), 95–112.

McArthur, Tom (ed.). 1995. *The Oxford Companion to the English Language*. Abridged edition. Oxford: Oxford University Press.

Melchers, Gunnel and Philip Shaw. 2013. *World Englishes*. 2nd edn. London: Routledge.

Mesthrie, Rajend (ed.). 2008. *Varieties of English 4: Africa, South and Southeast Asia*. Berlin: Mouton de Gruyter.

Milroy, James and Lesley Milroy. 1998. *Authority in language: investigating Standard English*. 3rd edition. London and New York: Routledge.

Moag, Rodney. 1982. English as a foreign, second, native, and basal language: a new taxonomy of English-using societies. In Pride (ed.), 11–50.

Mustapha, Abolaji. 2011. Redefining deviations in Nigerian English. In Udofot and Udoudom (eds.), 246–261.

Ndimele, Ozo-mekuri (ed.). 2007. *Convergence: English & Nigerian languages - a festschrift for Munzali A.Jibril*. The Linguistic Association of Nigeria in collaboration with M & J Grand Orbit Communications & Emhai Press, Port Harcourt.

Ngũgĩ wa Thiong'o. 1986. *Decolonising the mind: the politics of language in African literature*. London: Heinemann Education.

Nwagbara, Austin. 2008. Travelling thoughts, trailing texts: vehicle writings as discourse. In M. Bagwasi, M. Alimi and P. Ebewo (eds.), *English language and literature: cross cultural currents* 85–97. Newcastle-upon-Tyne: Cambridge Scholars Publishing.

Obiechina, Emmanuel. 1972. *Onitsha market literature*. London: Heinemann.

Ode, Godwin. 2015. Threats to mother tongues in Nigeria: strategies for revitalisation. In Ndimele (ed.), 22–38.

Odumuh, Adama. 1986. The future of English in Nigeria. In Unoh (ed.),

Odumuh, Adama. 1987. *Nigerian English (NigE): Selected essays.* Zaria: Ahmadu Bello University Press.

Ofulue, Christine. 2011. Kinship address terms in Nigerian English: some socio-cultural dilemmas. *Journal of the Nigeria English Studies Association* 14(1), 132–150.

Ogede, O.S. 1991. The Igbo roots of Olaudah Equiano. *Africa: Journal of the International African Institute* 61:1, 138–41.

Ogoanah, Felix. 2011. The pragmatic roles of as in in Nigerian English. *World Englishes* 30:2, 200–210.

Ogu, Julius. 1992. *A historical survey of English and the Nigerian situation.* Lagos: Kraft Books.

Ojarikre, Anthony. 2007. Aspects of the segmental phonology of Urhobo English. In Ndimele (ed.), 71–82.

Oji, N. 1988. *English grammar for advanced students.* Uruowulu-Obosi: Pacific Publishers.

Okafor, Nduka. 1971. *The development of universities in Nigeria.* London: Longman.

Okoro, Oko. 1986. Standard Nigerian English vs. errors: where to draw the line? *Lagos Review of English Studies* 8, 94–106.

Okoro, Oko. 2004. Codifying Nigerian English: some practical problems of labelling. In Segun Awonusi and. Babalola (eds.), 166–181.

Okoro, Oko (ed.). 2010. *Nigerian English in sociolinguistic perspectives: linguistic and literary paradgims. A festshcrift for Funso Akere.* Lagos: Pumark Nigeria Limited.

Okoro, Oko. 2011. *Exploring Nigerian English: A Guide to Usage.* Saarbrücken: VDM Verlag Dr Müller.

Okunrimeta, Uriel. 2011. Izon syntax and the English of Izon-English bilinguals. *World Englishes* 30:2, 211–228.

Okunsebor, Felix. 2015. The English language and spelling pronunciation: a case study of the phenomenon in Esan. Opeibi et al., (eds.),

Olofinjana, I. 2012. African nationalism: Agbebi's contribution. In 'Black History Month Series', accessible at https://israelolofinjana.wordpress.com.

Olukotun, Ayo. 2003. At the barricades: resurgent media in colonial Nigeria, 1900–1960. In Oyebade (ed.), 226–246.

Omachonu, Gideon. 2011. *Optimality account of stress in Standard British and Nigerian English.* Saarbrücken: LAP Lambert Academic Publishing.

Omolewa, Michael. 1979. The emergence of non-Standard English in Nigeria, 1842–1926. In Ubahakwe (ed.), 14–26.

Omodiaogbe, S.A. 1997. An error analysis of the English language of Education students in Edo and Delta States. University of Nigeria, Nsukka PhD thesis.

Omolayo, Segun. 2017. *"POP" errors in English – writers beware.* Multinational Concepts.

Omoniyi, Tope. 2006. West African Englishes. In Braj B .Kachru, Yamuna Kachru and Cecil L. Nelson, *The handbook of world Englishes,* 172–187. Oxford: Blackwell.

Onwuekwe, Chika. 2003. Constitutional development, 1914–1960: British legacy or local exigency? In Oyebade (ed.), 153–180.

Opanachi, Dorothy. 2013. Phonological problems of Igala learners of the English Language as L2. *Journal of Igbo Language and Linguistics* 6 & 7, 67–72.

Opeibi, Tunde, Josef Schmied, Tope Omoniyi and Kofo Adedeji (eds.). 2015. *Essays on language in societal transformation: a festschrift in honour of Segun Awonusi.* Göttingen: Cuvillier Verlag.

Oribhabor, Erita. 2010. The use of Naija in the media, arts, and entertainment. Proceedings of the Conference on Nigerian Pidgin, University of Ibadan, 8–9 July, 2009. www.ifra-nigeria.org).

Osofisan, Femi. 2001. Rotten English, rotten nation: an improvisation from the perspective of drama. In Femi Osofisan, *Literature and the pressures of freedom,* 123–163. Ibadan: Centre STAGE-AFRICA.

Osundare, Niyi. 2014. 'Don't talk like a book': variety under-differentiation in Nigerian English usage. In Akinjobi (ed.), 30–42.

Otsuji, Emi and Alistair Pennycook. 2010. Metrolingualism: fixity, fluidity and language in flux. *International Journal of Multilingualism* 7(3), 240–254.

Owadayo, Matthew. 1995. Samuel Ajayi Crowder. In J.A. Omoyajowo (ed.), *Makers of the Church in Nigeria.* Lagos: CSS Bookshops.

Owolabi, Kola and Ademola Dasylva (eds.). 2004. *Forms and functions of English and indigenous languages in Nigeria: a festschrift in honour of Ayo Banjo.* Ibadan: Group Publishers.

Oyebade, Adebayo (ed.). 2003. *The Foundations of Nigeria: Essays in Honor of Toyin Falola.* Trenton, NJ: Africa World Press.

Palmer, Frank R. 1990. *Modality and the English modals.* 2nd edn. London: Longman.

Pinon, R. and J. Hayden. 2010. The benefits of the English language for individuals and societies: quantitative indicators from Cameroon, Nigeria, Rwanda, Bangladesh and Pakistan. A custom report compiled by Euromonitor International for the British Council.

Pride, John (ed.). 1982. *New Englishes.* Rowley, MA: Newbury House.

Quirk, Randolph. 1990. Language varieties and standard language. *English Today* 21, 3–10.

Roach, Peter, James Hartman and Jane Setter (eds.). 2006. *Introduction to Daniel Jones, Cambridge English Pronouncing Dictionary.* 17th edn. Cambridge: Cambridge University Press.

Rotimi, Taiwo. 2012. *Language and Mobile Telecommunication in Nigeria. SMS as a Digital and Lingua-cultural Expression.* Ile-Ife: Obafemi Awolowo University Press.

Rubdy, Rani. 2001. 'Creative destruction: Singapore's Speak Good English Movement.' *World Englishes* 20, 341–355.

Rubdy, R. and L.Alsagoff. 2013. The cultural dynamics of globalization: problematizing hybridity. In R. Rubdy and L. Alsagoff (eds.), *The Global-Local Interface and Hybridity,* 1–14. Bristol: Multilingual Matters.

Sailaja, Pingali. 2009. *Indian English.* Edinburgh: Edinburgh University Press.

Salami, Ayo. 1968. Defining a Standard Nigerian English. *Journal of the Nigeria English Studies Association* 2(2), 99–106.

Sani, Mu'azu. 1989. *An introductory phonology of Hausa.* Kano: Triumph Publishing.

Schmied, Josef. 1991. *English in Africa: An introduction.* London: Longman Group.

Schneider, Edgar. 2003. The dynamics of new Englishes; from identity construction to dialect birth. *Language* 75:2, 233–281.

Schneider, Edgar. 2007. *Postcolonial English: varieties around the world.* Cambridge: Cambridge University Press.

Selinker, L. 1972. Interlanguage. *International Review of Applied Linguistics* 10, 209–231.

Simo Bobda, Augustin. 1995. The phonologies of Nigerian English and Cameroon English. In Bamgbose et al., (eds.), 248–268.

Simo Bobda, Augustin. 2007. Some segmental rules of Nigerian English phonology. *English World-Wide* 28(3), 279–310.

Simo Bobda, Augustin. 2010. Word stress in Cameroon and Nigerian Englishes. *World Englishes* 29(1), 59–74.

Sofunke, Biodun. 1990. National language policy for democratic Nigeria. In Emenanjo (ed.), 31–49.

Soneye, Taiwo and Ulrike Gut. 2011. H-deletion and h-insertion in Nigerian spoken English. Unpublished paper presented at the 28th Conference of the Nigeria English Studies Association, Benin, October 24–27, 2011.

Spencer, John (ed.). 1971. *The English Language in West Africa*. London: Longman.

Stevenson, K. 1974. On the teaching of spoken English. *Journal of the Nigeria English Studies Association* 6(1), 75–76.

Sunday, Adesina. 2011. Compound stress in Nigerian English. *English Today* 27(3), 43–51.

Taiwo, Oladele. 1979. Varieties of English in Nkem Nwankwo's novels. In Ubahakwe (ed.), 54–76.

Thomson, Sarah. 2001. *Language contact: an introduction*. Georgetown: Georgetown University Press.

Tiffen, Brian. 1974. The intelligibility of Nigerian English. University of London PhD thesis.

Trudgill, Peter and Jean Hannah. 2008. *International English*. 5th edn. London: Hodder Education.

Ubahakwe, Ebo. 1974. Bookish English among Nigerian students. *Journal of the Nigeria English Studies Association* 6(1), 38–51.

Ubahakwe, Ebo. 1979. Adapting the role of the English language in Nigerian education. In Ubahakwe (ed.), 276–296.

Ubahakwe, Ebo (ed.). 1979. *Varieties and functions of the English language in Nigeria*. Lagos: Africa Universities Press, in association with the Nigeria English Studies Association.

Udofot, Inyang. 2002. The intonation of Nigerian English. *Journal of West African Languages* 29(2), 35–47.

Udofot, Inyang. 2003. Stress and rhythm in the Nigerian accent of English. *English World-Wide* 24(2), 201–220.

Udofot, Inyang. 2004. Varieties of spoken Nigerian English. In Awonusi and Babalola (eds.), 93–113.

Udofot, Inyang. 2005. Emergent trends in English usage in Nigeria. A paper presented to the 22nd Annual Conference of the Nigeria English Studies Association.

Udofot, Inyang. 2007. A tonal analysis of spoken Nigerian English. *Journal of the Nigeria English Studies Association* 3(1), 58–68.

Udofot, Inyang. 2010. The English language and politics in Nigeria. *Journal of the Nigeria English Studies Association of Nigeria* 13(1), 5–14.

Udofot, Inyang and Juliet Udoudom (eds.). 2011. *English usage in Nigeria since 1842: a festschrift for Prof. David Eka*. Ikot Ekpene: Devconsort Services.

Ufomata, Titi. 1990. Acceptable models for TEFL (with special reference to Nigeria). In Susan Ramsaran (ed.), *Studies in the pronunciation of English,* 212–218. London: Routledge.

Ugorji, C. 2010. *Nigerian English phonology*. Frankfurt am Main: Peter Lang.

Umar, Hafsat. 2015. American versus British English: implications on L2 users of British English in Nigeria. A paper presented at the 31st Annual Conference of the Nigeria English Studies Association, Federal University of Lokoja, Lokoja

Unegbu, Osondu. 2015. The national language issue: pros and contra. A paper presented at the 31st Annual Conference of the Nigeria English Studies Association, Lokoja, 26–29 October.

UNESCO (United Nations Educational, Scientific and Cultural Organization). 2015. Adult literacy rate, population 15+ (both sexes, female, male). UNESCO Institute of Statistics, https://en.wikipedia.org/wiki/List_of countries_by_literacy_rate.

Unoh, Solomon. 1986 (ed.). *The use of English in communication*. Ibadan: Spectrum.

Walsh, N.G. 1967. Distinguishing types and varieties of English in Nigeria. In *Journal of the Nigeria English Studies Association* 2, 47–55.

Wells, John. 1982. *Accents of English*. Cambridge: Cambridge University Press.

Wells, John. 2006. *English intonation: an introduction*. Cambridge: Cambridge University Press.

Werner, Valentine and Robert Fuchs. 2016. The present perfect in Nigerian English. *English Language and Linguistics*, 1–25. Cambridge: Cambridge University Press.

WHO (World Health Organization). 2017. World health rankings, accessible at https: //www. worldlifeexpectancy.com/nigeria-life.expectancy.

Wolf, Hans-Georg. 2010. English and West African Englishes: differences and commonalties. In Tony Kirkpatrick (ed.), *The Routledge handbook of world Englishes*. London: Routledge.

Wolf, Hans-Georg and Herbert Igboanusi. 2003. A preliminary comparison of some lexical items in Nigerian English and Cameroon English. In Peter Lucko, Lothar Peter and Hans-Georg Wolf (eds.), *Studies in African varieties of English*, 69–81. Frankfurt-am-Main: Peter Lang.

Zachernuk, Philip. 2000. *Colonial subjects: an African intelligentsia and Atlantic ideas*. Charlottesville: University of Virginia Press.

The International Corpus of English-Nigeria is accessible at: https://sourceforge.net/projects/ice-nigeria

The Antconc software is accessible at: http://www.antlab.sci.waseda.ac.jp/software.html

A link featuring the voice of Sir Abubakar Tafawa Balewa, 'The Golden Voice of Africa', is: https://www.youtube.com/watch?v=b-cjdPiR4rk.

Index

https://doi.org/10.1515/9781501504600-009